What Are My Rights?

Q&A About Teens And The Law

Judge Tom Jacobs

16pt

Copyright Page from the Original Book

Copyright © 2019, 2011, 2006, 1997 by Thomas A. Jacobs, J.D.

All rights reserved under International and Pan-American Copyright Conventions. Unless otherwise noted, no part of this book may be reproduced, stored in a retrieval system, or transmitted in any form or by any means, electronic, mechanical, photocopying, or otherwise, without express written permission of the publisher, except for brief quotations or critical reviews. For more information, go to www.freespirit.com/permissions.

Free Spirit, Free Spirit Publishing, and associated logos are trademarks and/or registered trademarks of Free Spirit Publishing Inc. A complete listing of our logos and trademarks is available at www.freespirit.com.

Library of Congress Cataloging-in-Publication Data
Names: Jacobs, Thomas A., author.
Title: What are my rights? : Q&A about teens and the law / Tom A. Jacobs, J.D.
Description: Revised and updated fourth edition. | Minneapolis, MN : Free Spirit Publishing Inc., [2019]
   | Series: Teens & the law series | Includes bibliographical references and index.
Subjects: LCSH: Teenagers—Legal status, laws, etc.—United States—Juvenile literature. | Minors—
   United States—Juvenile literature. | Children's rights—United States—Juvenile literature.
   | CYAC: Teenagers—Legal status, laws, etc. | Children's rights. | Law.
Classification: LCC KF479 (ebook) | LCC KF479 .J334 2019 (print) | DDC 346.7301/30835—dc23
LC record available at https://lccn.loc.gov/2018036032

> Free Spirit Publishing does not have control over or assume responsibility for author or third-party websites and their content. At the time of this book's publication, all facts and figures cited within are the most current available. All website URLs are accurate and active; all publications, organizations, websites, and other resources exist as described in this book; and all have been verified as of December 2018. If you find an error or believe that a resource listed here is not as described, please contact Free Spirit Publishing. Parents, teachers, and other adults: We strongly urge you to monitor children's use of the internet.

Publisher's Note: The information contained in this book is not intended to supersede the advice of parents or legal counsel. Specific laws differ from one jurisdiction to another. Contact a local library, lawyer, or court to learn about the laws in your state or province.

The MADD "Contract for Life" on page 133 is reprinted by permission of Mandy Msuta, community relations coordinator at MADD Canada.

The names, ages, schools, and locations of all persons in *What Are My Rights?* are real, except where noted. They have been taken from public records and published court opinions.

Reading Level High School–Adult; Interest Level Ages 12 & up; Fountas & Pinnell Guided Reading Level Z+

Edited by Alison Behnke, Pamela Espeland, Jay E. Johnson, and Elizabeth Verdick
Cover and interior design by Emily Dyer and Tasha Kenyon

Free Spirit Publishing Inc.
6325 Sandburg Road, Suite 100
Minneapolis, MN 55427-3674
(612) 338-2068
help4kids@freespirit.com
www.freespirit.com

TABLE OF CONTENTS

DEDICATION	i
ACKNOWLEDGMENTS	ii
Foreword	v
Introduction	viii
CHAPTER 1: You and Your Family	1
CHAPTER 2: You and School	41
CHAPTER 3: You and the Internet	104
CHAPTER 4: You and Your Job	149
CHAPTER 5: You and Your Body	178
CHAPTER 6: Growing Up	239
CHAPTER 7: You and Other Important Rights	294
CHAPTER 8: Crimes and Punishments	351
CHAPTER 9: You and the Legal System	383
Appendix	441
Glossary	448
Selected Bibliography	464
About the Author	468
Other Great Resources from Free Spirit	470
Index	475

DEDICATION

This book is dedicated to my children: Matt, Alex, Natalie, Julie, and Colin. A part of their teen years lives within the pages of this book. Their mother and I survived their adolescence and cherish them now as our best friends. And I must not forget my grandchildren: Tiago, Levi, Hannah, Paige, Felix, Tomas, Jackson, Hudson, Parker, Chase, Austin, Taylor, and Kali. I encourage them to listen, read, and enjoy life.

ACKNOWLEDGMENTS

You would not be reading this book were it not for the following persons. Heartfelt appreciation and love are extended to my rock, Anne Johnson. Thanks also to my daughter and son-in-law, Natalie and Mike, for your assistance with this and earlier editions. In addition, Judge William Schafer III lit a spark in 1976 when he assigned me to write a pamphlet about extradition. The flame for research and writing continues to burn. Thanks, Bill.

Michelle Colla, Pamela Davis, Ken Reeves, Jami Taylor, Sue Tone, and Kathy Welch are also acknowledged for their contributions to the first edition. Also, I'm grateful to John and Mike Malone, Erin Gunn, John Staci, Rick Tilman, and Jennifer Pritchard for their input to this revision. The reference librarians at the Phoenix Public Library, Scottsdale City Library, Arizona State University College of Law Library, and State of Arizona Law Library are dedicated public servants who saved me untold hours of research time.

Thanks also to a special group of Girl Scouts—Troop 399, who reviewed and commented on the original work. This includes troop leader Maria del Mar Verdin, assistant Caroline Como, Scouts Andrea Arenas, Amanda Bernardo, Nicole Croci, Kristin Reynolds, Vanessa Schafer, Amanda and Jessica Scharlau, and Jamie Stewart, and Scout mom Kristen Scharlau.

Lana Malone deserves special mention for taking time to read the manuscript and pen a much-appreciated foreword. Our discussions about teens and the laws that affect them have contributed to this effort. I'm honored to call her a friend and fellow educator of young people. And I must mention Dr. Jenny L. Walker, who contributed the foreword for an earlier edition. Thanks to each of you.

Editor Jay E. Johnson put me through the worst month of my life—resulting in a book vastly improved from its earlier, self-published editions. Thanks, Jay. Editors Elizabeth Verdick and Pamela Espeland guided me through a challenging process resulting in the first and second editions of the book.

Alison Behnke helped shepherd the third and fourth editions to publication. Your dedication and hard work, Alison, are greatly appreciated. It has been a pleasure working with you again. And finally, the dedication and ongoing work by publicist Amanda Shofner must be recognized. Thanks, Amanda, for all you do.

Free Spirit founder and publisher Judy Galbraith and her support staff share in this effort, as well as graphic designers Emily Dyer, Marieka Heinlen, and Tasha Kenyon. Thanks for your wisdom and talent throughout this project.

Foreword

Your life is complex. You're navigating a maze of issues involving friends, sexuality, jobs, internet use, school, and family—to name just a few. And, on top of all that, you probably have questions about your legal rights, yet it's not always obvious where to find the answers. As someone who taught high school for twenty-three years—and also as a mother of two and grandmother of six—I know that many adults don't have the answers to all your questions. In fact, often we may not even realize that some of your concerns have been addressed by the courts. That's just one reason why *What Are My Rights?* by Judge Tom Jacobs is such an important and valuable source of information.

As you'll see from the table of contents, *What Are My Rights?* addresses a wide range of questions about your rights. The book also is written with insight and caring, which is not surprising given that Judge Tom has many years of experience as a judge in juvenile and family courts and also has five children and thirteen grandchildren of his own. Judge Tom addresses issues including adoption, divorce, rights and responsibilities at school and at work, social media, sexual harassment, drugs and alcohol, discrimination, and a multitude of other topics that he knows are of concern to teens and the adults who care about them. His discussions of legal decisions and their impact on teens' lives are current, clear, and well researched.

As a "digital native"—a young person who has never known what it's like to live in a world without texting, tweeting, Snapchat, and Instagram—you probably get a lot of your information online, not only from books. You're in luck! If you still have questions after you read *What Are My Rights?,* visit AsktheJudge.info, Judge Tom's website. Judge Tom and his daughter, attorney Natalie, answer questions that come straight from teens from around the world. If you *still* don't see the answer that you're

> looking for, you can ask them a question yourself.

I can say with conviction that this book is an incredible resource—primarily for you, but also for parents, teachers, counselors, and anyone else who works with young people. More important, this could be a life-changing book for teens who might have no one to turn to for answers. I've seen my students, my children, their friends, and other young people in my life struggle with issues concerning their rights and responsibilities. It would have been much easier for all of us if we'd had this book to read before the issues occurred. *What Are My Rights?* is written with a profound understanding of the lives of teens and of the legal system—a very powerful combination. Thanks to Judge Tom and his expertise, this book gives you the knowledge you need to navigate some of the concerns that might arise in your daily life.

Lana Malone
former French teacher (23 years)
Flagstaff Unified School District, Arizona

Introduction

As a teen, your relationship to the law is complex. It's also very important to nearly every part of your life. How much do you know about your rights and responsibilities? What are your thoughts on how the legal system treats you? What do you want to learn more about?

As you think about these questions, consider the following real-life scenario about teens and the law:

Conrad, age eighteen, had a history of depression and had attempted suicide in the past. He met seventeen-year-old Michelle online and they began a romantic relationship. Because they lived in different towns, they communicated mostly through texts and online messages. Then, through text messages, he told Michelle that he was thinking about ending his life.

Although Michelle first encouraged Conrad to get help, she later began encouraging him to go through with suicide. She said his family would understand and that she would help them through their grief. Michelle researched methods of suicide, and wrote to Conrad about hanging, suffocation, and carbon monoxide poisoning. She wrote messages including, "You're just making it harder on yourself by pushing it off, you just have to do it," and, "I thought you wanted to do this. The time is right and you're ready."

Conrad ended his life by inhaling carbon monoxide while sitting in the cab of his grandfather's truck. That day, he and Michelle had texted frequently. At one point she said, "If u don't do it now you're never gonna do it." Conrad's body was found the next day.

A criminal investigation was conducted into Conrad's death and Michelle's role in it. Michelle's lawyer argued that her messages to Conrad were protected as free speech. But did her speech cross the line and constitute a crime? What do you think? Michelle didn't participate directly in Conrad's death. Should she be held responsible for encouraging him to act? See chapter 3, for more about this case.

Scenarios like the one above, although an extreme example of digital abuse, are part of why it was so important to revise, update, and expand *What Are My Rights?* Teens have always faced unique challenges and have always needed to know their rights. But the internet and online communication—including issues such as cyberbullying and sexting—continue to add more complexity and new facets to teens' relationship to the law. Knowing about laws that directly affect teens can help you make better decisions about what to do—and what not to do. For example, being informed could help you decide whether or not to:

- cut class
- use a fake ID
- obey your teacher
- smoke cigarettes or marijuana
- bully someone online or by cell phone
- take action as a bystander to bullying or look the other way
- delete or forward a sexual image you receive
- gamble

- get a job
- stay out past curfew
- get into a fight

What Are My Rights? won't tell you everything you need to know about how laws are passed and enforced, and it won't tell you how the government works. It *will* tell you which laws affect you and why. It will also tell you what happens if you break the law and get caught. It will help you understand the law, recognize your responsibilities, and appreciate your rights. Each chapter has an introduction that orients you to certain issues, followed by a series of questions that raise topics concerning you and your friends.

Your rights are certainly nothing to take for granted. It wasn't all that long ago that young people had no recognizable rights. As recently as seventy-five years ago, children were mainly considered the property of their parents. Many children and teenagers spent twelve-hour days laboring in terrible, unsafe conditions because they had no protection under the law—and in some countries, this is still the case. Thankfully, things have changed in the

United States. You and other young people now have rights that protect you within your family, at school, online, on the job, at the doctor, and in your community.

> In 1899, the first juvenile court in the United States was established in Cook County, Illinois. The goal of the juvenile court was to focus on rehabilitation rather than punishment, and to guide young offenders toward being responsible, law-abiding adults. Before the juvenile justice system was created, children under the age of 7 were generally classified as "infants," meaning that they were too young to fully understand their actions. Therefore, they could not be guilty of felonies (serious crimes). Juveniles between the ages of 7 and 14 could stand trial only if the court determined that they knew the difference between right and wrong. Juveniles over the age of 14 could be charged and tried for their offenses. If convicted, they faced the same consequences as adults—including, in some cases, the death penalty. As you'll discover in

> the following pages, the status, rights, and responsibilities of children and teenagers have changed significantly since 1899.

Your state legislature and local officials are responsible for seeing that laws exist to protect and serve young people and the community as a whole. The authority to act for the people in passing laws and enforcing them in the nation's courts comes from the United States Constitution, the Bill of Rights,[1] and state constitutions (which closely follow the US Constitution). Just as federal and state laws regarding teenagers in the United States differ, the laws of Canada vary among its provinces. Some Canadian laws and related community resources are included in this book, along with US laws and resources.

Many teenagers have questions about the law—"Can I get in trouble for what I do on the computer at home?" "Can my teacher search my cell phone?"

---

[1] See chapter 2

"What if my parents die?"—but they don't know where to turn for answers. *What Are My Rights?* is designed to be your first stop for exploring these and other legal questions. It covers some childhood issues as well as concerns of the later teen years. The first chapters address parental authority, your rights at school, and issues of law while you're on the internet and at your job. Other chapters discuss rights of a more personal nature: dealing with your body and growing up. The final two chapters consider the more somber side of the law—the consequences of willful misconduct or bad judgment—and offer basic information about the legal system.

Throughout this book, you'll find "FYI" (For Your Information) sections with descriptions of resources—including other books, national organizations, and websites—that you can turn to for information and advice. You'll also find listings for toll-free telephone numbers and hotlines. But if an issue in this book applies to you, it's best to speak first with someone you know and trust. If possible, talk things over with your parents or guardians. Consider telling a teacher, a school counselor, or a youth leader at your place of worship. Or think of another adult you can talk to—someone who will listen, understand, and give you good advice. You probably know at least one adult who will help you and stand by you.

Are you interested in learning more about the cases in *What Are My Rights?*

The published opinions of all the country's appellate courts are found in a series of books called reporters. The series is divided into regions. For example, California decisions are found in the *Pacific Reporter,* while Maine decisions are located in the *Atlantic Reporter.* Each state also has its own set of reporters. This means that each decision may be found in both a regional reporter and a state reporter.

United States Supreme Court decisions can be found in several federal reporters. All of the Supreme Court cases in this book are located in either the *US Supreme Court Reports* or the *Supreme Court Reporter.* You can also find most Supreme Court decisions on the Court's website at supremecourt.gov. In addition, you can search online for the name of a case to find the written opinion or go to legal websites such as findlaw.com or justia.com. Plus, if you're interested in what goes on at the Supreme Court, you can take a look at www.oyez.org for daily events and recordings of oral arguments before the Court.

In this book, you'll also find true stories of teenagers who have spoken out or changed the law to benefit young people. You'll read about different ways you can stand up for yourself and invoke your rights. Knowledge is power. As you learn more about legal issues, think about what you might do to bring about positive change at home, at work, at school, and in your community.

CHAPTER 1

You and Your Family

"At our best level of existence, we are parts of a family, and at our highest level of achievement, we work to keep the family alive."
—Maya Angelou, American writer, activist, and actress

Did you know that almost 200 countries, including the United States and Canada, have signed a Declaration of the Rights of the Child? The United Nations passed the Declaration in 1959, and it calls upon all countries to guarantee you (and every young person):

- a childhood without adult responsibilities
- a happy family life
- a school that educates you according to your learning needs and interests
- a doctor who knows your name
- a safe neighborhood

- a chance to achieve and succeed in life

> "The rights to conceive and raise one's children have been deemed 'essential' ... 'basic civil rights' ... and 'rights far more precious ... than property rights.'"
> —US Supreme Court, *Stanley v. Illinois,* 92 S.Ct. 1208 (1972)

A teenagers' bill of rights might also include the right to be heard and listened to by others, the right to receive good guidance, and the right to receive fair treatment and reasonable discipline from authority figures.

The process of safeguarding yourself and your future starts at home. In fact, many of the rules you have to follow at home are rooted in the law. While some of these rules may seem unfair or overly strict, they're designed to protect you. Understanding your rights and responsibilities at home can bring you closer to reaching your goals in life.

In 2013, more than 5 million US children lived with a grandparent as their primary caretaker.

Source: *The Nation's Children 2015,* Child Welfare League of America

"WHAT DOES ADOPTION MEAN?"

Under special circumstances, you may receive a new parent or parents. If your parents die, for example, or agree to let someone else raise you, the court may allow that person to adopt you. Most of the time, it's young children or babies who are adopted, but in certain situations teenagers and even adults may be adopted. This often occurs in cases where there's a long-term relationship between a stepparent and stepchild or between adult and minor siblings.

More than 100,000 adoptions take place in the United States each year. These include children born in the United States as well as children brought into the United States from other countries. In most states, you must be at least eighteen to adopt a child. Some states require the adult to be ten years older than the child who is being adopted. Other states have no age restrictions. You don't have to be married to adopt a child. Single people—straight, gay, and lesbian—have become adoptive parents of children of all ages.

If your parents are divorced and your mother or father remarries, your new stepparent may adopt you if your other biological parent agrees. A stepparent adoption must also be approved by a judge. In many states, if you're over a certain age—usually ten to twelve years old—you must appear at the hearing and agree with the adoption. The judge will ask you if you want your stepfather or stepmother to be your legal parent, and if you want your last name to be changed to theirs.

During the adoption process, you may meet with a social worker and a lawyer. They, in turn, meet with your prospective new parent or parents and gather information to help the judge decide whether to allow the adoption. After a complete investigation, recommendations are made to the court. The investigation, called an adoptive home study, considers the motivation to adopt, finances, criminal history, family background, education, work history, and references from relatives and nonrelatives. If the court has any concerns, the adoption may be delayed. The bottom line in any adoption is whether it's best for the child. While most adoptions are granted, occasionally the judge may decide that it's not in the child's best interests.

> - In 2016, almost 118,000 children were waiting to be adopted in the United States.
> - In 2017, 41 American children were adopted in Canada; 20 in the Netherlands; and 12 in Ireland.
>
> **Sources:** *The AFCARS Report,* US Department of Health and Human Services (2017); US Department of State (2018)

If you were adopted when you were a baby, what are you entitled to know about the adoption and its circumstances? Privacy for birth parents, adoptive parents, and adopted children is still the general rule. Each state has its own laws regarding the disclosure of records. Depending on where you live, you may be able to find out nonidentifying information—information that tells you about your biological parents without revealing their names. Or, once you're an adult, you may be able to find out identifying information—including their names.

You may also be able to learn about your birth parents' medical history. Contact the court where the adoption took place to ask for this information. Some states operate a Confidential Intermediary (CI) Program. The CI attempts to make contact with the birth parents, adoptive parents, and adoptee. The sharing of confidential information may be arranged with consent from the people involved, as may contact among the parties. Do a Google search using the name of your state and the phrase "Confidential Intermediary" for details.

> **"Courts are not free to take children from parents simply by**

> deciding another home appears more advantageous."
> —US Supreme Court, *DeBoer v. DeBoer,* 114 S.Ct. 1 (1993)

FYI

Adopted: The Ultimate Teen Guide by Suzanne Buckingham Slade (Scarecrow Press, Inc., 2013). Presenting stories of adopted teens, *Adopted* addresses the questions, concerns, and issues that other adopted teens may face.

All the Broken Pieces by Ann E. Burg (Scholastic Paperbacks, 2012). This moving novel, written in verse, tells the story of a Vietnamese boy adopted by an American family. Matt Pin was airlifted to the United States when he was abandoned by his American soldier father and his Vietnamese mother wanted him to have a better life than she could provide. Now 12 years old and a star pitcher on his school's baseball team,

Matt wrestles with the present and the past.

Where Are My Birth Parents? A Guide for Teenage Adoptees by Karen Gravelle and Susan Fischer (Walker and Company, 1995). This book discusses how and why adopted children may try to locate and get to know their birth parents as well as explores the possible psychological benefits and problems associated with that process.

US Citizenship and Immigration Services
1-800-375-5283
uscis.gov

Contact the USCIS for information on international adoptions and immigration rules and regulations.

"WHAT IS FOSTER CARE? HOW LONG DOES IT LAST?"

Nearly half a million children live in foster homes, group homes, emergency receiving homes, or child-crisis centers across the United States. Young people are moved to out-of-home care for many reasons, including neglect, abandonment, or child abuse.[2] If the state learns that a child is being maltreated in some way, the child may be removed from the home. It's the state's responsibility to protect its children. If removed, a child is either placed with relatives, friends, or—as a last resort—into a foster home.

The people who operate foster homes are licensed, trained, and monitored by a state agency—usually Child Protective Services (CPS). If you're placed in foster care, you'll receive medical, dental, psychological, and educational services. An attorney and/or guardian may be appointed to look out for you and to discuss your situation and represent you in court. Depending on your age, you may have the opportunity to appear in court with your lawyer. The judge may want to hear from you directly.

The goal of every court and agency responsible for your care is to find you

---

[2] See chapter 5, for more information on abuse and neglect.

a permanent home. This may mean returning you to your parents when they're ready to provide safe care, placing you with relatives or friends, or finding you an adoptive home. A lot depends on why you were originally placed in foster care. If the problems have been solved and you can be safely returned to your parents, the court may allow it. Otherwise, after you've spent six to twelve months in foster care, other more permanent plans will be considered.

- In 2016, there were more than 436,000 children in foster care in the United States, including 117,000 waiting to be adopted. Approximately 23,000 foster children aged out of the system without being adopted. More than 57,000 children were adopted out of the foster care system in 2016.
- In 2018, the US Department of Health and Human Services reported an increase, due in part to the country's opioid epidemic, in child abuse fatalities. The 1,700 deaths in 2016 represented a 7% increase over the 1,589 deaths reported in 2015.

Sources: US Department of Health and Human Services (2017); National Foster Youth Institute (2017); KidsCount.org (2018)

State laws regarding your rights and your parents' rights have changed in the last decade or so. Parents are required to show by their actions, not words, that they intend to work toward your return. They must resolve whatever problem caused you to be placed in foster care—by, for example, getting counseling, going into drug rehabilitation, or taking parenting classes. If too much time passes without any positive results, alternative plans must be made. Although there's no time limit on a foster home placement, state and federal laws discuss a "permanent" home for all children. Each case is considered on an individual basis by the courts and social workers.

You don't lose any rights while you're in foster care. The agency responsible for you must see that all of your needs are met and that you're in a safe environment. You should receive medical and dental care, as well as schooling and recreation. In foster care, you have to follow house rules regarding hygiene, curfew, and study and recreation time.

Once you turn eighteen and become an adult, foster care may end. Some states allow you to remain in foster care if you're still in high school or if special circumstances exist. Otherwise, if you do still need care after you're eighteen, your state may provide assistance to young adults who age out of foster care, or Adult Protective Services may provide help.

FosterClub
fosterclub.com

Young people (24 or younger) who are or have been in foster care can join the FosterClub and meet and network with others who know what they have gone through. The site also has foster care facts, questions and answers, message boards, and contests.

"WHAT HAPPENS TO ME IF MY PARENTS GET A DIVORCE?"

If your parents get a divorce, it doesn't mean that they're no longer your parents, or that they no longer love you. Children are not the cause of their parents' divorce—and they have no reason to feel guilty or blame themselves. If your parents have divorced and you're struggling with feelings of guilt, sadness, or fear, get help so you can work things out in your life. Contact a school counselor, who may recommend that you talk to a therapist or other specialized professional. Or let your mother or father know that the divorce is bothering you, and that you need help dealing with it.

Can your parents force you to go to counseling if you're troubled by divorce (or any other issue)? Yes. They can arrange for the whole family to attend counseling or individual counseling for one or two of you. Since you have little choice but to go, keep an open mind.

It may seem awkward at first, but you'll soon find yourself opening up and feeling better. Relationship issues don't happen overnight, and healing also takes time. Talk with your friends and you'll see that you're not alone in your thoughts, fears, and concerns.

If your parents get a divorce, decisions have to be made that directly affect you. You may have questions: "Do I have to move?" "Will I be separated from my brothers and sisters?" "Will I get to see the parent I don't live with?" A court may help your parents with these decisions, and, depending on your age, you may be asked for your opinion on what *you* want to happen.

A lawyer may be appointed to represent you if your parents don't agree on visitation issues or where you should live. Tell your lawyer *exactly* what you feel about these issues and why. This is the *only* way to be sure that the judge considers your wishes before a decision is made.

The ultimate question in each divorce case is "What is in the child's best interests?" However, the states don't all follow the same laws in determining the answer. Some states give preference to the desires of the child; others don't. Some appoint lawyers or guardians to speak for children; others don't. In most cases, though, the results are the same, since "best interests" remains the goal in all jurisdictions. Both parents are considered in custody disputes about which parent you'll live with. In the past, the law tended to support automatic custody with the mother, but today fathers are often granted custody of their children.

Courts grant either sole custody to one parent, or joint or shared custody to both parents. In a *sole custody* situation, you'll live with one of your parents and visit the other (for example, on weekends, holidays, and during the summer). If your noncustodial parent lives out of state, you may spend all or part of the summer with that parent. The same is true for your brothers and sisters. Courts try to keep the children in a family together. If siblings are split up, arrangements may be made for frequent contact and visits.

Joint or *shared custody* requires both parents to agree on the living arrangements of the children. It allows both parents to share legal and physical custody of you and your brothers and sisters, with an agreed-upon division of time and responsibilities throughout the year. You may live with your mother during the school year, and with your father during the summer and holidays. Or, if your parents live close by, especially in the same school district, you may alternate weeks or months at each parent's home.

The rule in custody situations should be whatever works out best for all of you. Be sure to speak up and let your parents know how you feel about the arrangements. Whatever is decided, give it a try for a while. If you feel strongly one way or the other, tell your parents. It's best to get your feelings out in the open. Speaking up may help change things. You'll also be helping your siblings if they feel the same way but are worried about saying anything.

If you find yourself unable to talk to anyone about divorce and custody worries, visit your school or public library. You'll find books and pamphlets written especially for children and teens that will help answer some of your questions and concerns. Or look online for similar resources. Check one out—and maybe confide in a friend.

For a state-by-state chart about custody factors, see Appendix.

> Many cases have addressed custody and visitation issues and have made determinations including the following:
> • A parent's marijuana abuse (not the legal use of medical marijuana) could affect a court's decision about custody rights.*
> • It is the court's responsibility—not the responsibility of teenage children—to decide visitation terms and issues.**
> • A 13-year-old should be interviewed by the judge prior to granting the mother's request that visits with the father be terminated.***

Citations: **Daggett v. Sternick*, 109 A.3d 1137 (Maine 2015); ***Milligan v. Milligan*, 149 So.3d 623 (Alabama 2014); ****Zubizarreta v. Hemminger*, 967 NYS2d 423 (New York 2013)

The Divorce Workbook for Teens: Activities to Help You Move Beyond the Breakup by Lisa M. Schab (Instant Help Books, 2008). A wide range of suggestions and activities helps teens work through their feelings and thoughts about their parents' divorce.

My Parents Are Getting Divorced: How to Keep It Together When Your Mom and Dad Are Splitting Up by Florence Cadier and Melissa Daly (Amulet Books, 2004). Helpful information and guidance for young people going through their parents' divorce.

When Divorce Hits Home: Keeping Yourself Together When

Your Family Comes Apart by Beth Baruch Joselow and Thea Joselow (Authors Choice Press, 2000). Written by a mother-daughter team, this book is based on interviews with lots of kids who have been through the divorce of their parents.

"WHAT IS KIDNAPPING?"

Kidnapping is defined as knowingly restraining someone with a specific intent to do something. This may be to collect a ransom, use a person as a hostage, or have someone do involuntary work. Other intentions may be to injure a person or to interfere with the operation of an airplane, bus, train, or other form of transportation. Kidnapping may be a felony, depending on the circumstances. If someone is convicted of kidnapping, it's not uncommon for that person to receive a jail or prison sentence.

Custodial interference, sometimes called *parental kidnapping,* happens when one parent keeps a child from the parent who has legal custody. Statistics indicate that over 200,000 children are kidnapped by parents or other family members every year. Specific state and federal laws against parental kidnapping carry stiff sentences for violation.

> If you're a victim of kidnapping or custodial interference, or if your brother or sister is in danger of being kidnapped, *take immediate action.* Call the police or 911 for emergency assistance.

For example, say the court has placed you in the legal custody of your mother. Your father lives out of state and has holiday visits. After you spend two weeks with your father at Christmas, he decides not to return you to your mother. This is custodial interference and may be prosecuted as a crime.

If your parents agree that you can live with your father, however, they should ask the court to modify the custody order. Courts grant modification requests all the time. The key issue is what's best for you. If there's no risk of abuse or neglect, and the change is to your benefit, it will most likely be approved.

Let your opinion be heard in custody modification situations. Many courts want to know whether you agree with the change of custody. Feel free to write the court a letter. Or you may have the opportunity to go to court and speak with the judge. This is your chance to state your true feelings. If you're hesitant to speak up in your parents' presence, ask to talk to the judge alone. Many judges will allow this. You may be taken to the judge's office with your lawyer or guardian, where you can speak freely. The judge will make sure your statements remain confidential.

The point is that *you* are the most important person in the case. Your opinion matters and should be heard. The results may not be 100 percent to your satisfaction, but speaking up gives you the chance to share your views and to make sure your concerns are taken into account.

"IF MY PARENTS GET A DIVORCE, WILL I STILL GET TO VISIT MY GRANDPARENTS?"

Visitation is a big issue that gets decided in every divorce case. It starts with your parents. If your mother is given sole custody, your father will probably be granted visitation rights or parenting time. Likewise, if your father is given sole custody, your mother will usually be granted visitation. This means the noncustodial parent will be able to see you on a regular basis, with set times and days. Or it may be more flexible, depending on what your parents agree on. The court will review the terms and, based on what's in your best interests, approve or modify them.

Over the past few years, grandparents and great-grandparents have become active in asserting their requests for visits with grandchildren (and great-grandchildren) whose parents divorce. Many states have passed laws allowing grandparents to seek a court order for visits if they've been denied visitation by the parents. Some states require a minimum period of time to pass (three to six months) before the visits begin—a period where everyone can cool off after the divorce. Other courts require a hearing with an opportunity for parents to oppose grandparent visits if a good reason exists. If visits are granted, the court will usually set forth a schedule that all are required to follow. Each case is unique; there's no specific formula that's followed with identical results each time.

Stepparents may also seek visitation rights. For example, if your mother and stepfather get a divorce, does your former stepfather have any visitation rights? Can you continue to visit the stepparent who is now legally out of the picture? State legislatures are now considering laws addressing parents who find themselves in this situation. Most states, at this time, don't provide stepparents with visitation rights by law. Some courts, however, will look at the whole picture, including how long the stepparent has been involved in your life, your opinion about visitation, and any other relevant factors. Courts have granted former stepparents visitation with their stepchildren. Again, the bottom line is what's best for you.

"DO MY PARENTS HAVE TO SUPPORT ME AFTER THEY GET DIVORCED?"

Failure to pay child support is an ongoing issue before courts across the country. Thousands of single parents—most of whom are mothers—are receiving state and federal funds in the absence of financial assistance from the children's other parents (mostly fathers). Once brought before a judge, many parents who are delinquent on their payments start paying their child support as ordered by the court. Those who don't may be found in contempt of court and incarcerated.

What is this all about? Why are parents going to jail?

First, *all* parents have a legal duty and obligation to support their children. This includes divorced parents and those who never married. The *duty* to support a child means providing financial assistance to the custodial parent for the basic necessities of life—food, shelter, clothing, medical expenses, and education. The *obligation* may apply to either parent—mother or father. The court looks at the whole family situation, including both parents' earnings, standards of living, and debts, and the ages and needs of the children. Guidelines exist to help the court arrive at a fair child support figure. Once the amount is determined, the court makes an order and payments are scheduled to begin, usually on a monthly basis.

As children get older, support payments may be increased as the children's needs change and the cost of living rises. If a parent misses a payment or is occasionally late in paying, any dispute will probably be resolved without going back to court. However, if *no* payments are made, this becomes a serious matter. Nationwide, courts and law enforcement agencies have cracked down on parents who are behind in their payments. Why? In part, because taxpayers pay millions of dollars for families on welfare who aren't being supported by responsible parents.

- A Colorado court held that a 16-year-old boy may be liable for child support if he is proven to be the baby's father.*
- In cases from Arkansas** and Kansas,*** young parents have been held responsible for child support. The fathers were 12 and 13, while the mothers were 15 and 16. One case involved consenting teens while the other involved an older babysitter.

Citations: *Schierenbeck v. Minor*, 367 P.2d 333 (Colorado 1961); ***Hamm v. Office of Child Support Enforcement*, 985 SW2d 742 (Arkansas 1999); ****Hermesmann v. Seyer*, 847 P.2d 1273 (Kansas 1993)

States are trying various methods to get parents to pay their child support. Some states have gone public with billboards and wanted posters in an effort to embarrass "deadbeat" parents into paying. In Arizona, a parent who falls six months behind in child support payments can have his or her professional license (medical, law, therapist, etc.) or work permit or certificate suspended.

If your parents are divorced, their duty to support you continues until you turn eighteen or are emancipated.[3] Some states require child support to continue after your eighteenth birthday if you're still in high school. Once you graduate or get your general educational development (GED) diploma, if you are eighteen or over, the legal obligation to support you may end. A number of states also extend the support obligation beyond eighteen if you're physically or mentally disabled. Your parents may agree at the time of the divorce to cover your college or technical school expenses. This will obviously extend support past your eighteenth birthday, and such an agreement has been determined by the courts to be valid and enforceable.

Even if you're a teenage parent, you still have a duty and obligation to

---

[3] To learn about emancipation, see chapter 6.

support your child or children. Some states require the parents of a teenage mother or father to assist in the baby's support, but the birth parents, regardless of age, carry the primary responsibility.

"CAN I 'DIVORCE' MY PARENTS?"

A Florida boy named Gregory K. got a court order terminating his mother's parental rights and giving him the legal right to become part of a new family. His birth father didn't contest the adoption. In effect, Gregory "divorced" his parents.

This case was unusual because it was filed by a child with a lawyer's help. Usually, the state or a child welfare agency files this type of lawsuit on behalf of a child. However, when Gregory was eleven, he decided he wanted to remain in the foster home where he'd lived for nine months. Because he'd been neglected and abused by his parents, Gregory had been in foster care for two years. He hadn't seen his mother in eighteen months. He thought she'd forgotten about him. His new foster parents wanted to adopt him, and the court determined that this was best for Gregory.

Gregory's case opened the door for a whole new discussion and review of children's rights. Since then, state legislatures and courts across the country have paid closer attention to the reasonable and legitimate demands of minors. The emphasis now is on "permanency" for all children and teenagers in foster care. If kids are unable to return home or be placed with relatives, alternative permanent homes are sought. In appropriate cases, public and private agencies take legal action toward terminating parents' rights.

This doesn't mean that because you don't like being grounded, you can go to court and get new parents. This is a serious decision that's limited in its application. Only in the most extreme situation, and usually as a last resort, will the legal rights of a parent be terminated.

If things are seriously wrong in your family and you have questions or problems that you've been keeping to yourself, find someone you trust and can talk to. A school counselor, a teacher, a clergy member, or an adult friend or family member may be someone you can turn to. Don't let the situation get so out of control that your health and safety are at risk. Community groups or Child Protective Services (CPS) are good resources for assistance.

"WHO HAS THE RIGHT TO DISCIPLINE ME?"

"You can't tell me what to do." "I don't have to—you're not my parent!" "If you touch me, I'll call the police!" In the heat of an argument, you may say things like this to a parent, stepparent, guardian, or teacher. Who has the right to discipline you?

The law gives your parents control over your life until you become an adult. In fact, the US Supreme Court has stated that the custody, care, and nurturance of a child belong first to the parents and that it's their duty to

prepare you for independence.[4] This means that your parents can decide:
- what school you'll go to
- when you'll be able to drive
- what religion (if any) to raise you in
- when you can get a job
- if you can marry before you're eighteen

Your parents or guardians, however, are *not* free to discipline you beyond reason. Every state has child protection laws and an agency to investigate cases of child abuse, neglect, and abandonment. If Child Protective Services (CPS) determines that the discipline or punishment you receive is excessive or harmful, whether physically, sexually, or emotionally, they may remove you from your home to a safer environment.

Strict "rules of the house"—what you may consider harsh punishment—aren't sufficient for CPS or the police to get involved. The government cannot interfere with the duties of a parent to

---

[4] Exceptions to parental control are discussed in chapter 6.

raise a child unless abuse has occurred or the threat of abuse or neglect exists.

Abuse and neglect are specifically defined by state law.[5] *Abuse* may include physical, sexual, and emotional harm. *Neglect* may mean physical, emotional, or educational deprivation. Emotional neglect by a parent isn't easy to pin down or prove. Not all states recognize emotional harm to a child or teenager as requiring legal action or intervention. Typical symptoms of emotional harm include depression, poor performance at school, and antisocial or destructive behavior.

In a case from Iowa, a ten-year-old girl whose parents were divorced was removed from her mother's home. Following the divorce, the girl had become depressed and developed an eating disorder. Her mother provoked the child's negative feelings toward her father and encouraged her to eat in order to cope with her stress. At one point, the 5'3" girl weighed 290 pounds. The court considered this a form of

---

[5] See chapter 5, for more information on abuse and neglect.

emotional abuse and placed her in a residential treatment program.

Although emotional neglect is difficult to define, a California court stated that "persons of common intelligence would not have to guess whether someone was maltreating their child to the point of causing severe emotional harm."

The bottom line, however, is that you're required to follow the rules your parents set. If there's a disagreement—about driving or your curfew, for example—talk about it with your parents. Ask them to sit down with you and calmly discuss the situation. Maybe you can reach a compromise. If not, you'll still feel better for getting your feelings out in the open.

While you're at school, teachers and other school staff take the place of your parents. This is referred to as *in loco parentis,* meaning "in the place of a parent." Misconduct will result in some form of disciplinary action such as detention time, extra assignments, or lost privileges. In extreme cases, suspension or expulsion may occur. School policy may also permit paddling or spanking, which the US Supreme

Court has determined is not cruel and unusual punishment under the Eighth Amendment. School districts vary in the use of corporal punishment to discipline students.[6]

> Try these ideas for talking with your parents about disagreements or concerns you have:
> - Pick a quiet time.
> - Keep distractions to a minimum—turn off the TV, music, cell phones, and computers.
> - Don't start talks when your friends are over.
> - Stay calm and use respectful language. (Try to speak to your parents the same way you'd want them to talk to you.)
> - State your position and explain why you feel the way you do.
> - Ask your parents to state their position—and listen to what they say.

---

[6] See chapter 2.

"CAN MY PARENTS FORCE ME TO FOLLOW THEIR RELIGION?"

The First Amendment to the US Constitution guarantees all Americans freedom of religion. This isn't limited to adults. Children and teenagers enjoy the same right, which is balanced with the fundamental rights of parents to raise their children without government interference.

This means the government and the courts won't get involved if you and your parents disagree about religious beliefs or practices. As long as you're safe and your parents provide for your basic needs (food, shelter, clothing, and medical care), the state can't interfere with your family. Your parents are free to decide what church you attend (if any), how often, and what practices will be honored in the home.

If, however, you are at risk of being abused or neglected because of your parents' religious beliefs, the police or Child Protective Services (CPS) may step in to ensure your safety. For example, if you needed a blood transfusion or other urgent medical care, and your parents refused to give their consent due to their religious beliefs, the court could get involved. In a life-threatening situation, or one where there's a risk of permanent disability, the court has the right to order the appropriate medical care for you.

Occasionally, a hospital or doctor will ask the court to assist with difficult emergency cases. In 1944, the US Supreme Court stated that parents may be free to become martyrs themselves, but they are not free to make martyrs of their children (*Prince v. Massachusetts,* 321 US 158, Massachusetts 1944). In following that decision, a Minnesota court stated that "although one is free to believe what one will, religious freedom ends when one's conduct offends the law by, for example, endangering a child's life" (*Lundman v. McKown,* 530 N.W.2d 807, Minnesota 1995).

In that Minnesota case, an eleven-year-old boy was diagnosed with juvenile-onset diabetes. His parents were Christian Scientists, members of a religion that believes in prayer as the proper treatment for illness. The boy died because he was denied medical treatment. In discussing the difference between freedom to believe and freedom to act, the court upheld the government's right to restrict acts based on religious beliefs. In other words, people can't claim religion as a reason for not paying taxes, violating child labor laws, being married to more than one person at a time, or refusing medical care for their children.

As you get older and think about the role of religion in your life, talk with your parents. Share your ideas and feelings. Talk with your friends who may belong to different faiths. What is their relationship with their parents on the subject of religion? It won't be long before you're independent and able to worship as you choose.

"DO I NEED A GUARDIAN IF MY PARENTS DIE?"

A guardian is a person who takes the place of your parents. He or she has the same responsibilities as your mother or father, including caring for you and your social, educational, and medical needs. Likewise, you have an obligation to obey and respect your guardian.

A guardian is either appointed by a court or named by your parents in their will. Usually, a relative or close friend of the family—someone you know—is named as your guardian.

In order for someone to be named a court-appointed guardian, the person must be screened and investigated to determine whether he or she can handle the responsibilities involved. If the court finds that the appointment isn't in your best interests, it won't be made. Another person will then be considered. If no one is available to be your guardian, then the state—through Child Protective Services (CPS)—will be appointed.

A guardian may be permanent or act as a guardian for you until you turn eighteen. If you get married or are adopted before then, the guardianship ends. In some states, if you're a certain age, you'll have a say in who becomes your guardian. You may have the opportunity to approve or disapprove the guardianship or request a new one. There must be good, sound reasons for such a request, or the court will deny it.

Think About It, Talk About It

1. Make a list of the rules you have to follow at home and think about how they're related to the law.

2. Consider starting a peer support group for teens with common concerns about custody, visitation, and adoption. Invite a local counselor to one of your meetings to discuss some of the issues.

3. You've recently made friends with a new student at your school. One day, she tells you that she's supposed to be living with her mother in another state. Against her mother's wishes, she decided not to return home after visiting her father for the summer. Your friend is afraid of being arrested, pulled out of school, and returned to her mother against her will. What can you tell her? How can you help?

4. Discuss how you would approach your parents about their rules regarding what you can and can't see at the movie theater, what you're allowed and not allowed to read, or places you're permitted or not permitted to go.

CHAPTER 2

You and School

> "Education is our passport to the future, for tomorrow belongs to the people who prepare for it today."
> —Malcolm X, American civil rights activist

Since the advent of student rights in the 1960s, many on-and off-campus activities have been challenged in the courts. Students have sought and found refuge in the Bill of Rights, with a number of cases getting the attention of the US Supreme Court in Washington, DC.

Some of your peers have taken a stand regarding incidents at school as well as events that happen off-campus but are school-related. As a result, the courts have had to consider your individual rights. For example, the First Amendment guarantees freedom of speech, religion, and the press. First Amendment protection once applied only to adults, but it has since been extended to students.

The Fourth Amendment's protection from unreasonable searches and seizures applies to you too. The key word here is "unreasonable," as considered in the context of the school setting. Are your locker, cell phone, and backpack private and off-limits to school security or teachers? What about your car when it's parked on campus? Is a drug test to play sports or join the band an illegal search?

The Fifth Amendment, guaranteeing due process and protection against self-incrimination, is also on your side. But do you know what the amendment means and how it plays a role in your life? What is due process?

What does the Eighth Amendment's protection against cruel and unusual punishment have to do with you at school? Do you have any recourse if you're unjustly accused of something at school and expelled as a result?

These issues and more are discussed in this chapter. As you read, refer to the Bill of Rights below. Think about how these ten amendments to the US

Constitution apply to your school life. Although the Bill of Rights was written more than 200 years ago and is probably shorter than one of your homework assignments, it continues to be the foundation of all our rights and a model for democracies around the world.

"DO I HAVE TO GO TO SCHOOL?"

By law, all US children are required to be educated. This applies to elementary and high school students, regardless of immigration status. The Supreme Court decided in 1982 that children in the country illegally may enroll in public school. The court said that denying public education could impose a lifetime of hardship "on a class of children not accountable for their disabling status" (*Plyler v. Doe*, 102 S.Ct. 2382, 1982).

Public education is free, as is transportation to and from school (in most communities). Breakfast and lunch programs are provided for qualifying students. Private school education is also an option.

States differ on the minimum age at which you must begin your education. Some require children who are five or six years old by a certain date (September 1, for example) to start first grade. The rules vary slightly from state to state; see the chart in section entitled "Appendix: Compulsory School Attendance", for details. In most states, parents who fail to send their children to school may be charged with education neglect. Consequences include community service hours, counseling, fines, and/or jail.

> **"Education is the very foundation of good citizenship."**
> —US Supreme Court, *Brown v. Board of Education*, 74 S.Ct. 686 (1954)

There are a few exceptions to the general attendance laws. Some parents send their children to *charter schools*—smaller, specialized programs approved or licensed by the State Department of Education. Or, your parents may choose to homeschool you, in which case your progress may be tested in some states. In other words, you and your parents are largely free to decide the nature of your education and where you will attend school.

United States Bill of Rights

I. Congress shall make no law respecting an establishment of religion, or prohibiting the free exercise thereof; or abridging the freedom of speech, or of the press; or the right of the people peaceably to assemble, and to petition the Government for a redress of grievances.

II. A well regulated Militia, being necessary to the security of a free State, the right of the people to keep and bear Arms, shall not be infringed.

III. No Soldier shall, in time of peace be quartered in any house, without the consent of the Owner, nor in time of war, but in a manner to be prescribed by law.

IV. The right of the people to be secure in their persons, houses, papers, and effects, against unreasonable searches and seizures, shall not be violated, and no Warrants shall issue, but upon probable cause, supported by Oath or affirmation, and particularly describing the place to be searched, and the persons or things to be seized.

V. No person shall be held to answer for a capital, or otherwise infamous crime, unless on a presentment or indictment of a Grand Jury, except in cases arising in the land or naval forces, or in the Militia, when in actual service in time of War or in public danger; nor shall any person be subject for the same offence to be twice put in jeopardy of life or limb; nor shall be compelled in any criminal case to be a witness against himself; nor be deprived of life, liberty, or property, without due process of law; nor shall private property be taken for public use, without just compensation.

VI. In all criminal prosecutions, the accused shall enjoy the right to a speedy and public trial, by an impartial jury of the State and district wherein the crime shall have been committed, which district shall have been previously ascertained by law, and to be informed of the nature and cause of the accusation; to be confronted with the witnesses against him; to have compulsory process for obtaining witnesses in his favor, and to have the Assistance of Counsel for his defence.

VII. In suits at common law, where the value in controversy shall exceed twenty dollars, the right of trial by jury shall be preserved, and no fact tried by a jury shall be otherwise re-examined in any Court of the United States, than according to the rules of the common law.

VIII. Excessive bail shall not be required, nor excessive fines imposed, nor cruel and unusual punishments inflicted.

IX. The enumeration in the Constitution, of certain rights, shall not be construed to deny or disparage others retained by the people.

X. The powers not delegated to the United States by the Constitution,

> nor prohibited by it to the States, are reserved to the States respectively, or to the people.
> *(1791)*

> In 1951 Linda Brown was an African American third-grader in Kansas when her father tried to enroll her in an all-white school. The school denied her admission, so Linda's father sued the school district. Linda and her family won their case in 1954, when the Supreme Court found racial segregation to be discrimination and unconstitutional in *Brown v. Board of Education.* Linda went on to become an educator and civil rights advocate. She died in 2018 at age 75.

Exceptions are also made for students who fall into exempt categories, such as actors and actresses. Child labor laws allow young people to work certain hours during the school year,[7] but the laws specify that their

---

[7] See chapter 4.

educational needs must be met through a tutor or some other arrangement.

Before starting school or transferring from one school to another, you must be current on all required immunizations. The school will want to see a record of your shots or a letter from your doctor. Most schools have the forms you need to file. If you're not up to date on your shots, or if you don't have a doctor, talk with the school nurse or principal. Arrangements may be made with the local health department to give you the needed immunizations. In all states, you're required to be vaccinated against diphtheria, measles, rubella, and polio. (There may be exceptions to some immunization requirements based on parental preferences and/or religious grounds. Check your state law for specifics.)

- Public school districts are required by the federal McKinney-Vento Homeless Assistance Act (1987) to register homeless children.

- An estimated 2.4 million children experienced homelessness in the US in 2013.
- Approximately 1.3 million homeless children were attending public schools in 2015.
- In 2012, approximately 1.7 million young people were being homeschooled in the United States.
- In 2014–2015, 83% of US students graduated from high school in four years.

Sources: National Center for Education Statistics (2016 and 2017); National Center for Homeless Education (2014); National Center on Family Homelessness (2014); US Department of Education

"HOW LONG DO I HAVE TO STAY IN SCHOOL?"

As the chart in section entitled "Appendix: Compulsory School Attendance", shows, different states have defined different age ranges for compulsory school attendance. You can call any school or district office to find out what's required where you live. Some states have increased the minimum level of education to the twelfth grade. Other states are considering suspending driver's licenses for teens who don't go to school. Within some limits, you generally don't have to leave high school until you graduate. You're not excluded, for example, if you're a sophomore at age eighteen or nineteen. Some states set a maximum age for regular school attendance at twenty-one.

The law doesn't mandate that you attend a mainstream high school. If your interests lie elsewhere, or your study habits require something other than six hours a day in a classroom, other programs are available. Look into a trade school or vocational program in your area.

If you stop going to school before graduating, you can still earn your high school diploma. Once you've been out of school for six months, you're eligible to enroll in a general educational development (GED) program. When you pass the test and receive your diploma, you'll be able to continue with your education.

To get high school dropouts involved in education, communities have developed a variety of nontraditional programs. Some help teens with substance abuse issues, while others address teen parenthood or delinquency problems. Youth Challenge is a quasi-military federal program sponsored by the National Guard. It currently operates in twenty-eight states, Puerto Rico, and the District of Columbia. Youth Challenge presents a blend of classroom study, community service, and physical training in a seventeen-month program for sixteen-and seventeen-year-old dropouts who are drug-free and not involved with the court. (See ngycp.org for more information.)

If you're pregnant or have children, you may finish high school at your regular school, or the district may have a special program for teen parents. Check with your school counselor for more details.

The National and Community Service Act provides an opportunity to help pay for an education or for job training. The program is designed for young people who aren't in school, who have limited English language skills, and/or who are homeless or in foster care. You must be between ages sixteen and twenty-five to be eligible. Members perform community service work and are paid an allowance that may increase the longer you stay in the program. Check with a high school counselor or your local youth services bureau for information on how to apply.

Thinking About Dropping Out?
- In 2016, 50.4 million students attended public elementary and secondary schools; 35.4 million were in preK through eighth grade and 15 million were in high school.
- In 2015, 6% of 16-to 24-year-olds were considered high school dropouts (did not obtain a GED). That year, 86,000 people earned GED diplomas.
- The unemployment rate in 2016 among dropouts ages 20 to 24 years old was 17%, compared with 10% for those who finished high school and 5% for those with a college degree.

Regardless of your reason for leaving or wanting to leave school, there may be a program for teens in your situation. Continuing education programs exist for teen parents, students with substance abuse issues, working teens, and students with poor academic records. Contact a school counselor or district office for information about these opportunities.

Source: *Digest of Education Statistics* (2016)

"WHAT WILL HAPPEN TO ME IF I DITCH SCHOOL?"

State law requires you to be in school for a certain number of days each school year. There is also a maximum number of days allowed for unexcused absences. Once you hit that number, you may be suspended or expelled. Either consequence is serious and may significantly affect your education.

Missing school without an acceptable excuse is called *truancy.* Your school's assistant principal or attendance officer may be authorized to issue tickets, order you to appear in court, or even arrest you and take you before a judge if you don't show up for school. The laws differ around the country, but all states have mandatory attendance laws.

Emergencies such as illness or a death in the family are reasonable excuses for missing a class or a whole day of school. You may also receive permission to miss school to take a special trip or attend a family function. If you plan to be absent on certain days, let your teacher know in advance.

During the school year, J.M. missed 41 unexcused days of school and had failing grades in every class. When staff at his school were unable to contact his mother, the court got involved and made J.M. a ward of the court on the basis of juvenile neglect (specifically regarding J.M.'s education). This meant the judge could remove J.M. from his mother's custody if she didn't make sure he went to school every day.

Citation: *In re J.M.*, 334 P.3d 568 (Wyoming 2014)

Schools and courts are serious about school attendance. Some states have passed laws making parents accountable for their children's truancy. Parents may be fined or jailed if the truancy continues. In Colorado, a fifteen-year-old girl was ordered to spend a month in a detention center for missing forty-three days of school and being late to school nineteen times. Her parents were also sent to jail for ten days and fined $300.

"SHOULD I HAVE TO PASS A CIVICS TEST TO GRADUATE FROM HIGH SCHOOL?"

- How many US senators are there?
- What are the first ten amendments to the US Constitution called?
- Name one branch of government.

These are some of the 100 questions on a civics exam required of every applicant for US citizenship. In some states, lawmakers have proposed legislation to add a civics test as a requirement for graduation from high school.

An Arizona legislator commented on the bill, "Every single student ... across the United States of America should have basic knowledge and understanding of American government. Civics is just common sense." Arizona enacted the Civics Education Initiative (A.R.S. 15-701.01) in 2015, requiring high school students and people studying for their GED tests to correctly answer 60 of the 100 questions from the US citizenship test. If they fail, they can retake the test until they pass, at which point they'll receive their diploma. Other states—including Kentucky, Missouri, North Dakota, and South Carolina—have passed similar legislation.

"DO I HAVE TO OBEY MY TEACHER?"

At the beginning of each school year, you may be given a copy of your school's rules regarding what's expected and the consequences for noncompliance. When you break a school rule, you may face civil or criminal action—or both.

Civil action, in the context of school behavior, means that the school may discipline you. It can't lock you up or give you a criminal record, but the punishment may include suspension or expulsion. If what you did also violates your state's criminal laws, you may be charged with a crime (or delinquent act). This means you'll have to go to court[8] and may end up on probation. This may seem unfair, since you get punished by the school and again by the court. But this has been determined appropriate, with no violation of your constitutional protection from *double jeopardy* (being tried and sentenced twice for the same offense).

If you're sent home, suspended, or expelled for disruptive behavior, your parents will be notified. You're entitled to *due process,* meaning you have a right to be heard. You and your parents

---

[8] See chapter 8.

may meet with the principal to discuss your behavior and the consequences the school has imposed. This doesn't happen for every infraction—usually only those that carry serious penalties and inclusion in your school record. You may also be entitled to a hearing before the school board.

Corporal punishment (swats or paddling) in public schools is banned in more than thirty states. However, depending on where you live, it may be permissible in your school, as long as it's not excessive. Physical discipline isn't prohibited by the US Constitution, but it may be limited by state law or school policy. A reasonable amount of force may be used by school officials to break up fights, prevent damage to the school, take weapons from students, or act in self-defense.

Courts consider the following factors to determine if the discipline used at school was reasonable and not cruel or excessive:
- the student's age and maturity
- the student's past behavior
- the instrument used for discipline
- the motivation of the disciplinarian

- the availability of less severe discipline options

A federal court suggested the following guidelines for school authorities using corporal punishment:
- Students must be given advance notice as to what behavior merits corporal punishment.
- Corporal punishment must not be used for a first offense.
- A second school official must be present when the punishment is carried out.
- A written statement about the incident, punishment, and witnesses must be given to the student's parent.

> "The use of corporal punishment in this country as a means of disciplining schoolchildren dates back to the colonial period.... Teachers may impose reasonable but not excessive force to discipline a child."
> —US Supreme Court, *Ingraham v. Wright*, 97 S.Ct. 1401 (1977)

Because of their special position in the community, teachers are given extra protection under the law. Hitting a teacher is a serious crime (aggravated assault) and carries penalties including probation, community service hours, fines, and/or time in detention or a state juvenile institution.

School officials are authorized to discipline students for swearing or making obscene statements or gestures. Although you have the right of free expression, it's not without bounds. The US Supreme Court has held that if your activity is "materially and substantially" disruptive to the school, or if you infringe upon others' rights, restrictions may be imposed. Students should respect *all* school personnel and expect their respect in return.

Unless you're a student, you may not be allowed on school grounds or in a classroom without permission. Interfering with a class may result in charges and penalties for disorderly conduct and trespassing.

Following the February 2018 massacre of 17 students and

personnel at a high school in Parkland, Florida, thousands of students across the country participated in a 17-minute walk-out to protest gun violence. Wylie Greer was a 17-year-old attending Greenbrier High School in Arkansas. He and two classmates walked out of their classes and sat outside. When asked by the principal and dean of students to go back inside, they refused to return to class until the 17 minutes were up. Later in the day they were given a choice between a two-day in-school suspension or two swats with a wooden paddle. They each chose the swats, with their parents' consent. Afterward Wylie commented, "I believe that corporal punishment has no place in schools, even if it wasn't painful to me. The idea that violence should be used against someone who was protesting violence as a means to discipline them is appalling."

"WHAT IF I DAMAGE SCHOOL PROPERTY?"

All students are responsible for taking care of their books and school materials, including digital devices provided by the school. If yours are damaged or lost, you may have to pay replacement or repair costs. You'll also have to pay the repair costs if you commit vandalism at school, such as damaging your locker, breaking a window, or painting graffiti. Stealing or damaging school property may result in suspension or expulsion, as well as having your grades or diploma withheld until the situation is corrected.

If you seriously damage school property, you may be charged with criminal damage or reckless burning, depending on what you did. If someone is injured by your actions, assault or endangerment charges may also be filed against you. Intentional or irresponsible conduct at school can result in disciplinary action from both law enforcement and the school.

> During the 2015–2016 school year, 864,900 violent incidents were recorded in public schools. These incidents included robbery, physical attacks and fights with and without weapons, rape, and sexual assault.
> **Source:** National Center for Education Statistics (2015)

State laws often place financial responsibility for school damage on both students and their parents. In 1996, three twelve-year-olds (two girls and one boy) caused $50,000 worth of damage to an elementary school in Arizona. The children were sentenced to two years of probation, 300 hours of community service each, and $1,000 in restitution to cover the school's insurance deductible. They were also limited to five hours of television time a week while on probation, and they were expelled from their school.

"WHY CAN'T I WEAR WHAT I WANT TO SCHOOL?"

Not only has every parent in America been asked this question at one time or another, so have the nine justices of the US Supreme Court. As a result of a decision they made in 1969, you may be attending a school with a dress code, uniforms, or strict rules about T-shirts and protest buttons.

The case was called *Tinker v. Des Moines Independent Community School District* (89 S.Ct. 733). During the Vietnam War, a group of parents in Iowa protested the conflict by wearing black armbands around town. Worried that the parents' children or other students would do the same, the Des Moines school district passed a policy prohibiting all students from wearing armbands. Any student wearing one to school would be asked to remove it, and if he or she refused, suspension would follow. Three students wore armbands and were suspended. They took the matter to court.

The Supreme Court crafted a test that still determines whether students' freedom of speech and expression can be restricted. The court emphasized that students are "persons" under the Constitution in school as well as out of school. Their fundamental rights must be respected by the state.

The First Amendment protects not only pure speech (spoken or written speech) but also *symbolic speech,* such as a shirt with a slogan or a pin that conveys a particular message. Since the armband was a form of symbolic speech, it was protected by the First Amendment. However, the court determined that a student's freedom of expression at school isn't unlimited. If the expression is "materially or substantially" disruptive to the normal course of events at school, or if it impinges on the rights of others, it may be restricted.

> **"Schools function as a marketplace of ideas.... The 'robust exchange of ideas' is a special concern of the First Amendment."**

> —US Supreme Court, *Keyishian v. Board of Regents,* 87 S.Ct. 675 (1967)

In *Tinker,* the court held that simply wearing a black armband wasn't disruptive to school activities or the rights of other students. This decision opened the door for numerous other challenges regarding student activities on campus. Under the *Tinker* test, schools may prohibit certain items of clothing if it can be shown that wearing them is disruptive to the school environment or creates discipline problems. Certain colors, gang insignias, some sports logos, or displays of profanity on clothes have been banned. Generally, if a school's dress code promotes discipline or good health, it will survive a legal challenge.

> • In support of breast cancer awareness and one of his relatives, freshman Nick Morgan wore a bracelet that read "I ♥ Boobies! (Keep a Breast)." In 2010, a teacher told the New York 15-year-old to remove it while at school. Nick refused and was

given detention. Upon further consideration, the school recognized Nick's First Amendment rights. In 2013, in a similar challenge, a federal judge in Pennsylvania* upheld the wearing of the bracelets at school as freedom of expression that is not lewd or vulgar.

• An Ohio middle school banned baggy, low-slung pants as a safety hazard—too many boys were tripping at school. Towns in other states have banned the public display of underwear, with fines up to $250.

Citation: *B.H. v. Easton Area School District,* 725 F.3d 293 (Pennsylvania 2013)

The *Tinker* decision may also be relevant to a more recent form of protest at schools. In 2016, Colin Kaepernick, the San Francisco 49ers quarterback at the time, started a national conversation by kneeling on the sidelines during the national anthem before games. Kaepernick intended his act of protest to call attention to police mistreatment and violence toward black

Americans. The movement became widespread, inspiring others to protest and #TakeAKnee, including some of Kaepernick's fellow NFL players and other professional athletes as well as student athletes of all ages. While some schools have attempted to discipline students for kneeling in protest, no major court cases have taken place yet that specifically consider this issue. However, related cases from history suggest that the First Amendment's protections would apply. Under *Tinker's* "disruption test," which allows for peaceful protests and symbolic speech, students could silently protest by kneeling as long as their conduct did not disrupt the learning environment.

In response to the #TakeAKnee movement and its legal implications for students, the ACLU of Southern California stated, "Because the law is well-established in this area, and student protests—including those addressing deep and longstanding racial and economic inequities—are consistent with core constitutional values, students, teachers, coaches, and other relevant school personnel should understand that the First Amendment protects this form of student protest."

The same principle applies to hairstyles at school. In the case of *Olff v. East Side Union High School District* (92 S.Ct. 703, 1972) the Supreme Court said, "One's hairstyle, like one's taste for food, or one's liking for certain kinds of music, art, reading, or recreation is certainly fundamental in our constitutional scheme." Even fundamental rights are not absolute, however. In certain circumstances, they may be regulated or limited. If a school regulation (such as wearing a hat or hairnet when working in the school cafeteria, or around machinery in metal or wood shop) is related to safety or personal hygiene, it may be upheld as valid.

These rules also apply to private schools if the school receives any federal funding for programs or students. Otherwise, a private school may set its own rules as long as those rules don't discriminate on the basis of race, gender, religion, or nationality. Some states also prohibit discrimination based on sexual orientation.

Aside from the legal arguments about dress and personal appearance at school, your parents also have the authority to set rules for what you wear. Regardless of what is or isn't allowed at school, if your parents have rules about your appearance or dress, you're expected to follow them.

"CAN MY PROPERTY BE SEARCHED AND SEIZED?"

The Fourth Amendment protects you against unreasonable searches and seizures. Does this apply to you at school? Yes. Does it mean that your locker or backpack are off-limits to school personnel? No.

Your school has a responsibility to you and the community to provide you with an education in a safe environment, and to maintain order in the classroom and on campus. This can only be done when problems are kept to a minimum at school. Keeping guns, gangs, drugs, and violence out of schools is a priority across the nation. Strict rules regarding these activities are legal and enforceable.

Many sixth-to twelfth-grade students report high levels of crime (violent and nonviolent) in their schools. Nearly all students are aware of incidents of bullying, physical attack, or robbery on campus. Whether as victims or witnesses, students worry about school violence.

The leading case on search and seizure at school is *New Jersey v. T.L.O* (105 S.Ct. 733, 1985). This US Supreme Court decision set the standard for school searches. At a New Jersey high school, a teacher caught a freshman girl, T.L.O., smoking in the bathroom. T.L.O. was taken to the principal's office, where she denied any wrongdoing. The assistant principal demanded to see her purse and proceeded to open and search it. He found a pack of cigarettes, a small amount of marijuana, a marijuana pipe, empty plastic bags, a substantial number of $1 bills, an index card listing students who owed her money, and two letters that suggested she was dealing drugs. When the girl confessed to the police that she had been selling marijuana at school, she was charged and placed on probation.

The court debated whether the search of her purse was a violation of the Fourth Amendment. The court ruled that a school official may conduct a search of a student if there is a "reasonable suspicion" that a crime has been or is in the process of being committed, or that a school rule has been broken. "Reasonable suspicion" means more than a hunch that you're up to something unlawful or are about to break a school rule. Based on a totality of the circumstances—time, place, activity, your school record, age, and source of information—the search may pass the reasonable suspicion test. Since T.L.O. was seen smoking in the bathroom, the suspicion that she possessed cigarettes was reasonable. A search of her purse disclosed evidence of marijuana, creating enough reasonable suspicion to search further.

Although the court recognized that students have privacy rights at school, these rights are balanced with the school's need to maintain an environment where learning can take place. The court held that the standard to be applied in school searches is that of reasonableness. This covers not only your person, but your locker, desk, car, and backpack. Some cases have extended legal searches to off-campus incidents, if these incidents are reasonably related to the school.

A girl at an Arizona school was caught with ibuprofen, which the school said violated its antidrug policy. The girl claimed she got the pills from eighth-grader Savana Redding. Savana was taken to the principal's office and strip-searched by two female employees. No pills were found. The US Supreme Court found that the search was unreasonable and violated Savana's rights. The court concluded that "It does not require a constitutional scholar to conclude that a nude search of a 13-year-old child is an invasion of constitutional rights.... More than that: it is a violation of any known principle of human dignity."

Citation: *Safford Unified School District v. Redding,* 129 S.Ct. 2633 (Arizona 2009)

If you find yourself in a search situation at school, the principal and teachers have a right and a duty to question you. When you hear someone say they're "taking the Fifth," this doesn't apply at school unless the police are involved and the person is taken into custody. The "Fifth" here refers to the Fifth Amendment. It means you don't have to say anything that would help the police charge you with an offense; you have the right to remain silent if charges are or may be filed against you. School officials, however, aren't police officers (though your school may or may not have police officers on campus). They have the authority to investigate school violations, and they can question you. You may refuse to respond, which will delay the questioning until a parent arrives and advises you. If you maintain your silence, which is your right, the school may impose consequences.

Cases focusing on searches of juveniles have involved the following situations:

- In 2017, approximately 850 students at a Georgia high school were subjected to pat-down searches for illegal drugs. A case on behalf of the students, claiming that the searches were invasive and violated their civil rights, ended in a settlement.*
- An Arizona court ruled** that the odor of marijuana may justify a search with or without a warrant.
- A principal's warrantless search and seizure of a student's backpack was ruled permissible in an Oregon case.*** However, a warrantless search conducted by the school's uniformed resource officer was ruled illegal in a Washington case.†
- Police need a search warrant to place a GPS device on a person's car according to a ruling by a District of Columbia court.††
- A North Dakota court ruled that although it is a form of search, taking a warrantless DNA cheek swab from

a suspect does not violate the Fourth Amendment.†††

• An Arizona court found that under certain circumstances a juvenile on probation is subject to warrantless searches by the probation officer.‡

• In Pennsylvania, a court ruled that strip searches of juveniles entering detention centers are valid based on the need for safety and security of staff and inmates.‡‡

Citations: *K.A. v. Jeff Hobby, Sheriff* (US Middle District Court, Georgia); **State v. Sisco*, 373 P.3d 549 (Arizona 2016); ***State v. A.J.C.*, 326 P.3d 1195 (Oregon 2014); †*State v. Meneese*, 282 P.3d 83 (Washington 2012); ††*United States v. Jones*, 132 S.Ct. 945 (District of Columbia 2012); †††*State v. Alaniz*, 815 NW2d 234 (North Dakota 2012); ‡*State v. Adair*, 383 P.3d 1132 (Arizona 2016); ‡‡*J.B. v. Fassnacht*, 801 F.3d 336 (Pennsylvania 2015).

"CAN I BE SERVED WITH A SEARCH WARRANT?"

It is law enforcement's job to investigate criminal activity, and part of this process is the collection and preservation of evidence. Consequently, the police may search and seize evidence they believe is relevant to an alleged crime. Anyone, including a teenager, may be the subject of a search depending on the circumstances of the case.

With or without a search warrant, you and your room, car, backpack, locker, cell phone, or computer may be searched. If the evidence sought by the police is not in danger of being destroyed or hidden, they must obtain a search warrant from a judge based on probable cause that a crime has been committed and that you are involved in the investigation of this crime. So, yes, police (or other officials) could serve you with a search warrant. If this happens, notify your parents or guardians immediately.

"CAN I BE FORCED TO TAKE A DRUG TEST IF I GO OUT FOR SPORTS?"

The issue of drug testing at school concerns everyone on campus. While in session, your school is considered your temporary guardian. In that capacity, the school exercises a degree of supervision and control over you. This may include blood or urine tests to check for alcohol or drug use.

> In January 2011, New Jersey's Belvidere School District extended its random drug testing policy to middle school students. Like that of many districts, the policy's primary goals are deterrence and rehabilitation. Test results aren't made public, nor are they sent to the police for criminal prosecution; instead, students who test positive are offered counseling.

In addition to offering the standard courses, your school may sponsor a variety of clubs, organizations, and sports. No law automatically entitles you to participate in these activities. A student *right* is not the same as a student *privilege.* Therefore, the school may legally set standards for participation in the activity, including a minimum grade point average, a clean record regarding school infractions, and drug testing.

Like many other schools, Oregon's Vernonia School District adopted a Student Athlete Drug Policy in response to increased discipline problems and drug-related injuries among student athletes. The policy authorized random drug testing of students who participated in sports. The goals of the testing were to prevent drug use, protect students' health and safety, and provide assistance for avoiding or quitting drugs or alcohol.

In 1991, the district's policy was challenged by a seventh grader who signed up for football but refused to sign the drug-testing consent forms. After a four-year legal battle, the US Supreme Court ruled in support of the school district's policy. In fact, Justice Ruth Bader Ginsburg wrote that consideration should be given to extending the random testing to *all* students, not just athletes. Some schools use a low-tech version of the police Breathalyzer to screen students attending school dances and graduation night parties.

Minors in a school setting don't have the same expectation of privacy adults enjoy. Certain intrusions into your privacy go along with attending school, such as hearing tests, eye tests, and dental screenings. Student athletes have even less privacy due to the nature of school sports—public locker rooms, suiting up together, and so on. By choosing to go out for the team, students voluntarily subject themselves to greater regulation than is usually imposed on others.

In applying the reasonableness test, and by balancing the school's interest in a peaceful campus against the limited surrender of a student's privacy, the court determined that random drug testing for athletes is constitutional: "Deterring drug use by our nation's schoolchildren is … important."

In a 2013 report, 22% of high school students said they'd been offered, sold, or given illegal drugs on school property.
Source: National Center for Education Statistics (2015)

"DO I HAVE COMPLETE FREEDOM OF EXPRESSION IN SCHOOL?"

No one, whether a juvenile or adult (student or not), has *complete* freedom of expression. The government may place reasonable restrictions on our freedoms. For example, city laws about loud noise at night and dancing in the street have been found to be constitutional.

> **"Students and teachers do not shed their constitutional rights to freedom of speech or expression at the schoolhouse gate."**
> —US Supreme Court, *Tinker v. Des Moines Independent Community School District,* 89 S.Ct. 733 (1969)

Likewise, students and teachers aren't free to do anything they choose in the name of free speech or expression. Consider this example from the US Supreme Court in *Hazelwood School District v. Kuhlmeier* (1988):

My father "wasn't spending enough time with my mom, my sister, and I" before the divorce—he "was always out of town on business or out late playing cards with the guys" and "always argued about everything" with my mother.

Under the Equal Access Act of 1984, public school students are guaranteed the right to form extracurricular groups that engage in religious, political, or philosophical discourse. As long as no public school official participates, Bible clubs, atheist groups, the Young Republicans, the Young Democrats, and more are permitted. If some groups like these are permitted, a school cannot exclude other groups based on their positions or viewpoints.

These statements are from a high school journalism class article about the impact of divorce on young people and their families. Other articles covered teen pregnancy, sexual activity, and birth control. They were scheduled to be printed in the school newspaper. The principal, thinking that using the student's name in connection with the passage quoted above would offend her parents, and that the pregnant teens mentioned in another article could be easily identified, withheld the stories from publication. The principal was also concerned about exposing younger students at the school to material that might be inappropriate for their age. The newspaper staff filed a lawsuit, claiming a violation of their First Amendment freedom of expression.

Pledge of Allegiance: Sit or Stand?

In 1943, the US Supreme Court ruled that students do not have to stand or recite the Pledge of Allegiance at school.* While most US states do require public schools to take a moment during the day to say

> the Pledge, your right to free speech allows you to remain seated and/or silent if you choose. For example, 10-year-old Will Phillips of Arkansas refused to pledge to a country that discriminates against gay people, while 16-year-old Devin Booker of Arizona sat during the pledge in silent protest of police brutality.
> **Citation:** *West Virginia State Board of Education v. Barnette*, 63 S.Ct. 1178 (1943).

What do you think? Should the stories have been printed? Should there be a limit on what goes into your school newspaper?

The court ruled that since the paper wasn't a forum for public expression, but would be publicly distributed, the school could exercise control over its content. Teachers are charged with seeing that student activities and personal expression at school are consistent with the school's educational mission regarding fairness and respect. Offensive, vulgar, or racist speech, as well as speech that invades the privacy of another, may be censored in print, student government campaign speeches, and theater productions.

In another case concerning freedom of expression at school, a Missouri court spoke of balancing a school's interest in prohibiting profanity with a teacher's interest in using a certain method of teaching creative writing. Cecilia Lacks was a tenured teacher who taught English and journalism at a public high school. One of the assignments she gave her students was to write and perform short plays. The classroom productions were taped by a school employee. The school board viewed six of the plays and read two of the students' poems and found that they contained "extensive profanity," which violated school rules. They fired the creative-writing teacher. Lacks sued the school district for reinstatement and back wages—and she won.

The court recognized that schools have broad authority to prohibit student profanity. It further stated, however, that it's appropriate to consider the age and sophistication of the students, the relationship between the teaching method and educational objective, and the context and manner of the presentation. Because the context of the offensive language was part of a valid educational objective and not publicly distributed, the court decided it was improper to terminate the teacher. But the court also wrote, "A school must be able to set high standards for the student speech" that is generated at school. Schools may censor expression that is "poorly written ... biased or prejudiced, vulgar or profane, or unsuitable for immature audiences."

Exercising your freedom of expression can have serious consequences even when you don't end up in court. University of Alabama freshman Harley Barber, who was from New Jersey, posted a racist rant on Instagram on Martin Luther King Day in 2018. In the video she yelled, "I don't care if it's Martin Luther King Day.... I'm in the South now." She repeatedly used a racial slur while another girl laughed off-screen. The University of Alabama expelled Harley and she returned to New Jersey, where she and her family were met with death threats after her post went viral. Harley apologized, saying "I'm wrong and there's just no excuse for what I did."

Freedom of Expression and the Internet by Terri Dougherty (Lucent Books, 2010). Information about the complicated and often confusing issue of free speech online.

Free Speech edited by John Boaz (Greenhaven Press, 2006). Explores the challenges of free speech since September 11, 2001. Covers the Patriot Act, commercial free speech, and media consolidation.

Tinker v. Des Moines: Free Speech for Students by Susan Dudley Gold (Marshall Cavendish Benchmark, 2007). Takes a look at the landmark *Tinker* case and examines how it continues to affect students today.

"DO I HAVE TO PRAY AT SCHOOL?"

At a Rhode Island middle school graduation ceremony, a rabbi gave two prayers. Fourteen-year-old Deborah Weisman and her father objected to the prayers, but to no avail. School policy permitted principals to invite members of the clergy to offer prayers at graduation ceremonies.

Deborah challenged the practice as a violation of the Establishment Clause of the First Amendment. The purpose of the Establishment Clause is to maintain a strict separation between church and state. In other words, any government policy or practice must be *secular*—there is to be no state-sponsored religious exercise. States, including public schools, may not advance or inhibit religion, endorse one religion over another, or endorse religion in general. As the US Supreme Court stated in *Lee v. Weisman* (1992), "All creeds must be tolerated and none favored."

> **"Religious beliefs and religious expression are too precious to be either proscribed or prescribed by the State."**
> —US Supreme Court, *Lee v. Weisman*, 112 S.Ct. 2649 (1992)

Religions may be studied or compared with one another, but public schools may not single out one religion over others to teach, nor can the school implement religious practices. Likewise, public schools may not break for certain holy days over others. As a student, you may observe religious days, such as Rosh Hashanah, Good Friday, or Eid ul-Fitr. These days off from school won't be counted against you as unexcused absences. However, you must make up the work for those days, turn in assignments, and take any missed tests.

The government may not coerce anyone, including students, to support or participate in religious exercises. Nor is it the business of government to compose prayers for any group to recite, or arrange for prayers at a function that students are required or obligated to attend.

Deborah succeeded in her challenge. Although her case was too late to change her middle school graduation, it did affect her high school ceremony. The court's decision prohibiting prayer at public school events applies to every aspect of public school education—classes, assemblies, sporting events, and so on. A moment of silent meditation, without any religious overtone, is permissible. Private schools that don't receive federal money don't have these same restrictions.

"WHAT IS TITLE IX AND HOW DOES IT AFFECT ME?"

In 1972, Congress passed the Equal Opportunity in Education Act, popularly referred to as Title IX. The law's intended purpose is to eliminate gender-based discrimination in public schools as well as in private schools that receive federal funds.

Title IX applies to all educational activities, including sports, cheerleading, science and math courses, healthcare at school, band, and school clubs. Equal treatment of students regardless of gender involves a wide variety of factors, including provision of equipment, scheduling of games, locker rooms and practice facilities, medical care, scholarships, and more.

> **"No person in the United States shall, on the basis of sex, be excluded from participation in, be denied the benefits of, or be subjected to discrimination under any education program or activity receiving federal financial assistance."**
> —Equal Opportunity in Education Act, 1972

In addition to adhering to Title IX in public schools, some states have passed their own legislation prohibiting gender-based discrimination in athletic opportunities regardless of federal funding.

- In 2012, 17-year-old Erin DiMeglio of South Plantation High School in Florida became the state's

first female football player on a high school team. She was a third-string quarterback, a position she also played on the girls' flag football team.
- In the 2012 summer Olympics held in London, England, women representing the US brought home the majority of medals—58 in all, compared with the men's 46.
- Three facts everyone should know about Title IX:

1. While people often discuss Title IX mainly as it relates to sports, it also applies to all forms of gender-related sexual harassment and assault, domestic violence, dating violence, and stalking.

2. Title IX applies to public and private elementary schools, secondary schools, and school districts.

3. The law applies to students of any gender and prohibits discrimination based on gender identity and sexual orientation.

"WHAT IS AFFIRMATIVE ACTION AND HOW DOES IT AFFECT ME?"

Affirmative action policies are intentional efforts to promote the employment and education of groups that have historically been discriminated against and marginalized, including minority groups and women. The phrase originated in 1961 when President John F. Kennedy used it in an executive order that required government contractors to "take affirmative action to ensure that applicants are employed and treated during employment without regard to their race, creed, color, or national origin."

So, how does affirmative action apply to you as a teenager? It may have an impact on your continuing education. As you approach the end of high school, you might begin the process of applying to college or a university. Many of these institutions have sought diversity in their student populations through affirmative action. Schools have used quotas as well as

percentages based on race as a factor in accepting incoming students. These methods have been challenged and continue to be litigated in the courts. Three important Supreme Court cases regarding the evolution of affirmative action in education are listed below. For more information about each case, you can search online for the name of the case.
- *Regents of University of California v. Bakke,* 98 S.Ct. 2733 (1978): In this case, the Court upheld affirmative action but struck down the use of race-based quotas in admitting students.
- *Grutter v. Bollinger,* 124 S.Ct. 35 (2003): This case upheld the use of affirmative action based on racial preferences as one facet of choosing which students to admit.
- *Fisher v. University of Texas at Austin,* 133 S.Ct. 2411 (2013): In this case, the Court determined that taking race into consideration may be used as a method to accomplish diversity in a student population. The case was revisited in 2016 (136 S.Ct. 2198), at which point the

Court ruled that the university's race-conscious admissions program was lawful under the Constitution's Equal Protection Clause.

"I'M A STUDENT WITH A DISABILITY. WHAT RIGHTS DO I HAVE?"

Not that long ago, children with disabilities and learning differences were excluded from the same educational advantages given to other students. Beginning in 1975, a number of federal laws were passed by the US Congress that drastically improved the lives of children with disabilities. The Education for All Handicapped Children Act of 1975 and the Americans with Disabilities Act of 1990 (ADA) support the basic principle that *all* children are entitled to a "free, appropriate public education." Schools must take a child's disability into consideration when determining his or her needs and how to meet them.

> **"Our challenges don't define us. Our actions do."**

—Michael J. Fox, actor and author

If you're disabled, you're entitled to a complete evaluation to determine your "unique educational needs." Your school is required to develop an Individualized Education Program (IEP) designed to allow you to benefit from your education. Your parents may participate in developing this plan. It's reviewed regularly to make sure your performance reflects the goals of your IEP, and it may be adjusted accordingly.

> At an end-of-the-school-year ceremony, 11-year-old J.R.'s teachers and classmates gave him three awards: the Pigsty Award, a Procrastinator's Award, and a World's Worst Athlete Award. J.R. has dyslexia (a reading disorder) and dysgraphia (a writing disorder). He also has limited motor skills. He has received special education since kindergarten.
>
> Were the awards in bad taste, or in the spirit of fun? Is the school responsible for promoting equality

among students? Do "joke" awards like these discriminate?

> Here's what happened: J.R.'s father sued the school district for discrimination, and a settlement was reached. J.R. received public and private apologies, and the school district had to pay for four years of his college education and his family's attorney's fees.

Depending on your needs and your IEP, you might be *mainstreamed* into regular classes with the rest of your grade. If you're unable to attend mainstream classes, you may be transferred to a special school or taught at home. The school is required to provide whatever special services are needed to assist with your education, including psychological testing, speech therapy, and medical services. For a state-by-state chart about these special services, see section entitled "Compulsory Provision of Services for Special Education".

For students with disabilities, discipline at school is handled on a case-by-case basis. Your particular disability must be taken into consideration. You may not be suspended for more than ten days or expelled if your behavior is a result of your disability. The law requires that you be reevaluated to determine if a more appropriate school setting is necessary to meet your educational needs. In other words, you may be removed from the mainstream program and transferred to an alternative school.

Your attitude and willingness to cooperate with the services offered by your school will be a major factor in your academic and personal success.

- In 2011, a court granted 10-year-old Jordan Givens permission to take his trained German shepherd, Madison, to school. Jordan has autism, and being close to Madison keeps him calm in class.*
- In 2017, the Supreme Court recognized the right of a 5-year-old girl with cerebral palsy to bring her service dog, Wonder, to kindergarten to help her with daily activities.**

Citations: *Givens v. Hillsboro School District* (Oregon 2011); **Fry v. Napoleon Community School*, 137 S.Ct. 743 (Michigan 2017)

FYI

Americans with Disabilities Act by Susan Dudley Gold (Marshall Cavendish Benchmark, 2011). An examination of this important piece of legislation and its impact on US citizens who have disabilities.

Disability Resource Community
disabilityresource.org
This site offers a wealth of links to helpful resources for people with disabilities.

"CAN I GO TO SCHOOL IF I HAVE HIV OR AIDS?"

Ryan White was thirteen years old when he was diagnosed with HIV, the virus that causes AIDS. He had been infected by treatments for his hemophilia (a genetic disorder that prevents the blood from clotting correctly). In 1985, Ryan was barred from attending his high school in Indiana because school officials were afraid he might spread the virus to others. The family sued the school district, and in 1986 Ryan won the right to return to school. He learned to drive and, although the disease progressed, he never gave up. He spoke at schools and fund-raisers about misconceptions about AIDS. He died in 1990 at age eighteen. Soon after, Congress passed the Ryan White Comprehensive AIDS Resources Emergency Act of 1990, which funnels millions of dollars into AIDS research, education, and treatment.

Some school districts have attempted to keep children with HIV and AIDS from going to school. However, as long as health officials determine that a student presents no danger to others, attendance is approved. Research indicates that casual contact with someone infected with HIV isn't a health risk. If the student's behavior, on the other hand, presents a risk to others (for example, the student is prone to biting or fighting with others), he or she may be kept from regular classes, and a special education plan will be developed.

Think About It, Talk About It

1. You have a friend who plays school sports. What would you do if you found out that he or she smokes marijuana over the summer?

2. Would you tell your parents if a younger brother or sister started ditching classes at school? If not, what *would* you do?

3. Do you feel safe at your school? If not, what are some ways you could protect yourself or feel safer?

4. Would you like it if you had to wear a uniform to school? Do you think all schools should require students to wear uniforms? Why or why not?

5. What if you learned that your best friend tested positive for HIV? What would you say? What if other kids at school found out and started to avoid your friend? How would you respond?

6. Your family has moved and you've started your junior year at a new school. There are numerous clubs and activities but nothing for gay students. You approach the administration to see if you can start an LGBT club and are told no. What do you do next? What are your options?

CHAPTER 3

You and the Internet

> "Off-campus speech can become on-campus speech with the click of a mouse."
> —US District Court, *Doninger v. Niehoff,* 594 F.Supp.2d 211 (Connecticut 2009)

As a twenty-first-century teenager, you were born into a technology-rich "wired" world, heavily influenced by the internet. Our highly connected and web-focused culture has resulted in many exciting and useful ways to communicate, learn, socialize, stay informed, take action on causes that matter to you, entertain yourself, and foster your creativity. However, it also presents challenges for you and your friends—challenges your grandparents did not face. The growth of the internet has, for example, added new complexity to issues regarding your free expression as a student, both on and off school grounds.

You may have asked yourself some of the questions in this chapter. They cover issues that continue to be debated in classrooms, living rooms, and courtrooms across the country.

- Children ages 8 to 12 use social media an average of six hours a day; those between 13 and 18 use social media for up to nine hours a day.
- Tweens and teens multitask while studying; 70% listen to music, 60% text, and 50% use social media.
- In 2017 Washington State passed a law that encourages public schools to offer media literacy, digital citizenship, and internet safety resources. One goal of the law is to help students learn to analyze information from social media and television and think critically about what they're reading.

Sources: Commonsensemedia.org (2015); *New York Times Upfront* magazine (2017)

"IS THE INTERNET PROTECTED BY THE FIRST AMENDMENT?"

In 1997, the US Supreme Court stated that information and communication on the internet are protected by the First Amendment to the Constitution. This means you have a right to freedom of speech while online. This does not mean, however, that anything goes—that you can say anything you like to or about anyone without consequences. The First Amendment provides protection for speech that is reasonable.

The leading case governing student free speech is the 1969 *Tinker* decision. The Supreme Court ruled that student speech is protected as long as it doesn't disrupt the school environment or violate another person's rights. The *Tinker* test has been applied to most of the cases discussed in this chapter. What you do online or through the means of any electronic device—whether by email, in a blog, on a social networking site, or by cell phone—may be censored, and consequences may be imposed if your communication is found to be inappropriate under the *Tinker* ruling.

"WHAT IS CYBERBULLYING?"

The face of bullying has changed in recent years. While in-person bullying still takes place in classrooms, hallways, and buses, there is also a newer form of bullying: cyberbullying. Cyberbullying means bullying someone online or by cell phone. It might involve posting hurtful photos and messages to the internet or sending threatening text messages. The harassment that may happen face to face at school now continues 24-7 in cyberspace, where the effects—like those of all bullying—are long-lasting and often tragic.

Cyberbullying is a global problem. It has, in some cases, contributed to suicide. Sometimes people who bully others online think they're anonymous because they're alone with no witnesses present when they do the bullying.

However, the internet never forgets. Tracking systems can identify the computer or cell phone used to carry out the bullying and, in many cases, can also identify the person doing the cyberbullying.

Not only has cyberbullying been punished at school, in some instances, criminal charges have been brought or civil lawsuits filed against the teenager who did the cyberbullying as well as his or her parents. Students have been suspended, expelled, arrested, and detained as a result of their online and cell phone activities. Many teens and their parents have paid a heavy price for mean and thoughtless emails, texts, YouTube posts, and more.

One example of a cyberbullying case that carried enormous financial costs for a family involved a fourteen-year-old student named Justin. The eighth grader created a website at home called "Teacher Sux." He used the site to criticize teachers and make sexual comments about them. The consequences were emotionally and physically devastating to his algebra teacher, who had to take medical leave for the next year after Justin created a picture of the teacher that morphed into Hitler and asked for donations to "help pay a hit man." This teacher and her husband sued Justin's parents. A jury awarded $450,000 in damages to the teacher and $50,000 to her husband for loss of companionship (*J.S. v. Bethlehem Area School District*, 807 A.2d 847, Pennsylvania, 2002).

- In 2016, 33.8% of students ages 12 to 17 reported being cyberbullied. In the same survey, 12% reported that they had cyberbullied someone else.
- Six in 10 teens say cyberbullying is a major problem for people their age.
- In a study of 5,593 middle and high school students, 6% reported cyberbullying *themselves* (digital self-harm). Students reported that their reasons for doing this included to be funny or entertaining; because they were experiencing feelings of self-hatred; and to see if anyone noticed or reacted. Overall, boys were more likely to say their behavior was

a joke or a way to get attention, while girls were more likely to say they did it because they were depressed.

• To learn more about what you can do about cyberbullying, see the article "Activities for Teens: Ten Ideas for Youth to Educate Their Community About Cyberbullying" at cyberbullying.org.

Sources: Cyberbullying Research Center (2017); *Journal of Adolescent Health* (September 2017)

Bad Apple by Laura Ruby (HarperCollins, 2009). This YA novel introduces Tola, a high school student who must deal with a blog where her classmates publicly gossip about her.

Words Wound: Delete Cyberbullying and Make Kindness Go Viral by Justin W. Patchin and Sameer Hinduja (Free Spirit Publishing, 2013). Written specifically for teens to help them protect themselves and their peers, this book provides practical strategies for those who are being cyberbullied, witness cyberbullying, or want to make their school a safer place.

Define the Line
mcgill.ca/definetheline

This website suggests tips and tricks for staying safe online, being a good digital citizen, and avoiding cyberbullying behavior. (The site also addresses the issue of sexual violence on college campuses.)

NSTeens
nsteens.org

This program of the National Center for Missing and Exploited Children offers free internet safety resources. Find out how to stay in control of your online profile, and watch videos of real-life stories told by teens who have been victims of internet exploitation.

That's Not Cool
thatsnotcool.com

Get advice from other teens on how to deal with textual harassment, constant messaging, and more. Is

someone pressuring or harassing you? Tell them to back off by sending a callout card.
A Thin Line
athinline.org
This site from MTV presents facts, quizzes, real stories, and hypothetical scenarios about the line between digital use and digital abuse.

Before sending your next post, tweet, or email, think about the possible consequences for yourself and your family, and for the targeted person and his or her family. Even posts that are intended to be relatively harmless jokes or pranks can turn into big problems. In a small number of extreme cases, such as those of Phoebe Prince, Megan Meier, and Tyler Clementi, teens have even committed suicide as a result of the cyberbullying they faced. The people who bullied them probably never foresaw the way these cases would end. But *bullycides* are preventable. The bottom line regarding all online activity? **Think before you click, post, or send.**

If you're being bullied on Twitter, on your Facebook or Instagram page, via your cell phone, or through any other means—online or otherwise—*take action.* Don't keep it to yourself. Tell your parent, a teacher, a friend, or a friend's parents. Cyberbullying is against the law, whether through a specific cyberbullying statute or under your state's general harassment or stalking laws.

> If you live in the US, your state probably talks specifically about cyberbullying. In all states but Alaska and Wisconsin, either the term *cyberbullying* is included in a state law, or the state's criminal statutes regarding threatening, stalking, intimidation, or harassment include the phrase "electronic or online harassment." In Canada, the criminal code (Section 264) covers criminal harassment and stalking, and these laws generally cover electronic harassment. Some provinces are considering specific cyberbullying legislation.

> **Source:** Cyberbullying Research Center, www.cyberbullying.org (2018)

"CAN I GET IN TROUBLE AT SCHOOL FOR WHAT I WRITE ON MY COMPUTER AT HOME?"

The short answer is "it depends." If your comments amount to an actual threat to anyone or if they cause disruption at school, then yes—the school may discipline you.

In one case, eighteen-year-old Nick drew his inspiration from a creative writing class at Kentlake High School in Washington State. Students were asked to write their own obituaries. Nick took the project a step further when he posted a webpage from home containing mock obituaries of his friends. A local TV station called the webpage a hit list, and Nick was suspended. But the court found no evidence of a threat or intent to intimidate anyone and ruled in Nick's favor (*Emmett v. Kent School District*

No.415, 92 F.Supp.2d 1088, Washington, 2000).

Another high school student, Justin, was a seventeen-year-old senior at Hickory High School in Pennsylvania. He used his grandmother's computer to create and post a fake online profile of the school's principal.

Justin's parody profile contained silly questions, untrue answers, and crude language. It also included the principal's picture, which Justin had taken from the school's website. Justin sent the page link to several of his friends, and soon most of the student body had seen it. Justin was suspended for ten days and prohibited from attending his high school graduation ceremony.

Justin challenged the school's discipline and won. The court stated that an "internet page is not outside of the protections of the First Amendment." The court also ruled that Justin's parody did not disrupt the school environment or interfere with the school's mission. The school district appealed and the US Supreme Court declined to hear the case, leaving the lower court's ruling in place (*Layshock v. Hermitage School*

District, 496 F.Supp.2d 587, Pennsylvania, 2007).

Additional examples of off-campus speech resulting in consequences at school include:

• A 15-year-old freshman posted on Facebook, saying, "Plot twist, bomb isn't found and goes off tomorrow." The post led to a 10-day suspension followed by a 13-day expulsion. A federal court upheld the suspension, finding that the school did not violate the student's right to free speech or due process.*

• A high school senior posted a rap song on Facebook and YouTube, in which he threatened two teachers. The courts held that this expression was not protected by the First Amendment, and upheld the school board's decision to suspend the student and transfer him to an alternative school.**

• A 10th-grade student sent a string of violent and threatening instant messages to his friends about planning a school shooting. The court found a three-month expulsion to be justified under the *Tinker* disruption test.*** (The *Tinker* test is discussed in chapter 2 under "Why can't I wear what I want to school?")

Citations: **R.L. v. Central York School District,* 183 F.Supp.3d 625 (Pennsylvania 2016); ***Bell v. Itawamba County School Board,* 799 F.3d 379 (Mississippi 2015); ****Wymar v. Douglas County School District,* 728 F.3d 1062 (Nevada 2013)

"CAN A TEACHER MONITOR MY USE OF A SCHOOL COMPUTER?"

Most schools have an Acceptable Use Policy (AUP) included in either the Student Handbook or Code of Conduct. The AUP tells you what is allowed or prohibited at school regarding laptops, cell phones, and other electronic devices. Violating the policy will have consequences that may range from the loss of computer privileges to suspension or expulsion.

Joshua was a seventeen-year-old student in North Carolina. A few days after the Columbine killings—in which two students at a Colorado high school killed twelve other students, a teacher, and themselves—Joshua posted "The end is near" on his school's screensaver. He had permission to use the computers for schoolwork but not for personal posts. Joshua was expelled from school for one year. He was also charged with communicating a threat, and a jury found him guilty. He was sentenced to forty-five days in jail, one and a half years of probation, and forty-eight hours of community service. On appeal, the court reversed the conviction, ruling that there was no evidence of a willful threat to injure anyone or damage property. Although Joshua eventually won in court, he still spent some time in jail (*State v. Mortimer,* 542 S.E.2d 330, North Carolina, 2001).

The duty to comply with AUPs applies to educators and administrators as well as students. For example, schools that provide students with laptops and allow them to take these computers home must respect students' privacy.

Some students at Harriton Senior High School in Pennsylvania found out what it felt like to have that privacy compromised. They were given laptops to use for their schoolwork, not knowing school personnel could activate the computers' microphones and webcams without students being alerted that they were on. An assistant principal told fifteen-year-old Blake Robbins that he was suspected of selling drugs, based on a photograph taken with his laptop. (The photo showed candy—not drugs—on a desk in Blake's bedroom.) A subsequent investigation revealed that Blake had been photographed hundreds of times in a two-week period, sometimes while he was asleep. More than 50,000 screen shots and webcam images were taken, involving approximately forty students. The school later explained that these features allowed them to find missing computers. Students and their families filed lawsuits against the school for invasion of privacy, resulting in a settlement for $610,000. The school also ended its tracking program for missing computers. No criminal charges were filed, since the Federal Bureau of Investigation (FBI) found no criminal intent or wrongdoing by the school.

"CAN I GO TO JAIL FOR CYBERBULLYING?"

Yes, you can—whether you're convicted or not. That's because you can be arrested and taken to jail when you're caught. It may be a few hours or a few days before you're taken before a judge. After that, you may or may not be released before your next court date. Many juveniles and adults spend time in jail or detention waiting for their day in court.

Consider the following examples of cyberbullying and its consequences for the people involved.

> **"There is no constitutional right to be a bully."**
> —3rd Circuit Court of Appeals, *Sypniewski v. Warren Hills Regional Board of Education*, 307 F.3d 243 (New Jersey 2002)

Keeley Houghton and Emily Moore were fourteen years old when Keeley took a dislike to Emily. She assaulted and threatened Emily and wrote on her Facebook page, "Keeley is going to murder the bitch." Keeley pleaded guilty to online harassment. She was sentenced to three months in a young offenders' institution. The judge commented at her sentencing, "Bullies are by their nature cowards, in school and society. The evil odious effects of being bullied stay with you for life."

Some insurance companies now offer special cyberbullying insurance to protect parents (and families) against financial harm that might be caused by their child's online activities. Most traditional home insurance policies do *not* cover incidents of cyberbullying. In fact, many specifically exclude coverage for costs or damages caused by what they call "electronic aggression."

In another case, a Pennsylvania boy posted sexually graphic pictures of himself online. He was around thirteen at the time, and probably forgot all about the images until five years later when some internet surfers found the pictures and decided to taunt the boy with them. Eighteen-year-old Matthew Bean of New Jersey was part of this "electronic mob"—even though he'd never even met the other teen. Bean sent the pictures to the teen's teachers and college administrators. The group made posts including "lets make this kid want to die." The police traced the posts to Bean, who pleaded guilty to cyberstalking. He was sentenced to forty-five days in federal prison, five years of probation, and a $2,000 fine.

If you're charged with cyberbullying or one of its elements (online harassment, stalking, or threatening) and you're found guilty, you could be suspended or expelled from school, placed on probation, required to perform community service—and/or sentenced for months or years in jail or prison.

> One form of online harassment is known as "revenge porn." This is defined as "the distribution of sexually explicit images or video of individuals

without their consent." In one month alone (January 2017), Facebook received 51,000 reports of revenge porn and disabled more than 14,000 accounts for posting such images. Examples of revenge porn include:

- A 19-year-old woman in Texas was blackmailed into having sex with three other teens after an ex-boyfriend threatened to release an explicit video of her.
- A 20-something woman in Pennsylvania had unknown men come to her home after an ex posted her photos and address with an invitation to "come hook up."
- When Leah Juliett was 14, she sent four semi-nude photos to a boy she liked. The following year she discovered they had been leaked online. In 2017, as a 20-year-old sophomore in college, Leah organized a March Against Revenge Porn in Brooklyn, New York.

Currently, 40 states plus the District of Columbia have enacted laws against revenge porn. For example, in 2016, Arizona passed a law prohibiting sharing, posting, or otherwise "disclosing" a nude or sexual image of someone "with the intent to harm, harass, intimidate, threaten, or coerce the depicted person." Under this law, the act is a felony, punishable by incarceration and fines. (A.R.S. 13-1425, 2016)

StopBullying.gov
stopbullying.gov
This resource provides information from various federal agencies on how kids, teens, young adults, parents, educators, and others can prevent and stop bullying.

"WILL MY POSTS ON SOCIAL MEDIA HURT ME LATER ON?"

When Katie Evans was an eighteen-year-old high school senior in Florida, she wrote a critical note about her English teacher and posted it on Facebook. Her comment read, "Ms. Sarah Phelps is the worst teacher I've ever met! To those select students who have had the displeasure of having Ms. Sarah Phelps, or simply knowing her and her insane antics: Here is the place to express your feelings of hatred."

Katie added a photo of her teacher from the school's yearbook, and invited others to add their comments. Only three students posted their thoughts—and all were in favor of Ms. Phelps and critical of Katie. Two days later, Katie took down the post. Ms. Phelps never saw what Katie wrote, and Katie remained in her class for the rest of the semester.

About two months after Katie had taken down her Facebook post, the principal saw a copy of Katie's writing and gave her a three-day suspension for cyberbullying and harassing a staff member. Katie was also dropped from her Advanced Placement classes. She did, however, graduate on schedule with her class.

Katie filed a lawsuit against her high school principal for violating her free speech. She asked for removal of the suspension from her permanent school record. Katie was concerned about her future applications for jobs, graduate school programs, and scholarships. She realized that her future success might be affected by the reference to her as a "cyberbully" in an official record. A Florida court ruled in Katie's favor. The judge stated that Katie's Facebook post had not been threatening, disruptive, or vulgar, and was within her First Amendment rights.

Katie's case is just one example of the many ways social networking posts can lead to difficulty, extra work, or even more serious trouble down the road—even if you win in court. Consider these other real-life scenarios.

> Google your own name every now and then to see if anyone else has posted something offensive about you online or something that might be taken the wrong way if seen by others. Try to have such items removed—especially before applying for an important position or program. Facebook, Instagram, YouTube, and

> other social networking sites have safety controls and policies in place regarding the removal of offensive or undesired material. If you see a questionable comment or post, tell your parents right away. Websites such as wiredsafety.org and netsmartz.org also have tips on cleaning up your online profile.

Sixteen-year-old cheerleader Victoria Lindsay was badly beaten by a group of her classmates in Florida. The group recorded the incident and posted the video on YouTube and MySpace.

All of Victoria's attackers—who ranged in age from fourteen to eighteen—were prosecuted and faced trial as adults. The footage of the assault, showing the girls beating Victoria, was crucial evidence in the case. In effect, it served as the next best thing to an impartial eyewitness. Five of the girls entered guilty pleas and were sentenced to probation, community service hours, and restitution. One of them received fifteen days in jail.

Joshua Lipton was a college student in Rhode Island when he caused a near-fatal three-car collision. He had been drinking and was speeding at the time of the crash. Before Joshua's court date, and while one of the victims remained hospitalized, Joshua went to a Halloween party dressed as a prisoner. He posted pictures from the party on his Facebook page. The prosecutor used the pictures in a presentation to the judge at Joshua's sentencing. The judge admitted being influenced by the pictures and decided that Joshua's actions and his attitude supported a two-year prison term.

Twenty-year-old Hadley Jons was selected as a juror on a trial in Michigan. While the prosecution was still presenting their side of the case, Hadley wrote on Facebook at home that it was "gonna be fun to tell the defendant they're GUILTY." Her post was caught before the trial ended. Hadley was removed from the jury and found in contempt of court. She was sentenced to write an essay on the Sixth Amendment and a defendant's right to a fair trial. She was also fined $250.

Hadley had sworn to be an impartial juror and not to decide the case before all evidence was presented by both the prosecution and the defense.

Online behavior may often seem harmless or temporary, but it can have long-term consequences. In 2017, 10 high school seniors from across the United States were scheduled to start college at Harvard University in the fall. Then school administrators discovered that these teens were members of a private Facebook chat that had formed as an offshoot of the official Harvard Class of 2021 Facebook group. In the private group chat, the teens had posted racist and anti-Semitic comments and memes and made jokes about child molestation, suicide, and pedophilia. After finding this information, the university's administration determined that the students were not a good fit for the Harvard community and withdrew their offers of admission.

"CAN I BE PROSECUTED FOR COMMENTS I MAKE ONLINE?"

While still not commonplace, it is no longer unusual for criminal charges to be filed in cases involving internet use. There may not be an internet-specific law on which to base a charge, but the act of harassment, threatening, intimidation, or bullying using electronic communication may be cause for criminal prosecution.

In 2011, for instance, two North Carolina teenagers were charged with misdemeanor cyberbullying. Justin Ray Jackson, age seventeen, and Joshua Aaron Temple, age eighteen, created a Facebook page on which they threatened a fifteen-year-old classmate. They wrote that they were going to harm the boy, and Justin added "that he was bringing a gun to school to hunt [the teen]." North Carolina law makes it a crime to intimidate or torment a minor through the use of the internet. Joshua and Justin were released to their parents. Both teens were suspended from school for ten days. They completed community service and the case was closed.

> The following cases provide a few examples of the intersection between online activity and the law.
>
> • Do you remember reading about Michelle Carter, age 17, and her boyfriend, 18-year-old Conrad Roy III in section entitled "Introduction"? After Conrad ended his life, Michelle was convicted of involuntary manslaughter for her role in his death. In 2017, she was sentenced to two and a half years in prison and five years of probation.*
>
> • As a condition of probation after committing assault, A.S., age 17, was ordered by a judge to provide the passwords to her accounts and submit to searches—with no warrant needed—by her probation officer and law enforcement.** The court ruled that her environment and lifestyle justified observing her online activities and that this was a key way for the court to monitor "conduct which can endanger her, conduct which will be a violation of probation terms and

conditions." The court said this probation term related to her "future criminality and rehabilitation."

• A juvenile who sexually molested a 6-year-old girl was placed on probation and restricted from using electronic and digital devices unless he had permission from his probation officer.*** He was required to submit these devices for warrantless searches. These terms were approved by an appellate court, holding that they were "essential to [his] rehabilitation, in deterring him from reoffending."

Citations: *Commonwealth v. Michelle Carter* (Massachusetts 2017); **In re A.S., 200 Cal. Rptr.* 3d 100 (California 2016); ****In re George F.,* 248 Cal. App. 4th 734 (California 2016)

In a Florida case, Taylor Wynn, age sixteen, and McKenzie Barker, age fifteen, created a fake Facebook account using the name and photo of a former friend at school. They altered the girl's photo by attaching the image of a woman's nude body to the picture of her face and posted comments suggesting that the girl was willing to perform various sex acts with local men. The bullied girl suffered weeks of ridicule at school until the page was taken down. Taylor and McKenzie were arrested and charged with felony aggravated stalking. They explained that they did it as a joke because they didn't like the other girl anymore and they thought it would be funny. An agreement was reached with the bullied teen, her parents, and the prosecutor: Taylor and McKenzie would admit what they had done, and a Neighborhood Accountability Board would determine their punishment. This is a diversion program[9] allowing the girls to avoid prosecution and criminal records.

Some teens charged with cyberbullying and related online crimes have been able to clear their records, depending on the facts of the case as well as state laws and policies. But that doesn't mean you can say anything online and get away with it. If the

---

[9] See chapter 9, for information on diversion.

content you post online—on your own site or someone else's—constitutes a threat of harm to a person or to property, it may violate a criminal law. Every state has laws regarding threatening, stalking, and harassment. For details, Google the word you're curious about (such as "stalking") and your state's name.

"CAN I GET IN TROUBLE FOR USING MY CELL PHONE AND THE INTERNET DURING TEST TAKING AND PAPER WRITING?"

The age-old problem of cheating at school has an online twist. The widespread use of cell phones has led some students to devise creative ways to cheat during exams. A Common Sense Media survey showed that 35 percent of teens with cell phones reported using their phones to cheat at least once. Methods of cheating include storing information on a phone to use during a test, texting friends for answers, taking pictures of tests to send or sell to other students, and searching the internet for answers during a test.

The internet has also made it easier to commit plagiarism. Some students admit downloading complete papers or reports from the internet and turning them in as their own. Others say they have copied chunks of text from websites and used them in assignments or papers as if they were the authors of this material.

The bottom line regarding digital ethics is that cheating is cheating—regardless of the method. Students who are caught violating school policies on cheating may face suspension or expulsion.

"CAN A TEACHER TAKE MY CELL PHONE AND READ MY MESSAGES?"

Many schools have rules about the use of cell phones and other digital devices at school. You can find your school's policy in your Student Handbook. Generally, school rules limit the use of phones during class and other school activities. Consequences for violating the policy include confiscation of the phone until the end of class or the day. Continued violations may result in longer periods of confiscation and/or require the presence of a parent to get the phone back.

A teacher or an administrator who takes your phone doesn't necessarily have full access to it. The general practice is that if the teacher has reasonable suspicion that a rule or law has been broken, the phone may be searched for evidence supporting the suspicion.

A school security officer at Monarch High School in Colorado saw a student smoking in the school parking lot. He took the sixteen-year-old to the principal's office, where the student's cell phone was taken away. School officials read his messages, transcribing some of them and placed them in the student's file. The student and his parents challenged the school's action, claiming an invasion of privacy and a violation of the Fourth Amendment's protection against unreasonable searches and seizures. The case was settled when the school district agreed to limit searches of cell phones and to obtain permission from students or parents before checking text messages. However, if reasonable suspicion exists of an imminent threat to public safety, school authorities can proceed without permission. A similar policy exists at many schools. Even if the confiscation of the phone is legal, a search of the phone's contents may not hold up if challenged in a court of law.

In another case, R.W. was a seventh grader at Mississippi's Southaven Middle School, which prohibited the use of cell phones at school. R.W. was in class one day when he looked at his phone to read a text message from his father. The teacher took his phone. Later, the teacher and other school officials read R.W.'s messages and looked at his pictures. One picture showed R.W. reportedly throwing gang signs, and another showed a friend of R.W.'s holding a BB gun. R.W. said that he was just goofing around at home. However, school officials claimed he "was a threat to school safety" and expelled him. A federal court felt a jury should decide the case and commented that "there are limits ... upon the power of school officials to police the private lives of their students." The case was settled through mediation.

"CAN I GET INTO TROUBLE FOR 'SEXTING'?"

Sexting is the practice of sending nude or semi-nude pictures of yourself to someone else by cell phone—text messaging with sexual content. In some states, depending on the language of a state's anti-sexting law, sexually graphic text alone—without photos—may also constitute sexting and be illegal.

> In 2016, 18.7% of kids between 12 and 17 said they'd received a naked or semi-nude image from someone through electronic means. In addition, 12% reported sending an explicit image of themselves to someone else. For more information on staying safe and making good decisions, see the article "Sexting: Advice for Teens" at cyberbullying.org.

> **Source:** Cyberbullying Research Center

Some teens have paid a high price for this behavior. Jessica Logan's text message had a tragic outcome. When Jessica was a senior at Sycamore High School in Ohio, she sent nude pictures of herself to her boyfriend. After they broke up, he sent the photos to a few of his friends. Before long, hundreds of students at several schools had viewed the photos. The harassment Jessica endured was relentless. People called her a slut and a whore, teased her, and threw things at her. She became depressed and started skipping school. Finally Jessica decided to go on local television—anonymously—to tell her story. "I just want to make sure no one else will have to go through this again," she explained. Two months later, Jessica hanged herself in her bedroom closet.

Phillip Alpert was an eighteen-year-old high school student in Florida when he and his sixteen-year-old girlfriend split up. While they were dating, she had sent him nude pictures of herself. After the breakup, Phillip became angry and sent the pictures to more than seventy people, including his ex-girlfriend's parents, grandparents, and teachers.

Because Phillip's ex-girlfriend was not legally an adult (in most states you must be at least eighteen years old), Phillip was charged with and convicted of sending child pornography. He was sentenced to five years of probation and required to register as a sex offender until he's forty-three years old. In a 2009 interview, Phillip said, "A lot of my friends have not stood by me ... people don't want to talk to me anymore."

Child pornography is a crime. In most states it is a felony to send, receive, or even possess sexual photos of teenagers or children. And child pornography laws aren't limited to cell phone texting. Using any form of communication (email, instant messaging, and so on) to send and/or receive sexual content involving minors may have dire consequences. Your life will drastically change if you're caught violating existing child pornography laws or the newer sexting laws that some states have passed. This includes nonconsensual posts or what is sometimes called "revenge porn." (See section entitled "CAN I GO TO JAIL FOR CYBERBULLYING?" for more information.)

Because numerous teens have been charged with sexting or possession of child pornography as a result of their school or the police searching their cell phones, be sure to know your rights. Know when the police can and cannot read your text messages. Generally, if the police have probable cause to believe a crime has been committed, they can search a cell phone with or without a search warrant. If you are arrested, the police may confiscate your phone and look through it for evidence of criminal activity.

How private is your cell phone? What rights do others have to search it? The following two cases considered aspects of these questions:

- US courts have addressed cell phone privacy for students as well as persons arrested and in custody. The Supreme Court has ruled that, in most cases, a search warrant is needed to search an arrestee's cell phone.

• An Arizona court ruled that adults have a reasonable expectation of privacy regarding their phones, stating that "cell phones are intrinsically private, and the failure to password protect access to them is not an invitation for others to snoop." However, this does not apply to parents who monitor their children's digital devices.**

Citations: *Riley v. California,* 134 S.Ct. 1609 (2014); ***State v. Peoples,* 378 P.3d 421 (Arizona 2016)

Think About It, Talk About It

1. Aaron was in eighth grade at Weedsport Middle School in New York. On his parent's computer, he designed an animated icon for his AOL instant message page. It depicted a hand-drawn pistol shooting at a person's head. Underneath the drawing were the words, "Kill Mr. VanderMolen" (Aaron's English teacher). Over the next few weeks, Aaron's friends, classmates, and others on his buddy list saw this artwork when he chatted with them online. School administrators eventually discovered the icon, and Aaron was suspended for a semester and kicked off the baseball team. He and his parents challenged the discipline in court (*Wisniewski v. Board of Education of Weedsport Central School District,* 494 F.3d 34, New York, 2007). What do you think happened in his case? Did the court rule for or against Aaron? Why?

2. Seventeen-year-old Ashleigh Hall met Peter Cartwright on Facebook. Attracted by a picture of a young, bare-chested man, she soon agreed to meet him in person. Peter told her his father would pick her up near her home.

Peter Cartwright was actually thirty-three-year-old Peter Chapman, a convicted sex offender. He raped and strangled Ashleigh, burying her body in a nearby field. Chapman was caught the next day. He confessed to the murder and was sentenced to life in prison.

Have you ever friended a stranger online or shared personal information with someone you've never met in person? What do you think are the risks of doing this? What steps might you take to help keep yourself as safe as possible?

3. When Hope Witsell was a middle school student in Florida, she sent a topless photo of herself to a boy she liked at school. Her text was intercepted by a student who had borrowed the boy's cell phone. The image soon spread through Hope's school and even to other schools. Hope's parents grounded her for the summer, and she was suspended for one week from school. Following months of taunting—some of it online or using cell phones—Hope hanged herself from the canopy of her bed. She was thirteen.

If you knew someone who was being bullied online or through text messages—or if you knew a person who was cyberbullying someone else—what would you do? As a bystander, what do you think your responsibilities are?

4. Avery Doninger was a sixteen-year-old junior at Connecticut's Lewis S. Mills High School. She was the class secretary and planned to run for the same office in her senior year. Upset at the school's cancellation of an end-of-year event, Avery sent out a message on her personal blog—from home—urging the community to speak out in favor of the event. In her post she referred to the administration as "douchebags." As a consequence, Avery was prohibited from running for class office. She and her mother sued the school district claiming a violation of her freedom of expression.

As a class officer or athlete, do you consider yourself a role model at school? When you make posts online, what kinds of questions, if any, do you ask yourself first? Has your online activity ever gotten you in trouble? How do you think the court ruled in Avery's case?

Answers

In Aaron's case (question #1), the court supported the school's discipline of Aaron. They found his words to constitute an immediate threat of injury to a specific person. The US Supreme Court declined to hear the case when Aaron appealed the lower court's ruling.

The court also ruled in the school's favor in Avery's case (question #4). Although written at home, Avery's blog was considered on-campus speech since it invited and promoted community activity that would influence a school matter. She and her mother lost their case, and the school's discipline was upheld.

Staying Safe Online Contract
There are many benefits of social networking, online research, and other internet activities. Just be aware of the potential risks and remember to use your common sense whenever you're online. Consider signing this contract with an adult you trust as a reminder to exercise caution online.

1. I will immediately tell a parent or another adult I trust if something online is confusing or uncomfortable, or seems scary or threatening.

2. I will never give out my full name, address, telephone number, school name or location, password, or other identifying information when I'm online. If someone asks for this information, I will first discuss this with a parent.

3. I will never agree to meet someone I've met online, unless a parent consents or goes with me. If we meet, it will be in a public place during the day.

4. I will not respond to any scary message or one that uses threats or words that make me uncomfortable. I will make a copy of the message and show a trusted adult.

5. I will not send any hurtful messages online to anyone or post any inappropriate photos of myself. If someone asks for photos of me, I'll talk to a parent or another adult right away.

6. I will not give my username or password to anyone I don't know in person.

7. I will not open a new online account or download any software without telling my parents.

8. I will not give out a credit card number online without my parent's permission.

Young Person
_____
Date _____

Parent/Guardian
_____
Date _____

CHAPTER 4

You and Your Job

> "There is no substitute for hard work, 23 or 24 hours a day. And there is no substitute for patience and acceptance."
> —Cesar Chavez, American labor leader and civil rights activist

Many teenagers have jobs to help support their families, earn extra spending money, or save for college. You and your friends or classmates might be working after school, on weekends, or during the summer. How many hours can you legally work while you're in school? What about curfew? How do you cash your paycheck? Can you open a bank account? Do you have to pay taxes now that you're employed? These are natural questions for any teen who has a job or is thinking of getting one.

This chapter covers a variety of issues related to jobs and your legal rights in the working world. Coworkers, friends, and your parents may also be able to answer your questions and give you advice.

"HOW DO LABOR LAWS AFFECT ME WHEN I LOOK FOR WORK AND GET A JOB?"

Guess when this headline appeared: "Grim Report on Child Labor—200,000 Kids Will Be Hurt on [the] Job This Year."

During the 1800s? Early 1900s? In fact, the above headline was from a 1990 report on child labor violations in America (the *American Youth Work Center Report).*

We've come a long way from the days when some children worked as many as twelve to fifteen hours per day in sweatshop conditions, and today strict federal and state laws exist to protect minors from hazardous jobs. While accidents and injuries continue to affect young people at work (as well as adult workers), the law provides many more protections for underage employees than it did in years past.

> In 2017, 35% of teens between 16 and 19 had summer jobs. The previous year, the US Department of Labor reported that 42.1% of teens between 16 and 19 were enrolled in summer school.
> **Source:** US Bureau of Labor Statistics (2017); Drexel University (2018)

In 1938, Congress passed the Fair Labor Standards Act, which spelled out specific do's and don'ts for employers. The law addresses three areas of child labor: age restrictions, hours of employment, and hazardous jobs. The states have their own child labor laws that, for the most part, mirror the federal law.

If you're a full-time student, much of the law doesn't apply to you, because you're working only after school, on weekends, and during the summer. You don't need to be concerned about employment contracts, unemployment compensation, health insurance, or other long-term benefits. Once you graduate from high school or college and join the workforce full time, however, these issues will be important to you.

Unless you're eighteen, certain jobs will be off-limits to you. These include logging, railroading, and mining. You also can't work with power-driven machinery, dynamite, dangerous chemicals, or radioactive materials. Once you're eighteen, most restrictions are lifted under state and federal laws.

- In Florida, you must be 16 before you can wrestle an alligator.*
- If you're 11 to 13, you may work as a golf caddie for one round of 18 holes each day in Kentucky.**
- In Massachusetts, you must be 15 to get a license to perform as a contortionist or acrobat.***
- In Arizona, you can check out, package, and carry out liquor for a customer once you turn 16, as long as an adult supervisor is on the premises.†

Citations: *FSA 450.061; **K.R.S. 339.225; ***Mass. Gen. Law 149 Sec.105; †A.R.S. 4-244, 2017

States may also have limits on other hazardous and nonhazardous jobs. In some cases, the age restrictions are lowered. For example, you may deliver papers, bag groceries, or wait tables at a younger age. You may work in a family business before you're eighteen. If your family owns a farm, you may be restricted from operating certain equipment until you're sixteen or eighteen. Some states, cities, and towns also restrict door-to-door sales by minors (to a minimum age and between certain hours).

In addition to age restrictions, prohibited job categories, and limits on working conditions, there are rules about the number of hours you can work. These include:
- no school hours
- when school is in session, no more than eighteen hours per week, and only three hours each day

- when school is out, no more than forty hours per week, and no more than eight hours each day

If you're considering a job that's a little out of the ordinary or has unusual hours, check the library or the internet for the labor laws in your area. They vary among the states and may not follow the federal law described above. In fact, your state may have stricter laws regarding certain jobs. You'll need a Social Security number and possibly a work permit or an employment certificate before you start your job. Your employer will let you know if a permit or other documentation is required.

Can you be fired for no reason? In most cases, the answer is yes. Unless you have a contract with your employer, you're considered an *employee-at-will*. This means your boss can let you go for any nondiscriminatory reason.

Employers may not discriminate against you on the basis of disability, race, color, gender, or religion. The Civil Rights Act of 1964 and the Americans with Disabilities Act of 1990 (ADA) protect you from unlawful discrimination.

Recognizing that 43 million Americans have physical and mental disabilities, the US Congress intended the ADA to provide a clear mandate for the elimination of discrimination against individuals with disabilities. The ADA was amended in 2008, broadening the definition of *disability*.

The ADA requires equal opportunity and treatment for people with disabilities in private and public employment. It also applies to services offered by state and local governments, and places of public accommodation. The ADA covers employers with at least fifteen employees, so it may not apply to you. In addition, the Act doesn't guarantee that you will not lose your position. It only requires employers to reasonably accommodate your disability regarding work schedule, job assignment, and the purchase of specialized equipment. If accommodation creates an undue hardship on the employer, the Act doesn't apply.

The law, however, doesn't require employers to hire you. You still must qualify for any job, and you must be able to do the work once you start. If you believe you have been discriminated against at work or in applying for a job, do something about it. First, discuss your concerns with the employer. You may want to tell your parents to see if they can help you resolve the problem. If these steps are unsuccessful, contact the local office of the Equal Employment Opportunity Commission (EEOC) to review your case.

Summer Jobs Worldwide, 2012: Make the Most of the Summer Break by Susan Griffith (Crimson Publishing, 2012). This resource lists summer jobs in countries from Andorra to Uganda.

Teen Guide Job Search: 10 Easy Steps to Your Future by Donald Wilkes and Viola Hamilton-Wilkes (iUniverse, Inc., 2007). Offers advice on learning what your likes and dislikes are, putting together a résumé, employment sources, dressing for success, preparing for interviews, and on-the-job do's and don'ts.

What Color Is Your Parachute? for Teens: Discover Yourself, Design Your Future, and Plan for Your Dream Job by Carol Christen (Ten Speed Press, 2015). This guide features activities and advice on personal and job-related interests, motivation, interviewing, social media, internships, and more.

Young Worker Health and Safety Website

youngworkers.org

This site from the Young Workers Project provides information regarding safety, workers' compensation, and workplace harassment and discrimination. While the site's focus is on laws specific to California, it also provides valuable information for all teen workers and links for young people in other states.

"WHAT ARE MY RIGHTS AS A WORKING TEENAGER?"

You may feel that you have few rights as a teenager and even fewer while at work. You get the worst hours (usually Friday and Saturday nights) and the dirtiest assignments (cleanup!), and you have to wear a ridiculous shirt and hat—and all for minimum wage. In spite of this bleak picture, you and adults have almost the same rights on the job.

One of your most important rights is the protection you have against discrimination. This means it's against the law for any employer to hire, fire, promote, or pay you based on your race, gender, religion, color, or disability. Your qualifications and job performance are the only valid factors to be considered in evaluating you. The Civil Rights Act of 1964 assures you of these protections, and the law applies to teenagers as well as adults.

Due to federal and state laws about child labor, you may be restricted from certain jobs due to your age (see section entitled ""HOW DO LABOR LAWS AFFECT ME WHEN I LOOK FOR WORK AND GET A JOB?""). This may be a form of discrimination, but it's not illegal. Since most teenagers work only part time, they don't qualify for health insurance, paid vacation, sick leave, or retirement plans. As a part-time employee, however, you are entitled to a safe workplace, and possibly workers' compensation if you get injured on the job. Workers' compensation would assist you with medical bills and lost time at work.

As a full-or part-time employee, you may be drug tested or searched by your employer. It's the employer's responsibility to maintain a safe workplace. If you're suspected of alcohol or drug use, a reasonable search at work is permissible. Your employer may also conduct searches of your backpack or purse for merchandise. In addition, you may have to follow a dress code while at work. It's not discriminatory or illegal if the business requires a uniform or prohibits tattoos or certain hairstyles. Your personal appearance is important to any business, particularly those that serve the public.

Whether you're single or married, your employer can't fire you because you become pregnant. The same is true if you have an abortion. If you've worked full time for at least one year, you're entitled to maternity leave under the Family and Medical Leave Act (FMLA) of 1993. Although there's no guarantee that you'll be paid during your leave, you won't lose your job because of your absence. This applies to mothers and fathers alike.

FMLA also allows eligible employees to take up to twelve weeks of unpaid leave for childbirth, adoption, or the placement of a foster child in the home. It also applies if you are providing for the care of a spouse, child, or parent with a serious medical condition, or for your own medical care. Most teenagers don't qualify, since eligibility requires one year of employment, with at least 1,250 hours worked that year. The Act applies to employers of more than fifty employees, which also eliminates a number of teen parents.

If you believe you've been illegally discriminated against by your employer, take action. First, talk with your parents. They may suggest meeting with your employer to attempt to work things out. If this is unsuccessful, you may want to contact a lawyer with a background in employment law. You can also register a complaint with the Equal Employment Opportunity Commission (EEOC) or, as a last resort, file a lawsuit. You have rights and the responsibility to assert them, so don't be afraid to stand up for yourself.

> Samantha Elauf was 17 when she applied and interviewed for a job at an Abercrombie & Fitch store in Oklahoma. Samantha is Muslim, and as part of her faith she wears a headscarf called a hijab. The store's employee dress code prohibited any head coverings and Samantha was not hired. She challenged the decision, claiming it violated her beliefs and discriminated against her based on religion. In 2015, the Supreme Court ruled in Samantha's favor. In an 8-1 decision, the Court concluded that an employer may not make an applicant's religious practice or apparel a factor in hiring decisions, and that Abercrombie & Fitch's decision to deny Samantha a job based on her hijab violated the Civil Rights Act of 1964, which prohibits employment discrimination based on race, color,

religion, sex, or national origin. This law applies to teenagers as well as adults in the workplace.

Citation: *E.E.O.C. v. Abercrombie & Fitch,* 135 S.Ct. 2028 (2015)

"WHAT IF I'M SEXUALLY HARASSED AT WORK?"

Sexual harassment is defined as any unwelcome sexual advances, requests for sexual favors, and other verbal or physical conduct of a sexual nature. Sexual harassment is a form of discrimination, and it is against the law.

Regardless of your age, you have rights at work. Offensive language or gestures that create a hostile or abusive work environment don't have to be tolerated. If you're harassed by someone, report it immediately. At the very least, tell your parents or guardian. For more information on this subject, take a look at the federal government's Youth@Work Initiative at eeoc.gov/youth.

In 1998, the Supreme Court ruled on a case involving a teenage lifeguard in Florida (*Faragher v. City of Boca Raton,* 118 S.Ct. 2275, Florida, 1998). Beth Ann Faragher had been subjected to uninvited and offensive touching and comments from her supervisors. The court said that supervisors are responsible for maintaining a productive, safe workplace, and that a hostile or abusive environment of sexual harassment is never permissible.

A McDonald's restaurant in Colorado agreed to pay $505,000 to settle claims that a group of teenage girls were subjected to unwanted touching and lewd comments by a male supervisor. In another case, a large movie theater chain in North Carolina paid $765,000 to settle claims that a male supervisor sexually harassed a group of male teenage employees.

"WHAT DO I PUT ON A JOB APPLICATION IF I'M ASKED ABOUT PRIOR ARRESTS?"

You should write the truth. The exact phrasing of the question on the application is important. There's a difference between being *arrested* for a crime and being *convicted* of a crime. You may be arrested by the police, with no further action taken. Even if you're not charged with a crime and are released from custody, the arrest may remain on your record. This means the arrest may show up in a computer check with local police or through the FBI.

If you answer no on a job application when, in fact, you were arrested, you'll have to explain the situation. Employers are reluctant to hire someone who isn't straightforward and honest. After indicating that you were arrested, you might further volunteer that charges were never filed or that an error was made. Explain in a short statement whatever happened at the time of the incident.

On the other hand, the question on the application might be whether you've ever been *convicted* of a crime. Generally, there's no getting around this question—either you were convicted (found guilty of the charge) or you weren't. (Some states use the term *adjudicated* instead of *convicted*.) Simply answer the question. If you feel an explanation should be made, you can add a brief statement.

Having a record may prevent you from getting certain jobs. Depending on the type of job and the nature of your record, an employer can legally decline to hire you. For example, if you have two speeding tickets and you apply to be a messenger for a local company, you're not likely to get the job because of insurance restrictions. Once you're hired for a job, however, you qualify for certain rights and you can't be discriminated against.

"IF I WORK, WILL I BE MAKING MINIMUM WAGE?"

The Fair Labor Standards Act establishes an hourly minimum wage for the US workforce. When the Act was passed in 1938, the minimum wage was 25 cents per hour. Currently, the federal minimum wage is $7.25 per hour. If you're under age twenty, you may be paid $4.25 per hour for the first three months, as a training wage for new employees.

States may set a higher minimum wage than the federal figure, but they cannot go lower. For example, the state minimum wage in California is $11 per hour. In Washington State, it's $12. However, employees under the age of sixteen in Washington may be paid 85 percent of the state minimum wage ($10.20). What you're paid may also depend on the specific job and employer.

If you're a restaurant server, your first paycheck may have surprised you. If you did the math in your head before getting paid, the figure you calculated was probably higher than the one on your check. This is because your tips may be considered as wages. If you make more than $30 in tips each month, your boss may pay you less than the minimum wage, but no less than $2.13 per hour.

Can a worker who is paid by the hour earn more for overtime hours? Yes. For every hour more than forty hours that an employee works each week, the law requires that he or she be paid "time-and-a-half," which is one and a half times the employee's regular hourly rate. This may not apply to you or your friends, because most teens work fewer than forty hours each week. In fact, the law limits you to fewer than forty hours per week while you're in school.

Here's how the federal minimum wage has changed over the years:

1950	$0.75
1970	$1.45
1980	$3.10
1990	$3.80
1997	$5.15
2008	$6.55
2009	$7.25 (where it remained as of January 2019)

See dol.gov for current information and state specifics.

"DO I HAVE TO PAY INCOME TAXES?"

Given the size of your paycheck, you may think that you don't have to worry about taxes. "How could I owe income tax on the peanuts I earn?" Well, neither the federal government nor state governments feel this way. If you earn any amount of money throughout the year, you may have to pay a tax to the state or federal government, or both.

State income tax laws differ, so you'll have to check the rules where you live. A few states—Alaska, Florida, Nevada, South Dakota, Texas, Washington, and Wyoming—have no individual income tax. The federal tax laws, however, apply to everyone who earns an income. If you earn at least $6,300 during the year (January through December), you're required to file with the federal government's Internal Revenue Service (IRS). Many teens working part time don't earn this much.

You may, however, want to file an income tax return in order to claim a refund of any amounts withheld from your check by your employer. While you work, your employer may withhold part of your paycheck. This adds up over the course of the year. When you do your taxes, you'll either owe the government or receive a refund. If you overpaid (too much was withheld from your checks), you'll get the difference back. If you underpaid, you'll owe the difference, which is due by April 15 of each year.

State and federal tax forms come with instructions, but talk with your parents before you try to fill out the forms. Tax laws are complicated, and it's easy to make a mistake. If you have to file, you'll probably use the "EZ" form or e-File online (unless you're married or your income was over a certain amount). As you continue to work and your income increases, you may want to consult with a tax service or an accountant for assistance.

Internal Revenue Service (IRS)
irs.gov

Federal tax information is available 24-7 from the IRS. To find the number in your area, contact your local IRS office or look in a tax form instruction booklet (available at many government offices, post offices, banks, and libraries). Or visit irs.gov to download tax forms and instructions, view tax rules for students, and more. The IRS also posts YouTube videos about tax-related topics including part-time and summer jobs, using tax forms, and much more.

"CAN I OPEN MY OWN BANK ACCOUNT?"

> Kids in some states, including Ohio, Pennsylvania, and South Carolina, may open bank accounts and withdraw and deposit money without a parent's consent.

Between expenses for transportation, personal items, and entertainment, you may be living from paycheck to paycheck. But if you're in the habit of setting $5 or $10 aside each payday, you might want to consider opening your own bank account. Ask your parents for advice on this—if you live at home, you're still subject to their rules. Unless you're emancipated,[10] your parents can decide what you do with your money, including how much you can keep, what you can spend it on, and how much goes into the bank.

> In 2018, Arizona enacted a law authorizing the creation of a personal finance proficiency seal for high school graduates. If a student demonstrates proficiency in personal finance (according to guidelines set by state education officials) and maintains a 3.0 GPA, the seal is applied to the student's diploma and noted in his or her transcript.
> **Citation:** Arizona Revised Statute 15-260

Some banks offer special savings programs to students. For example, they

---

[10] See chapter 6.

may waive their monthly service fees for minors with accounts. This could save you anywhere from $5 to $100 each year. Also, find out what interest rate the bank pays on a savings account. Most banks are within a fraction of a percent of each other, but shopping around may be to your advantage.

A checking account can be a good way to keep a record of your expenses. It's also safer than carrying around a large amount of cash. Some checking accounts pay you interest, while others charge monthly fees for certain transactions. There may be a fee for going into the bank and dealing with a teller, or for using an automatic teller machine (ATM) outside the bank. Make sure you find out about all the fees the bank charges for your type of account. Fees can add up quickly, and you may lose any benefits of having the account.

Money Basics for Young Adults by Don Chambers (Healthy Wealth, 2011.) A comprehensive guide to money matters, this book explains how to open a bank account, manage a credit card, create a budget, and more.

Bank It

bankit.com/youth

Take a virtual stroll through the town of Bankitville, stopping at such common sites as a bank, mall, and car dealership. At each stop, you'll receive tips for dealing with money and questions you can ask your parents.

When you open up a bank account, check your monthly statement for accuracy, and learn how to balance your checkbook. Banks occasionally make mistakes, and these should be brought to their attention immediately. As the amount of money in your account increases, consider investing in stocks, bonds, or mutual funds that can help your money grow. You'll need a Social Security number and the consent of a parent or guardian to make an investment.

"CAN I START MY OWN BUSINESS?"

The general answer is yes. Because many employers won't hire anyone younger than fifteen or sixteen, entrepreneurial teens have found that starting a business is a great way to join the workforce and earn money.

Before starting a business, research the laws in your state regarding businesses owned by minors. Not only do state laws differ, but cities also have their own requirements for retail and service businesses. You may have to get a license to conduct your business as well as a tax number from your city and/or state so you can report your earnings and pay the appropriate taxes.

If you aren't eighteen, a parent or guardian will be required to cosign any papers you need to start your new business. Also, your earnings from the business may not, under your state laws, be entirely yours to keep. Your parents are legally responsible for you until you're eighteen (or until you're emancipated).[11] This means your parents may control your income or require you to save some of it.

The New Totally Awesome Business Book for Kids by Arthur Bochner and Rose Bochner (Newmarket Press, 2007). A revised edition of a book originally written by a financial expert and her 12-year-old son, this book suggests super business ideas for kids and tips for being a young entrepreneur.

Start It Up: The Complete Teen Business Guide to Turning Your Passions Into Pay by Kenrya Rankin (Zest Books, 2011). Practical tips, inspirational quotes, and more on how to transform your talents and hobbies into a profitable business.

The Survival Guide for Money Smarts: Earn, Save, Spend, Give by Eric Braun and Sandy Donovan (Free Spirit Publishing, 2016). This

---

[11] See chapter 6.

book provides the basics of financial literacy and money management for kids—from earning and saving money to spending and donating it.

- There are approximately 25 million teens in the United States. The average annual income of a 12-to 14-year-old is $2,767, while a 15-to 17-year-old earns an average of $4,923.
- Teens spend money on goods including food, clothing, music downloads, movies, and video games. An estimated $264 billion is spent each year by (and for) teenagers.

Sources: ChildStats.gov (2016); Statistic Brain Research Institute (2017)

Think About It, Talk About It

1. Last summer you started your own lawn maintenance business, and you did pretty well. You plan to expand this year and need to hire a helper.

As a boss, do you have to follow all the labor laws? What should you pay your employee? What if he or she doesn't do the job right?

2. You're a server at a restaurant and you like your job, but you have a few questions. Your first paycheck was a surprise—it was short almost forty dollars—and the other employees told you that the boss deducts for broken dishes, misorders, and unpaid checks.

What should you do? With the deductions, you're making only two dollars per hour plus tips. Do you have to put up with these rules?

3. You opened a checking account last year, and things went okay—until recently. Lately you've been writing checks and overdrawing your account by about ten dollars (sometimes more, sometimes less). You've had three overdrafts in the past three months, and your mother is threatening to close your account.

What should you do?

CHAPTER 5

You and Your Body

> "The right to be let alone—the most comprehensive of rights and the right most valued by civilized men."
> —US Supreme Court, *Olmstead v. United States*, 48 S.Ct. 564 (1928)

It's your life, and how you live it is your decision. This chapter will help prepare you for the consequences of personal decisions and privacy rights as they affect your body, health, and physical wellbeing. As a teen, you make many choices, some of which involve health and hygiene issues, sexual behavior, disease or disability, and your overall right to privacy.

Your right to privacy extends to marriage, having children, birth control, family relationships, and education. Teenagers often have a lot of questions when it comes to their health and physical well-being. They wonder about their rights to seek medical care, and whether birth control, abortions, and substance abuse counseling are available to them without parental consent.

These and other personal issues are important to you, your family, and your friends. Even if the situations described in this chapter don't apply specifically to you, you may know someone who needs help. The more you know about your rights, the better equipped you'll be to help yourself and others.

"CAN I GO TO THE DOCTOR WITHOUT MY PARENTS' PERMISSION?"

Most doctors, healthcare professionals, and hospitals require written permission from your parents or legal guardian before seeing you. There are, however, some exceptions to this rule.

The first exception is called *medical neglect*. Since your parents are responsible for your care, if they refuse to take you to the doctor, or if they fail to give you medicine that your doctor has prescribed, the state may step in to make sure your medical needs are met. If you, a sibling, or a friend is a victim of medical neglect, it should be reported to the police or Child Protective Services (CPS). If there's a risk of bodily harm or injury, or someone's life is in danger, the state will get involved. When you call CPS, ask to speak with a social worker and fully explain the situation. You can also call 1-800-4-A-CHILD (1-800-422-4453), which is a national twenty-four-hour helpline, or you can search Google for the name of your state and the phrase "Child Protective Services."

If you're under eighteen and don't live at home, you may be able to obtain medical care without your parents' consent. You're allowed to go to the doctor on your own, for example, if you're emancipated (legally free) under the laws of your state,[12] or if you're married or a parent. You can arrange for your own healthcare if you're pregnant or were sexually

---

[12] See chapter 6.

assaulted—whether your parents know about your circumstances or not.

If your parents are unavailable in an emergency situation and you need medical care or surgery, healthcare professionals may treat you. If your parents are going out of town, they should leave written consent for the person you're staying with to take you to the doctor if necessary.

Due to an increase in substance abuse by young people, a number of states have lowered the minimum age for receiving treatment and counseling without parental consent. In some states, a twelve-year-old may independently obtain alcohol and drug counseling. If you're in a treatment program under these circumstances, your identity is kept confidential and is disclosed to others only with your consent.

Teenagers can also receive healthcare on their own for the diagnosis and treatment of sexually transmitted diseases (STDs) such as herpes, gonorrhea, and syphilis. In most parts of the country, you have these same rights regarding diagnosis for HIV and AIDS. At very little or no cost, you may go to a clinic for diagnosis and counseling. Some family planning clinics, for example, charge twenty dollars for an HIV/STD test and counseling. The cost for treatment may also be on a sliding scale basis (in which the fee is adjusted depending on how much you're able to pay), or you may be eligible for public assistance.

For specific information on your state's laws about seeking medical care, contact your library, health department, or family doctor. Check out the issue of healthcare costs. For example, who is legally responsible for your bills if you seek treatment without your parents' consent? Find this out in advance! The number for your local public health agency is online, or you can call directory assistance (411 in the US) and ask for the number.

- According to the Centers for Disease Control and Prevention (CDC), 8,451 young people between the ages of 13 and 24 were diagnosed with HIV in 2016 in the United States. This

represented 21% of all the new diagnoses in the US that year.
- There are an estimated 20 million new cases a year of reported STDs and STIs (sexually transmitted infections). One half of these are among 15-to 24-year-olds.
- The CDC reported that in 2016 a record number of new STD cases were reported, with more than 2 million cases of chlamydia, gonorrhea, and syphilis.

Source: Centers for Disease Control and Prevention (2017 and 2018)

FYI

My Life After Now by Jessica Verdi (Sourcebooks, 2013). This poignant story follows a 16-year-old girl whose life changes forever when she discovers she's HIV-positive.

Teenagers, HIV, and AIDS: Insights from Youths Living with the Virus edited by Maureen E. Lyon and Lawrence J. D'Angelo (Praeger,

2006). Essays from experts as well as statements from HIV-positive teens present information about the virus, how to deal with a diagnosis, and how to support a friend who's living with HIV or AIDS.

The Body: The Complete HIV/AIDS Resource
thebody.com

Information, resources, support organizations, hotlines, insight from experts, forums for connecting with others, and much more. A comprehensive, up-to-the-minute site.

HIV Positive!
hivpositivemagazine.com

The website for the nationally recognized magazine is a great way to find help, statistics, and updates on medical progress in the field of HIV research.

I Wanna Know!
iwannaknow.org

A website maintained by the American Sexual Health Association, this is a reliable resource for information on sexuality and STDs. Learn how to prevent STDs, ask an expert questions via email, and check out other straight-talk sites listed on the links page.

National Prevention Information Network (from the Centers for Disease Control and Prevention)
npin.cdc.gov

This website provides information and support on a variety of health topics, including HIV/AIDS. While it is intended mainly for health professionals, the site contains a wealth of statistics, links, and other resources. The CDC also has an information hotline at 1-800-CDC-INFO (1-800-232-4636).

"CAN I DONATE MY BLOOD AND ORGANS?"

Generally, you can't give blood until you're eighteen. Once you're an adult, the decision is yours. A few states allow younger teens to donate blood with written consent from their parents and/or a doctor.

You might also have to meet certain health and minimum weight requirements before you're allowed to donate. For example, the American Red Cross requires you to weigh at least 110 pounds. If you're HIV-positive, they won't accept your donation. It's always best to check with your family doctor if you have any concerns. Discuss your thoughts and plans with your parents too.

Although some blood banks pay donors each time they come in, teens are generally not eligible. If you're emancipated[13] and your state law permits payment to minors, you can keep the payment. If you're not emancipated, your parents have a say about any money you receive.

You may also donate your organs when you die. If you're eighteen, you may advise the National Kidney Foundation, for example, that you wish to be a kidney donor. When you apply for your driver's license, there's a question regarding organ donation, and

---

[13] See chapter 6.

your donor status is marked on your license.

American Red Cross
1-800-733-2767
redcross.org

At the Red Cross website you can find information about being a blood donor, or contact your local blood bank or plasma center. Many blood centers also have information about organ and tissue donations.

"WHAT CAN I DO IF I'M BEING ABUSED OR NEGLECTED?"

Each year in the United States, approximately 3.6 million reports of child abuse and neglect are made regarding more than 6 million children (leading to 3.2 million investigations). Five children die *every day* at the hands of their parents or caregivers.

Abuse may be:

- physical (acts that cause physical injury)
- sexual (sexual activity that provides gratification or financial benefit to the *perpetrator,* or the person committing the abuse, such as sexual conduct, prostitution, pornography, or sexual exploitation)
- emotional (acts or omissions that cause emotional distress and/or mental disorders in a child)

Neglect may be:
- physical (including abandonment and/or failure to provide supervision, healthcare, adequate food, clothing, or shelter)
- emotional (including inadequate nurturance or a disregard for a child's emotional or developmental needs)
- educational (including permitting chronic truancy or otherwise disregarding the child's educational needs)

Child abuse and neglect are against the law. If you witness or hear about an incident of abuse or neglect, you should report it to the police or Child Protective Services (CPS). Every state has mandatory reporting laws spelling out the legal obligations of teachers, doctors, social workers, and others who are responsible for the care, custody, and control of children. A *required reporter* under state law who fails to report suspected child abuse or neglect has violated the law and may be charged with a misdemeanor or felony.

CPS is a state government agency charged with the duty to investigate abuse, neglect, and abandonment cases. In most states, CPS provides services to families to help them solve their problems and stay together. For example, parents may discipline their child, but if the punishments are excessive—for example, leaving welts or bruises—the police and courts may get involved to protect the child. If a child is removed from the home and placed in foster care, services are offered to assist in reuniting the family. If the parents are unsuccessful in their efforts to have their child returned to them, or if they refuse to cooperate, the child may stay with relatives or remain in foster care or an adoptive home.

The following cases highlight how seriously family and juvenile courts consider the welfare and best interests of children.

- A mother's parental rights to her daughter were terminated based on her neglect in protecting her from or reporting sexual abuse by others.*
- A child who has not been abused may become a ward of the court based on the physical abuse of his siblings.**
- A father was found guilty of neglecting his 2-year-old son by exposing him to multiple drug transactions on the street. He held the boy for 20 minutes while conducting drug deals in a neighborhood known for drug violence.***
- A mother left her 6-year-old daughter home alone overnight. The court did not accept her explanation that the child was "supervised" by the home alarm system. The facts supported a finding of neglect.†
- A court determined that a father's inability and failure to provide

suitable housing for his children amounted to neglect. The court ruled that the children would become wards of the court.††

Citations: *Traci E. v. Dep't of Child Safety,* 2017 WL 976996 (Arizona 2017); **Michele T. v. Dep't of Child Safety,* 2016 WL 5799473 (Arizona 2016); ***Thompson v. State,* 139 So. 377 (Florida 2014); †*T.J. v. Missouri Department of Social Services,* 305 S.W.3d 469 (Missouri 2010); ††*Michael S. v. Dep't of Child Safety,* 2017 WL 1024499 (Arizona 2017)

If you're in danger, or you know someone who's injured or has been abused at home, tell someone you trust. A teacher, school nurse, or police officer will be able to help. If a friend tells you that he or she has been sexually molested, tell a responsible adult. You're protected under the law when reporting suspected abuse or neglect. As long as you're truthful in reporting, the law protects you from liability. You may also report anonymously (without giving your name), although identifying yourself might help the investigation.

> - An estimated 676,000 cases of child maltreatment were reported in 2016. Neglect is the most common form of child maltreatment.
> - In 2016, there were an estimated 1,750 deaths from abuse and neglect, with 70% of these victims under the age of 3.
> - Among juvenile victims of sexual abuse, 90% know the person who abuses them.
>
> **Sources:** rainn.org; ChildHelp.org; KidsCount.org; Centers for Disease Control and Prevention; US Department of Health and Human Services

FYI

Childhelp National Child Abuse Hotline
1-800-4-A-CHILD (1-800-422-4453)
childhelp.org
Crisis counseling, referrals, information, and support for US and

Canadian teens, children, and adult survivors.

Child Welfare Information Gateway

1-800-394-3366

childwelfare.gov

Referrals and resource information, sponsored by the US Department of Health and Human Services. Open 9:30a.m.–5:30p.m. EST.

National Domestic Violence Hotline

1-800-799-SAFE (1-800-799-7233)

thehotline.org

Callers can be connected directly to help in their communities, including emergency services and shelters, as well as receive information and referrals, counseling, and assistance in reporting abuse. Calls to the hotline are confidential, and callers may remain anonymous if they wish.

"CAN I GET BIRTH CONTROL?"

If you choose to be sexually active, it's important to know your rights regarding birth control. Regardless of your age, the law allows you to obtain birth control, whether prescription or nonprescription. Condoms, foam, and spermicidal gels are available from drugstores, pharmacies, and grocery stores without a prescription. With a doctor's prescription, you can get birth control pills, an IUD, or a diaphragm.

The law doesn't require your parents' consent for birth control. Public health agencies (many of which are based in county or city hospitals) or family planning clinics may be able to assist you. Costs vary from no fee to sliding scale fees, depending on your income, or you may be charged higher amounts based on the services you use.

If you're sexually active, be aware of the consequences of unprotected sex and of pregnancy. You can contact a local clinic or agency for information and counseling. If the agency receives federal money for family planning services, it's required by law to maintain your confidentiality. Planned Parenthood is one such agency. When first contacting the agency, feel free to ask about their policies regarding your privacy rights.

- In a 2017 CDC study surveying 15-to 19-year-olds, 42.4% of never-married girls and 44.2% of never-married boys reported having had sexual intercourse at least once. These figures represented a slight decline since 2002 (from 45.5% of girls and 45.7% of boys).
- The same CDC study found that among the 57.6% of teen girls and 55.8% of teen boys who reported not having had sex yet, their reasons for waiting included because it was against their morals and religion, they hadn't found the right person, or they didn't want to risk pregnancy.
- In 2016, about 209,000 babies were born to teens ages 15 to 19. That number was down 9% compared with 2015, primarily due to more

teens waiting to have sex and more effective use of contraception.

Sources: Centers for Disease Control and Prevention (2017); US Department of Health and Human Services (2016)

Your school may offer sex education classes. Although you can't be forced or required to take such a class, learning the facts about sex from an objective and informative course can help you make intelligent decisions about sex. Discuss the sex education class option with your parents. You may also be able to review an outline of the course before deciding whether to take it. Keep in mind that not every school will offer comprehensive or objective classes. For example, studies have shown that abstinence-only education is ineffective, but it may be all that's available at your school.

Changing Bodies, Changing Lives: A Book for Teens on Sex

and Relationships by Ruth Bell (Three Rivers Press, 1998) This classic book offers frank, straightforward information—without judgment—on birth control, sexually transmitted diseases, pregnancy, and more.

S.E.X.: The All-You-Need-to-Know Sexuality Guide to Get You Through Your Teens and Twenties by Heather Corinna (Da Capo Press, 2016). This book spells out what you need and want to know about sex, providing comprehensive and accurate information in clear, straightforward language and without judgment.

Sexuality and Teens: What You Should Know About Sex, Abstinence, Birth Control, Pregnancy, and STDs (Issues in Focus Today) by Stephen Feinstein (Enslow Publishers, 2009). A balanced look at sexuality, contraception, and more.

Info for Teens
plannedparenthood.org/teens
This site from Planned Parenthood incorporates advice from teen

contributors and provides solid information on sexuality so that teens are empowered to make responsible choices.

Sex, Etc.

sexetc.org

A website by and for teens, this is a great place to read about the experiences of others who are going through some of the same things you might be. Get the scoop on dating, relationships, sex, STDs, and more.

TeensHealth

kidshealth.org/en/teens/sexual-health

Teens will find information about STDs (including the top five myths about them), tips for talking with a sexual partner about condoms, HIV and AIDS, and birth control.

In 2007, a Portland, Maine, middle school voted to provide birth control to students with parental permission. The full range of contraceptives was made available through the school's health center for 6th to 8th graders.

"CAN I GET AN ABORTION WITHOUT TELLING MY PARENTS?"

In 1973, Justice Harry Blackmun wrote the majority opinion for the US Supreme Court in *Roe v. Wade* (93 S.Ct. 705), the now-famous abortion decision. He wrote that the Fourteenth Amendment's protection of liberty is broad enough to include a woman's decision regarding her pregnancy: "[T]he right of personal privacy includes the abortion decision ... but ... this right is not unqualified."

The court balanced your right to privacy against the state's interest in protecting a *viable fetus*—a fetus that could survive outside of its mother before natural birth. Consequently, during the first trimester of pregnancy (which ends approximately twelve weeks after conception) you may obtain an abortion. During the second trimester, states may impose restrictions regarding the life and health of the mother; during the final trimester, states may prohibit abortion altogether.

> In 2014, approximately 652,600 abortions were performed in the United States. Girls under the age of 15 had 0.3% of the reported abortions, and girls ages 15 to 19 had 10.4% of the total. Among 15to 19-year-olds, this represented a 49% drop in their abortion rate since 2005.
> **Source:** Centers for Disease Control and Prevention (2017)

In a later case, *Bellotti v. Baird* (96 S.Ct. 2857, 1976), these abortion rights were extended to teen mothers. Whether you're single, married, separated, or divorced—regardless of your age—you may get an abortion.

The issue of parental consent has also been raised and decided. A state may require either a parent or a court to consent to a minor's abortion. In requiring a parent's consent or notification, the law must also include what is called a *judicial bypass* procedure. If a parent refuses to give consent, or if notifying the parent would endanger the minor, the parent may be bypassed and consent obtained from a court. In other words, neither your parents nor the father of the child has absolute veto power over your decision. Nor can your parents force you to have an abortion. Your privacy rights allow you to make the final decision.

Under the appropriate circumstances, you may petition the court directly for its consent. The judge will meet with you and possibly your lawyer (if one has been assigned to represent you) to discuss the situation. You may also have a counselor with you. It's the court's job to make sure you understand the decision to abort and you have received counseling regarding the alternatives to abortion. Even if the judge finds that you lack the maturity to make an intelligent decision, consent may still be given based on what's in your best interests.

Before making a decision, take time to learn about your options. Talk with someone you trust. If you decide against abortion, contact a local family planning agency to get information about foster care and adoption. You have the right to keep your child, sometimes with the help of the state (depending on your age), just as you have the right to place your child up for adoption.[14] Consider *all* your options before deciding what to do.

Abortion: Opposing Viewpoints Series edited by David M. Haugen (Greenhaven Press, 2010). Multiple authors discuss the controversies surrounding abortion and public policy. Covers *Roe v. Wade,* stem-cell research, ethics, and legislation.

Planned Parenthood Locator Service
1-800-230-7526
plannedparenthood.org

Call this number or visit the website to find the Planned Parenthood office nearest you. They offer counseling on birth control, abortion, alternative placement options (foster care and adoption), and more. The service is free and confidential;

---

[14] See chapter 1.

parental consent isn't required. A translator service is also provided.

"WHAT IS RAPE?"

"Was it rape?" "I told him no, but he wouldn't stop!" "I've known him for years—I thought he respected me." These are common statements from victims of rape. In the last several decades, people have become more aware of issues surrounding rape, sexual assault, and consent. Yet rape and sexual assault continue to be significant issues and incidents of both remain underreported.

Rape means having sexual intercourse with someone forcibly and without his or her consent. Rape can occur between a male and a female or two people of the same gender; either a male or a female may commit rape. In *gang rape,* a person is raped by several different people. Reports indicate that in the US, an average of 321,500 people age twelve and older are victims of rape and sexual assault each year.

It may also be considered rape, and therefore a crime, if both parties consent to sex but one person is under a certain age. Some states have established a minimum age at which a person can legally consent to having intercourse. If you have sex with someone under the legal age limit, even if it's with the consent of the underage person, you've broken the law. A violation is referred to as *statutory rape,* which is a felony.

If the victim of a rape is injured, or if the incident involves a weapon, threats, or violence, the act becomes *aggravated rape.* This crime carries a greater penalty than other forms of rape.

Rape statistics from the latest reporting year (2014) show that:
- 1,944 juveniles were arrested for rape.
- 33% were under age 15.
- 67% were ages 15–17.
- every 98 seconds someone is sexually assaulted in the US, and every 8 minutes, that victim is a child.

Sources: *Juvenile Offenders and Victims: A National Report,* National Center for Juvenile Justice (2014); rainn.org (Rape, Abuse and Incest National Network)

F Y I

Frequently Asked Questions About Date Rape by Tamra B. Orr (Rosen Publishing Group, 2007). This book explains what date rape is and makes it clear that the victim is never at fault.

Past Forgiving by Gloria D. Miklowitz (Simon & Schuster, 1995). Fifteen-year-old Alexandra finds that her boyfriend, Cliff, demands all of her time, isolates her by his jealousy, and finally becomes physically abusive. A compelling novel, honest in its exploration of date rape and how love can go wrong.

Sexual Assault: The Ultimate Teen Guide by Olivia Ghafoerkhan (Rowman & Littlefield Publishers, 2017). This book educates readers on sexual assault (including numerous myths about it), while also showing them how to help both themselves and their friends.

RAINN (Rape, Abuse and Incest National Network)
1-800-656-HOPE (1-800-656-4673)
rainn.org

RAINN is the nation's largest anti-sexual-assault organization and operates the National Sexual Assault Hotline. Calls are routed to a rape crisis center in the caller's area code.

In cases of *date rape*, victims usually know their offenders. The offender can be a longtime friend or casual acquaintance. Drugs and alcohol often contribute to date rapes. Some experts suspect that only one out of ten date rapes is reported. Because of low reporting, and the even lower incidence of prosecution and conviction, education may be the most effective way to deal with date rape.

Many high schools and colleges offer orientation programs aimed at rape awareness and prevention. Some college fraternities and sororities conduct similar programs. They advise students to always be on the alert, to walk with friends at night, and to carry pepper spray, mace, or a whistle. Students are also advised to remain sober to lessen the risk of rape. Additionally, efforts are being made to educate young men and women about consent, which can be defined as "a knowing and voluntary agreement to engage in specific sexual activity at the time of the activity."[15]

If you're a victim of rape or a rape attempt, *get help.* Call a crisis line, tell your parents, or tell a friend, and report the crime to the police. Provide as much identifying information about the perpetrator as you can: a physical description, make and color of car, and any other details you can recall. More details will increase the chance for an arrest and conviction. If you suffer visible injuries in the assault, let the police, a doctor, or a friend take pictures of you. This type of physical evidence is invaluable at trial.

---

[15] Source: Northwestern University code of conduct

- In 2015, about 321,000 incidents of sexual assault were reported to the police. An estimated 70% of incidents are not reported to the police, 71% of victims know their assailant, and only 6% of rapists spend time in jail or prison.
- People between the ages of 12 and 34 are at the highest risk of sexual violence.

Source: Rape, Abuse and Incest National Network

"DO I LOSE ANY RIGHTS IF I'M PREGNANT?"

Not so long ago, the answer to this question was a definite yes. In the 1970s, you could have been asked to drop out of school if you were an unwed pregnant minor, or you could have lost your job for taking maternity leave.

The law now allows you to continue your education if you're pregnant. You can't be discriminated against because you're pregnant or because you've had an abortion. Some school districts offer programs for pregnant teens, allowing them to obtain prenatal care and parenting classes while also staying on track with academic schoolwork. Check to see if your district offers these opportunities.

You can also obtain prenatal medical care with or without your parents' consent. If your parents know about the pregnancy and are supportive, all the better. But if they don't know, or if they oppose it, you can still get the medical attention you and the baby need.[16]

In 1978, the Pregnancy Discrimination Act regarding employment was passed. The Act applies to you whether you're a teenager or an adult. It prohibits any discrimination based solely on your medical condition resulting from an abortion or a pregnancy. If you're a full-time employee, you can take maternity leave (often without pay) without fear of losing your job. This affects few

---

[16] See chapter 5.

teenagers because most aren't employed full time. Depending on the circumstances, however, maternity leave may apply to teenage parents. States may have their own laws on this subject, so check into your local rules or contact the Equal Employment Opportunity Office (EEOC).

The courts have gone one step further in eliminating discrimination against women in the workplace. The Supreme Court ruled in 1991 that employers can't exclude women of childbearing age from jobs that pose reproductive hazards, such as industrial jobs. Gender-based discrimination, whether to protect the mother or her future children, is unlawful.

National Campaign to Prevent Teen and Unplanned Pregnancy
(202) 478-8500
thenationalcampaign.org
This site presents research and facts about teen pregnancy. Read others' stories, learn about STDs, and much more.

National Responsible Fatherhood Clearinghouse

fatherhood.gov

This website from the US Department of Health and Human Services offers strategies to encourage, strengthen, and support fathers of all ages in their parenting journeys.

Text4baby

text4baby.org

This free cell phone text messaging service, available in English and Spanish, is intended for women or teens who are pregnant or are new moms. Timed to the date of the baby's birth (or the projected due date), texts are sent three times a week with information on how to have a healthy pregnancy and a healthy infant. People can sign up by texting BABY (or BEBE for Spanish) to 511411.

"WHAT IF I'M DEPRESSED OR THINKING ABOUT SUICIDE?"

Everyone, regardless of age or circumstances, occasionally feels overwhelmed, stressed out, or sad. Sadness, loneliness, or feelings of alienation from family and friends can hit anyone at any time.

Whatever is troubling you—no matter how big the problem—help is available. Trained professionals can be reached at any time. Their services are confidential and nonjudgmental, and their purpose is to listen to you and offer suggestions to help you deal with what's going on in your life.

- Suicide is the third leading cause of death for kids ages 10 to 24 in the United States. In 2014, 425 US middle school students (ages 10 to 14) took their own lives.
- Nationwide, 16% of students report that they have seriously considered suicide.

- Girls are twice as likely as boys to think about suicide, while boys are four times more likely to die by suicide.
- A study in 2015 of a half-million teens ages 13 to 18 indicated 36% reported feeling very sad or hopeless, having thoughts of suicide, or planning or attempting suicide, compared with 32% in 2009. The same study found that 19% of teens used electronic devices (including smartphones) for 5 hours or more each day, compared with 8% in 2009. Experts are not yet sure whether a clear link exists between these findings but say that more research is needed.
- In April 2017, American rapper Logic released his song "1-800-273-8255"—the phone number of the National Suicide Prevention Lifeline. In August of that year, he performed the song at MTV's Video Music Awards. He played the song again at the Grammy Awards in February 2018. Following all three dates, calls to the lifeline increased dramatically for a period of time.

> **Sources:** Centers for Disease Control and Prevention (2017); *Clinical Psychological Science* (November 2017)

You may have a friend or an acquaintance who's feeling depressed or suicidal. Or perhaps he or she has already dealt with depression and could help you get through yours. Reach out and discuss the problem with someone you trust. If you're concerned about a friend, offer to help. If the situation is serious and you think your friend may hurt himself or herself, take action. Tell your parents, your friend's parents, or another responsible adult. Every state has laws regarding emergency mental healthcare. A brief placement in a hospital (twenty-four to seventy-two hours) for evaluation can start the healing process. In 2018, the American Academy of Pediatrics (AAP) issued new guidelines urging doctors to screen all young people ages twelve to twenty-one for depression annually at routine checkups or other office visits, and to treat the disorder earlier and more aggressively. The AAP argued that early detection and treatment of adolescent depression could help prevent suicide.

Whatever the issue—whether it's bullying, relationship problems, family issues, drugs, or something else—help is nearby. See the following FYI section for hotlines staffed with trained counselors. Call for help if you're suffering from depression or thinking about suicide.

Boy Meets Depression: Or Life Sucks and Then You Live by Kevin Breel (Harmony Books, 2015). In this book a young mental health activist demystifies depression with a personal account of his own struggle. He writes to bring hope and light to people in pain.

The Power to Prevent Suicide: A Guide for Teens Helping Teens by Richard E. Nelson and Judith C. Galas (Free Spirit Publishing, 2006). This book helps teens understand the causes of suicide, recognize the signs, and reach out to save a life.

When Nothing Matters Anymore: A Survival Guide for Depressed Teens by Bev Cobain (Free Spirit Publishing, 2007). Describes causes and types of depression, treatment options, and ideas for staying healthy. Includes real teen stories, survival tips, and resources.

American Association of Suicidology

(202) 237-2280

suicidology.org

This organization provides information, statistics, research, and education for those involved with suicide prevention or those touched by suicide.

Boys Town National Hotline

1-800-448-3000

boystown.org

Boys Town offers compassionate care for at-risk kids around the country. Parents, teens, and families can call the Boys Town 24-7 hotline to speak with trained counselors for help with depression, abuse, relationships, chemical dependency, and more.

Kids Help Phone

1-800-668-6868

kidshelpphone.ca

A toll-free Canadian telephone counseling service for young people ages 4–19.

National Runaway Safeline

1-800-RUNAWAY (1-800-786-2929)

1800runaway.org

Immediate crisis intervention, support, and referrals for runaways and those who are in crisis. Help is available for teens and adults.

National Suicide Prevention Lifeline

1-800-273-TALK (1-800-273-8255)

This 24-hour, toll-free, confidential suicide prevention hotline is available to anyone in suicidal crisis or emotional distress.

Crisis Text Line

crisistextline.org

If you need help and someone to talk to, text the word HOME to 741741. You'll be connected with a trained counselor.

Center for Native American Youth
(202) 736-2905
www.cnay.org
A national advocacy organization working to improve the health, safety, and overall well-being of Native Americans who are age 24 and under, with special emphasis on suicide prevention.

Suicide Awareness Voices of Education (SAVE)
save.org
Frequently asked questions, danger signs, support for suicide survivors, and more.

The Trevor Project
1-866-488-7386
thetrevorproject.org
The Trevor Project provides LGBT (lesbian, gay, bisexual, and transgender) teens with resources including a nationwide 24-7 crisis intervention hotline and advocacy programs that help create a safe, supportive, and positive environment for everyone.

Note: If you live outside the US and are feeling suicidal or troubled, here are some numbers you can call to speak with someone:

In Britain, call the Samaritans.org at 116 123.

In Canada, call the Kids Help Phone at 1-800-668-6868, or text CONNECT to 686868.

In Australia, phone 13 11 14 or go to lifeline.org.au.

"WHEN CAN I GET A TATTOO?"

You've probably had many conversations (or battles) with your parents about your choice of hairstyle, hair color, jewelry, and clothes. When it comes to body tattoos, piercing, and branding, your parents may have laid down the law and said no way.

Legally, you must be eighteen before getting a tattoo in most states. Adults who violate existing laws by tattooing a minor, or consenting to a tattoo in violation of the law, are subject to penalties. Branding and piercing body parts may also be regulated by state laws.

Once you become an adult, you can decide how to express and present yourself to others. Think it through before you act. Although laser treatment is available to remove ink from a tattoo, the skin area is never 100 percent restored to its original state. Branding is even more difficult, if not impossible, to erase or reverse. Keep in mind that many employers, including national franchises, can legally choose not to hire people who have visible markings. So before you tattoo or brand your fingers, hands, arms, or face, talk with some friends and/or adults who have tattoos and ask them about their experiences. Contact the local job bank or a work placement counselor at school to find out what personal adornments are acceptable in your area.

- In Illinois, an adult who pretends to be a minor's parent and consents to a tattoo or piercing for the minor is guilty of a crime.*

- An Arizona law makes tattooing a minor without a parent or guardian present a felony, subject to 1.5 years in jail.**

Citations: *720 ILCS 5/12-10.3 (2011); **A.R.S. 13-3721 (1999)

"HOW OLD DO I HAVE TO BE TO SMOKE?"

Tobacco—whether in the form of cigarettes, snuff, smokeless (chewing) tobacco, or liquid nicotine—is a subject of great concern to adults and teens. Several states have successfully sued the tobacco industry to recover the rising healthcare costs blamed on smoking. Tobacco companies are under pressure from the US Food and Drug Administration (FDA) regarding the dangers of nicotine, its relationship to lung disease and other respiratory ailments, and its addictive properties.

In most states, you must be eighteen to smoke and buy tobacco products. A 1997 FDA ruling requires stores to ask for photo identification before selling cigarettes or chewing tobacco to anyone who looks younger than twenty-seven. If you're caught violating the law, you and any adult involved can be prosecuted.

Even if you don't smoke or chew tobacco, breathing secondhand smoke has been proven to be a health hazard. Consequently, many public buildings across the nation offer smoke-free environments or separate no-smoking sections. Some cities have also banned smoking in all restaurants, bars, and other private businesses. If you're caught smoking in a restricted area, you may be cited. If you're also underage, you'll receive a second citation.

In 2003, a new smoking product emerged when a Chinese pharmacist invented the electronic cigarette, or e-cigarette. Designed to help smokers quit the habit, some e-cigarettes contain nicotine and other dangerous ingredients. E-cigarettes may also be a gateway to smoking real cigarettes. Some states restrict e-cigarettes to adults.

Teenagers often think it's okay to light up because their parents and friends smoke. Some parents condone their children's smoking and even buy cigarettes for them. If you or a friend is in this situation, take a look at the statistics and decide for yourself if your health and future well-being are worth the risk.

- An estimated 3,200 young people age 18 or younger begin smoking cigarettes each day. At current rates, about 1 out of every 13 US children will eventually die prematurely from a tobacco-related illness.
- From 2011 to 2016, cigarette smoking declined among middle and high school students, while use of e-cigarettes and vaporizers increased. A 2015 study reported that 4.3% of middle school students and 11.3% of high school students said they had used e-cigarettes in the preceding 30 days.
- Every year, 7,300 nonsmokers die of lung cancer from secondhand smoke.

- Tobacco smoke contains at least 70 cancer-causing substances.
- Smokers lose an average of 15 years of life.
- Between 2012 and 2017, e-cigarette marketing and packaging that looked similar to those for kid-friendly products, such as juice boxes, candy, or cookies, led to over 8,200 liquid nicotine exposures among children younger than 6. In extreme cases, consuming nicotine in e-liquid products can lead to cardiac arrest, seizures, coma, respiratory failure, and death among children.

Sources: Centers for Disease Control and Prevention (2018); *Trends in Tobacco Use* (2017); American Lung Association; Monitoring the Future.org (2015); National Poison Data System (2017); American Academy of Pediatrics (2017)

American Cancer Society
1-800-227-2345

cancer.org

Call the toll-free number to be connected with the American Cancer Society office nearest you. Call or go online for information about the Great American Smokeout program, how to get help quitting smoking, and information about cancer treatment and prevention.

American Lung Association
1-800-LUNGUSA (1-800-586-4872)
lung.org

Contact the American Lung Association for information about lung health, smoking, air pollution, current national research reports, and much more.

Nicotine Anonymous
1-877-TRY-NICA (1-877-879-6422)
nicotine-anonymous.org

This organization offers support toward eliminating nicotine from your life. Check their website to find a meeting in your area. If one isn't available, Nicotine Anonymous also offers meetings by phone and online.

Above the Influence
abovetheinfluence.com

Sponsored by the National Youth Anti-Drug Media Campaign, this site helps teens become more aware of the influences and pressures around them to smoke, drink, and participate in other risky behaviors.

The BADvertising Institute badvertising.org

The powerful images at this site will make you think twice about cigarette advertising and motivate you to quit smoking (or never start).

NoTobacco.org
notobacco.org

Find research on the effects of smoking, tips for quitting, and creative anti-tobacco posters.

"WHEN CAN I HAVE A BEER?"

You must be twenty-one in most states to buy or drink beer, wine, or any other alcoholic beverage. If you break the law and are caught drinking, you may be fined and assigned community service hours. The person who sells or gives you alcohol may also be prosecuted.

Being legally *intoxicated* means your blood alcohol level is over your state's limit. Even if you aren't legally drunk, you can still get into trouble for being *under the influence* of alcohol, which means your senses are affected. You may find yourself in dangerous situations and unable to make good choices when you have drugs or alcohol in your system. Poor decisions made under the influence may have a drastic impact on the rest of your life.

- The FBI reported that in 2016, 5,059 people under the age of 18 were arrested for driving under the influence (DUI).
- A 2017 study found that one-third of high school students reported drinking at least some alcohol in the preceding 30 days.
- In the same 2017 study, among the 62.6% of students nationwide who drove within 30 days of the study, 5.5% drove after drinking alcohol. In addition, 16.5% of students had ridden one or more times in a car

driven by someone who had been drinking alcohol.

Sources: FBI.gov (2016); Centers for Disease Control and Prevention (2018); National Institute on Drug Abuse

Between concerned family members, school, and community events, you've probably heard a lot about the dangers of alcohol. The statistics speak for themselves. The medical facts are equally clear: alcohol damages your brain cells, inflames the stomach lining, kills liver cells, blocks memory, dulls your senses, and has been linked to birth defects in infants.

Al-Anon and Alateen
1-888-4AL-ANON (1-888-425-2666)
al-anon.alateen.org

Al-Anon is a worldwide organization that provides support to families and friends of alcoholics; Alateen is for younger family members who are affected by someone else's drinking.

Request their free packet of teen materials.

Alcoholics Anonymous

(212) 870-3400

aa.org

Since its founding in 1935, AA has helped millions of men and women around the world stop drinking.

MentalHelp.Net

1-888-993-3112

mentalhelp.net

Tons of links to websites with self-help information on a wide variety of health issues including alcohol and drug abuse, as well as a 24-hour hotline to help those struggling with addiction.

"WHAT IF I USE OR SELL MARIJUANA?"

The federal government and some state legislatures have passed laws against the use, sale, and possession of marijuana for recreational use. Other states (Alaska, California, Colorado, Maine, Massachusetts, Nevada, Oregon,

Vermont, and Washington, as well as the District of Columbia) have legalized recreational marijuana for people age twenty-one or older, with limits placed on when, where, and how much marijuana can be purchased. Also, over two dozen states (including those that have legalized recreational marijuana) have passed laws authorizing doctors to prescribe small amounts of marijuana for personal medicinal use.

Violation of any drug law will result in some form of legal action. If a first offense involves a small amount of marijuana, you may be placed in a diversion program.[17] This means you'll be required to attend drug information classes and possibly participate in random drug testing. After you complete the terms, your case will be closed, with no arrest or juvenile record. If you fail to fulfill the diversion program's requirements, formal charges may be filed. If you're convicted of a drug violation, penalties may include detention time, probation, and

---

[17] See chapter 9.

suspension or loss of your driver's license.

> Alexis Bortell is a 12-year-old girl who suffers from severe epilepsy. Her family moved from Texas to Colorado, where they could legally obtain cannabis oil to treat Alexis's epilepsy and prevent her seizures. In 2017, Alexis joined four other plaintiffs in a lawsuit against the federal government, claiming that the Controlled Substances Act—a federal law that makes medical marijuana illegal except in certain states—is unconstitutional.
>
> Alexis explained her involvement with the case as follows: "Every time I look around my classroom, I think about what my classmates will be when we grow up. But there's nothing I can be because the government thinks I'm bad. I know they're wrong. I do hope we can win this case. If that happens, maybe I can be a doctor, or, if I need to, run for legislature."

Many teens claim they turn to drugs to avoid pressure, relieve stress, and help handle depression. But drugs, including marijuana, are a health risk. For example, marijuana contains up to 400 chemicals that can pose major health hazards. Believing that pot is the least dangerous of recreational drugs, more young people are using it—despite statistics showing that marijuana use often leads to experimentation with harder drugs.

A conviction on a marijuana charge goes on your record (through a local and national computer system that records arrests, convictions, and sentences) and can follow you throughout your life. Teenage drug use or experimentation can jeopardize future job opportunities.

Synthetic cannabis or marijuana, commonly called K2 or spice, has become a popular drug. Spice is a mixture of dried herbs, spices, and flowers sprayed with chemical compounds similar to the THC (tetrahydrocannabinol) found in marijuana. Because of the chemicals' side effects, some states are making the use and possession of spice illegal.

If you have a problem with drugs or alcohol, get help. Medical care and counseling are available, and you may not need your parents' consent to participate. A phone call to a local teen hotline or to any of the twelve-step programs in your community (such as Alcoholics Anonymous, Narcotics Anonymous, Cocaine Anonymous) is a first step toward recovery and a drug-free life. Look online or in the phone book's white pages for local listings.

Early warning signs indicating a problem include:
- You have new friends who abuse alcohol or other drugs.
- Your grades drop, you fail tests, or you miss a lot of classes.
- You withdraw from family and friends; you become isolated and lie about your drinking and drug use.
- You experience mood swings, depression, and a loss of interest in your usual activities.

To encourage teenagers to take steps against substance abuse and addiction as early as possible, state legislatures have lowered the minimum age for obtaining help for alcohol and other drug use. If you're afraid to go to your parents for help, ask your school nurse or counselor, or call a confidential hotline.

• Young people's brains keep developing well into their 20s. Alcohol can alter this development, potentially affecting both the brain's structure and its function.

• About 31% of teens who "vape" using electronic cigarettes (e-cigarettes) will start smoking within 6 months, compared with about 8% of teens who do not use e-cigarettes.

• Between 2014 and 2015, drug overdose deaths of 15-to 19-year-olds (mainly from heroin) rose 19%. About two-thirds of the victims were boys.

• To test your knowledge about substance abuse, take a drug and alcohol quiz at teens.drugabuse.gov/2017IQChallenge.

Sources: National Institute on Drug Abuse (2016); Centers for Disease Control and Prevention (2017)

- In a 2017 survey, 5.9% of high school seniors reported that they used marijuana daily, and 6.8% said they had used prescription stimulants for nonmedical reasons in the previous year.
- Approximately 19,000 people died in 2016 from overdosing on prescription opioid pain relievers.

Source: National Institute on Drug Abuse (NIDA) "Monitoring the Future" Survey (2017)

F Y I

D.A.R.E. (Drug Abuse Resistance Education)
1-800-223-DARE (1-800-223-3273)
dare.org
Information on D.A.R.E.'s anti-drug, anti-violence message for kids,

parents, educators, and D.A.R.E. officers.

Marijuana Anonymous
1-800-766-6779
marijuana-anonymous.org
Information and local referrals.

Narcotics Anonymous
(818) 773-9999
na.org
Find NA meetings in your area, information about recovering from drug addiction, and more.

Phoenix House
1-888-671-9392
phoenixhouse.org
Referral network that provides information on specific drugs and treatment options, and referrals to public and private treatment programs, self-help groups, and crisis centers.

Substance Abuse and Mental Health Services Administration Treatment Referral Helpline
1-800-662-HELP (1-800-662-4357)
samhsa.gov/treatment
A hotline for information, referrals, and crisis counseling, sponsored by

the US Department of Health and Human Services.
NIDA for Teens
teens.drugabuse.gov
This site from the National Institute on Drug Abuse presents science-based facts about how drugs affect the brain and body, for ages 11 to 15.

Think About It, Talk About It

1. Summer is near, and the weather is warm. One of your friends has stopped hanging out with you. You and your other friends and classmates dress in shorts and T-shirts, but he's always in jeans and long-sleeved shirts.

You suspect that he's being abused. What should you do?

2. Your brother is nineteen and pretty much does what he wants. Although you have to be twenty-one to buy alcohol in your state, anyone can easily get it. Your brother drinks, smokes, and uses marijuana. He says he's an adult, and if he's old enough to go to war and die, he's entitled to do as he pleases.

In a way, this makes sense, doesn't it? Why or why not?

3. What would you say to a friend who told you he or she would like to quit smoking but can't?

4. Your best friend confides in you that he has an STD. Friday night is his first date with a girl he's wanted to take out all year. Although he doesn't plan or expect to get intimate with her, he wants to be honest and upfront about himself. He asks you for advice. What do you tell him?

5. You see a page in your best friend's journal and discover a poem about depression and wanting to die by suicide. What should you do?

CHAPTER 6

Growing Up

> "You have to do your own growing no matter how tall your grandfather was."
> —Abraham Lincoln, 16th president of the United States

As you approach eighteen, you'll start to think more about your future. Whether that includes continuing your education, getting a job, traveling, interning, or a combination of all four, you'll need to do some planning. You'll also benefit from an awareness of your rights and obligations.

Adulthood means taking on new responsibilities. Your relationships with others, whether personal, professional, or social, go through many changes. Once you legally become an adult, you stand on your own. You own the consequences of your successes and failures.

- In mid-2018, an estimated 20.9 million young people ages 16 to 24 were employed. Of those, 26% had jobs in leisure and hospitality (including food services), while 18% worked in retail trade.
- In 2015, just over 26% of teens ages 16 to 19 reported doing volunteer work during the past year.
- In 2016, the college enrollment rate for recent high school graduates was nearly 70%.

Sources: US Bureau of Labor Statistics; careerbuilder.com

This chapter discusses a variety of subjects related to growing up. You'll learn about traffic laws, the right to change your name, the meaning of emancipation (and the ups and downs of being independent of your parents), getting your own place, and your rights and duties regarding the government in terms of voting, military service, and running for public office. If possible, talk about these subjects with your parents and friends. An important part of growing up is knowing when to ask questions and seek help.

"WHEN WILL I BE AN ADULT?"

Anyone under the age of eighteen is referred to as a minor, a child, a juvenile, or an adolescent. The term used depends on the situation. Once you turn eighteen, you're legally an adult, with all of the rights and obligations of adulthood.

> **"Constitutional rights do not mature and come into being magically only when one attains the state-defined age of majority. Minors, as well as adults, are protected by the Constitution and possess constitutional rights."**
> —US Supreme Court, *Planned Parenthood v. Danforth*, 96 S.Ct. 2831 (1976)

Turning eighteen, the "age of majority" in most states, entitles you to complete independence—in most situations. You can enjoy the freedom to move away from home, buy a car, work full time, travel, marry, vote, and join the armed services. In other words, major decisions about your life are yours to make.

This is not to say that your parents are automatically excluded, especially if they continue to support you. There's nothing magical about turning eighteen. And the legal rights you enjoy as an adult are balanced with certain obligations and responsibilities.

"WHAT DOES EMANCIPATION MEAN?"

At some point before your eighteenth birthday, you'll probably think about being free—that's *emancipation*. But what does it mean exactly? What are the legal consequences of being "free" from your parents? Are there any drawbacks to emancipation?

An emancipated person is legally free from his or her parents or legal guardian. This means your parents are no longer responsible for you or your actions, and you no longer have the right to be taken care of by them. The legal consequences of emancipation are the same as though you were eighteen.

A teenager becomes emancipated either by a court order (if your state has an emancipation law) or by certain other circumstances. Not all states have emancipation laws. If your state does, take a look at the law and follow its requirements in seeking emancipation, and the court will either grant or deny your request. For example, you may have to show the court that you have a job, live on your own, and pay your bills, and that your parents don't claim you as a dependent on their taxes. The court may then declare you a legally free teenager. Your lifestyle is taken into consideration in determining whether you're emancipated or not.

> In 2016, a teenager named Caitlyn filed a petition for emancipation from her parents so that she would be financially independent and therefore would qualify for need-based financial aid when applying to college. She was part of a middle-class family and was financially dependent on her parents, similar to many other teens. Her

> parents provided her with health insurance, housing, food, and more. (Caitlyn also worked throughout the year to earn her own money.)
>
> The court denied her emancipation request, finding that "it is in Caitlyn's best interests that her parents continue to support her, as their child, financially, 'emotionally and physically.'"
>
> **Citation:** *In re Caitlyn B.*, 2017 WL 1279023 (Arizona 2017)

If your state doesn't have an emancipation law, you still may become legally free from your parents before you're eighteen. If you join the armed services or get married, you're considered independent of your parents. Most states acknowledge your independence if either of these events occur before you reach the age of majority.

Teenagers who run away or are kicked out of their homes aren't legally emancipated. Their parents may still be held responsible for their actions and will continue to have authority over them.[18]

Responsibility shifts from your parents or guardians to you once you're emancipated. You still may not have all the rights and privileges of adulthood (being able to vote, enter into contracts, buy property, and so on), but the experience of living independently while you're sixteen or seventeen will be a learning experience in preparation for your complete independence.

If you're emancipated and face a problem or situation that's new to you, get some advice. Talk with someone you trust before you act or make a decision.

"CAN I CHANGE MY NAME?"

Once in a while, you might think about changing your name. (Some parents have saddled their kids with terrible, embarrassing names.) For any number of reasons, a different first, middle, or last name might seem like a good idea.

---

[18] See chapter 8.

Some countries have official lists of approved names for all newborns. When a mother in Iceland named her baby Blaer, meaning "light breeze," the authorities objected since it wasn't considered a proper feminine name. For years her daughter went by "Girl" in official and legal communications, until she took the matter to court. In 2013, at age 15, Blaer won the right to use the name her mother gave her.

Before state laws were passed regarding name changes, any person, including a minor, could change his or her name simply by using the new name. Today, most states require you to be eighteen to obtain a legal name change. Other states allow underage persons to apply if parental consent is given. You can apply to your local court (which may be the family, juvenile, or probate court, depending on your state). The court will consider your reasons for seeking a name change. If you're doing it to avoid paying bills, for example, your request will be denied. As long as you're not breaking the law or attempting to hide something, the name change will be allowed. The court will issue an order indicating the new name and will send a copy of the order to you.

Other opportunities to change your name occur when you get married or adopted. When women get married, they often change their last names. However, a bride may choose to keep her original surname (sometimes called a *maiden name*), or use both her husband's name and her own name, sometimes in a hyphenated form. Some brides and grooms both adopt a hyphenated name. Your marriage license and/or certificate will reflect any name changes.

When you're adopted, you have the opportunity to obtain an entirely new name—first, middle, and last. Your adoptive parents will decide on the names for you, but if you're a teenager, you'll most likely have a say. At the final adoption hearing, the judge will go over your new name with you. That's the time to speak up. If you don't agree or you want something different, tell your parents and the court. Once the adoption is granted, a new birth certificate will be issued stating your new legal name.

A number of other circumstances might also lead to changing your name. A change of last name may be appropriate if a parent's misconduct (criminal acts, for example) places a child at risk. A child may be allowed to add a stepparent's last name to his or her name, to reinforce a new identity and relieve anxieties. Sometimes the courts have ruled against name changes for teens.

If you legally change your name while you're a teenager, you and/or your parents need to notify all parties who have you officially listed under your old name. Provide a copy of the court order changing your name to your school, doctor, bank, insurance company, and employer. You'll also need to get a new driver's license or state ID card, and new credit cards if they were issued in your previous name. Changing your name carries with it an obligation to let the appropriate people know your new name to avoid confusion.

- As a middle school student in North Carolina, Jennifer Thornburg opposed dissecting animals in science class. At age 19, she legally changed her name to CutOut Dissection.com.
- When Courtney Blair Schwebel was a teenager, some people picked on him because of his name. In his early 20s, he officially changed it to one word: "Fun." Fun says that his new name "helps me cheer up ... people are very happy to see me."
- Upon seeing an ultrasound scan, a New Zealand couple realized their baby was "for real." They decided to name him "4Real." When the government rejected their request, the couple named the baby "Superman" instead.

"WHEN CAN I GET MY OWN APARTMENT?"

If you're under eighteen, most landlords won't rent to you without a parent or guardian cosigning the lease. This may be age discrimination, but it isn't illegal. Owners and landlords usually require a legally responsible adult to be on the lease or rental agreement.

Once you've moved in, you're required to pay the monthly rent and whatever additional expenses are spelled out in your agreement. This may include the first and last month's rent, utilities (gas, electric, water), the phone bill, an internet connection, and a security or damage deposit. If your name is on the lease, you're legally responsible for the apartment and for paying the expenses for the entire term of the lease.

You'll be given firm dates for paying your rent and the terms for any damage to the property. If you leave the place in the same condition as when you moved in, your security deposit will be refunded. Read your lease agreement carefully before signing it, and don't forget to keep a copy for yourself. Go over it with your parents and read the fine print.

If you have valuable personal property in your new place, consider buying renter's insurance. It may seem like an unnecessary expense, but if someone breaks in and takes your clothes, digital devices, and sporting equipment, you'll be left empty-handed unless you have insurance. If you're covered, you'll be able to replace what's been stolen.

"CAN I HAVE A GUN?"

As a general rule, firearms may not be sold to minors. Your parents must agree before you can have a gun, ammunition, or any toy gun that shoots a dangerous or explosive substance. BB guns, air rifles, and pistols may be considered weapons and should be used only under adult supervision.

Check with your local sporting goods store or game and fish department about the laws in your area. If you're given the chance to take a firearms safety course, sign up—even if you think you're familiar with weapons. If a friend wants to go hunting or target practicing with you, ask him or her to also take the class.

- In 2013, South Dakota became the first state to pass a law that allows teachers and other school employees to carry a gun while at work, with the permission of the local law enforcement agency.*

- Anyone in Alabama who sells, lends, or gives a pistol or a bowie knife to a minor has broken the law.**
- Children's toys depicting torture or torture instruments are restricted in Maryland.***
- In New York City, it's illegal to sell a box cutter to anyone under 21.†
- Cap guns are okay in Virginia, but firearms that discharge blanks or ball charges are restricted.††

Citations: *S.D. Laws 13-64-1; **Ala. 13A-11-57; ***Md. 24-302; † N.Y. Admin. Code 10-134.1; ††VA. 18.2-284

You're probably aware of the rules about weapons (like guns and knives) at school. Even if a friend asks you to hold a weapon or store it in your locker, don't. Under the law, school authorities may search your locker, and if you possess a weapon, even for a brief time, you're at fault. Zero-tolerance policies may result in your expulsion from school.

Kim Peters was a seventeen-year-old senior at Willow Canyon High School in Arizona. Her school, like many others, enforced a zero-tolerance policy on weapons—whether real weapons or realistic-looking replicas. Kim had started competitive skeet shooting in her freshman year and aspired to make the US Olympic team. She juggled a busy schedule including twelve hours each week at the shooting range. One day Kim was running late for school and parked in a nonstudent area. A security guard was writing her a ticket when he saw two unopened boxes of shotgun shells in the backseat. Kim was cited for violating the school's ban on possessing a dangerous instrument on campus and received a four-day suspension.

When it comes to guns (and gun look-alikes), the bottom line is to know the laws in your state, community, and school—and follow them.

- On February 14, 2018, a gunman murdered 14 students and three adults at Marjory Stoneman Douglas High School in Parkland, Florida. The following month, student activists organized March for Our Lives, a demonstration calling for tighter gun control. Held in Washington, DC, on March 24, the event drew hundreds of thousands of attendees, with many thousands more participating in similar protests across the United States and beyond.
- Following the 2012 massacre of 20 6-and 7-year-olds and six adults in a Newtown, Connecticut, school, many students across the US observed a moment of silence to honor the victims.
- In 2016, guns killed 3,128 children and teens. That's enough to fill 156 classrooms of 20 children each.
- One survey found that 56% of teens feel the Second Amendment of the US Constitution (see section entitled ""DO I HAVE TO GO TO SCHOOL?"") should remain in place

but that new laws should address issues including access to assault weapons and high-capacity ammunition clips.

Sources: Children's Defense Fund; StageofLife.com

FYI

Gun Violence: Opposing Viewpoints Series edited by Noel Merino (Greenhaven Press, 2015). Various authors debate how serious the problem of gun violence is, which factors contribute to gun violence, whether private gun ownership policies reduce gun violence, and which laws and regulations should govern guns.

SHOT: 101 Survivors of Gun Violence in America by Kathy Shorr (powerHouse Books, 2017). This book presents a photographic experience to encourage dialogue about gun violence.

"WHEN CAN I VOTE?"

It wasn't all that long ago that the right to vote in this country became universal. In your grandparents' lifetime, millions of Americans were prevented from voting. Some states had what was called a *poll* or *head tax.* Adults who wished to vote were required to pay a tax; those who couldn't afford the tax were unable to vote. Literacy tests were also required, and those who couldn't pass the test were denied the right to vote. Between 1964 and 1966, both the poll tax and voter registration tests were eliminated and declared unconstitutional. The Voting Rights Act of 1965 and the US Supreme Court opened the door to full voter participation to all US citizens. (However, a 2013 Supreme Court decision—*Shelby County v. Holder,* 133 S.Ct. 2612—struck down certain parts of the 1965 act.)

"Nobody will ever deprive the American people of the right to vote except the American people

> **themselves—and the only way they could do this is by not voting."**
> —President Franklin D. Roosevelt, 1944

In 1971, the 26th Amendment to the US Constitution was passed. It granted the right to vote to all citizens eighteen years of age or older. This applies to you and is without any restrictions. You merely need to register where you live and exercise your right by voting at every opportunity. This is one of the greatest rights Americans have. It allows us to choose our leaders and speak our minds on the issues before us—but not just on a national level. Don't think of local, city, town, or county elections as insignificant or unimportant. Decisions made by these elected officials affect your life too.

Information about how and where to register to vote is available at your local elections office or post office. A registrar might also be available to come to your home. California has "high school voter weeks," when you may register to vote at school during the last two weeks of September and April. Take advantage of this kind of registration opportunity, and then vote when elections are held. If you know in advance that you'll be away from your voting precinct on election day, arrange for an absentee ballot. Your local elections office or registrar can help you.

According to a Pew Research Center analysis, the majority of voters in the 2016 presidential election were millennials (people born between 1981 and 1996) and Gen Xers (people born between 1965 and 1980). Of the 137.5 million votes cast, 69.6 million represented members of this relatively new voting bloc.

Every Vote Matters: The Power of Your Voice, from Student Elections to the Supreme Court by Tom Jacobs and Natalie Jacobs (Free Spirit Publishing, 2016). Through explanations of significant Supreme Court cases that came down to a vote of five to four, this book demonstrates the importance of every voice and shows that voting in all elections is a crucial element of participation in democracy.

iCivics

icivics.org

Believing that the success of any democratic system depends on the active participation of its citizens, iCivics engages students in meaningful civic learning. Its mission is to ensure that every student receives a high-quality civic education and becomes involved both in the classroom and beyond.

Kids Voting USA

kidsvotingusa.org

This nonprofit, nonpartisan organization enables children and teens to visit official polling sites on election days and cast their own ballots on the same issues and candidates the adults are voting for. Speakers from the organization are available to come to your school and address civics and social studies classes.

March for Our Lives

marchforourlives.com

Formed by student activists who were survivors of the 2018 shooting at Marjory Stoneman Douglas High School, March for Our Lives members have campaigned across the United States in support of stricter gun control laws, voter participation, and more.

Rock the Vote
rockthevote.com

Seize the power of the youth vote to create political and social change.

"CAN I RUN FOR PUBLIC OFFICE?"

Once you're eighteen, you may be eligible to hold various public offices. All three branches of government have positions filled by elected officials. The *executive* branch includes state governors and the US president; the *legislative* branch includes state representatives and senators as well as Congress; and the *judicial* branch includes elected and appointed judges as well as public defenders and prosecutors. City, county, and town offices are also staffed by elected officials.

Due to variations from state to state, you'll have to check the exact requirements of the office you're interested in. Age and residency requirements may affect your decision to run. For example, to run for president of the United States, you must be thirty-five years old, be a natural-born US citizen, and have been a US resident for at least fourteen years.

You might want to start out by exploring opportunities on the local level of government. You can get involved while still in school. Join a student club or local political organization (such as the Young Democrats, Young Republicans, or groups affiliated with the Reform Party, Green Party, or other political organizations). Volunteer to help with a local campaign—stuffing envelopes, working a phone bank, or distributing literature. Learning all aspects of a campaign will come in handy down the road if you do choose to run for office.

> DeQuan Isom was 12 years old when he announced his plans to run for president—even though the US Constitution requires candidates to be 35 years old. DeQuan is now a young adult. He attends college in North Carolina, where he's studying political science. He still has ambitions of holding public office in the future. He is also a licensed minister.

"WILL I GET DRAFTED?"

Throughout US history, young men have been called for military service. From colonial times through the Vietnam War, eligible males over eighteen have been drafted. In 1973, the government ended the draft, replacing it with a "stand-by draft" for men and voluntary service for men and women. The Military Selective Service Act requires all males to register with the Selective Service System within thirty days of their eighteenth birthday and remain registered up to age twenty-six. This rule does not apply to women. Registration provides the government with a list of men to call up for service in the event of a national emergency. Failure to register is a crime with a penalty of five years in prison and/or a $250,000 fine.

Men and women may join the army, navy, air force, marines, national guard, or coast guard. If you're interested, contact your local recruiter. He or she will give you complete information about enlisting, including benefits, length of service, and opportunities for education and travel.

You may be ineligible to join the armed services because of your age. Not all branches will take you if you're under eighteen, unless you have your parents' consent or you're emancipated. You may also need your high school diploma or GED certificate to enlist. The armed forces limit the number of enlistees with GED or online diplomas. Some branches won't take you if you're on probation or parole or if you have a juvenile record. You may need to ask the court to destroy your record, which, if granted, will clear the way for your enlistment.[19] These are all questions to discuss with your recruiter.

If, by reason of religious training or belief, you object to military training and service, you may be excused from active duty. The US Constitution and the Bill of Rights protect your right to be a *conscientious objector.* You must still register with the Selective Service System, but you may be permitted to serve through noncombat civilian service. Discuss this with your parents before deciding what to do.

"WHEN CAN I GET MARRIED?"

If you're eighteen, you may marry without anyone's permission. If you're under eighteen, you'll need permission from your parents or guardians and/or the court. States have different requirements about underage persons obtaining marriage licenses. Some states

---

[19] See chapter 9.

require a blood test and/or counseling before issuing a license.

There may also be restrictions on whom you can marry. For example, marrying certain relatives (such as first or second cousins) is against federal law, but exactly which other relatives you may or may not marry varies from state to state. State laws also exist regarding the ages at which minors can marry, and whose consent they need.

- In most US states, minors can marry with judicial consent, parental consent, or both. In some states, the minimum age at which minors can marry even with this permission is 16 or 17.
- In some states, minors younger than 16 can marry with judicial and/or parental consent. For example, Massachusetts allows girls to marry at the age of 12 and boys to marry at the age of 14 if they have the consent of either their parents or a judge.
- More than 2 million marriages took place in 2016.

> - Between 2000 and 2015, more than 205,000 minors got married in the US.
> - In 2014, there were more than 57,000 15-to 17-year-olds married in the United States.
>
> **Sources:** National Center for Health Statistics; US Census Bureau; Pew Research Center

If you get married as a teenager, you're considered emancipated. You're legally free from your parents, and they're no longer responsible for you. Likewise, you're no longer under their authority. Some states, noting the high incidence of divorce among married teens, reinstate the parent-child relationship if a married teenager gets divorced and returns home.

US law used to prevent same-sex couples from marrying. However, in 2015, the Supreme Court ruled that same-sex couples have a fundamental and constitutional right to marry. In the case *Obergefell v. Hodges,* the Court held that "the nature of

marriage is that, through its enduring bond, two persons together can find other freedoms, such as expression, intimacy, and spirituality. This is true for all persons, whatever their sexual orientation."
Citation: 135 S.Ct. 2584

As an emancipated, married teen, you should be able to obtain medical care on your own. And you may find it easier to enter into certain contracts and business relationships. Renting an apartment and obtaining credit may be easier, for example. (Alcohol remains off-limits until you turn twenty-one, however.)

"WHAT RIGHTS DO TEEN PARENTS HAVE?"

The law doesn't distinguish between teen parents and adult parents. A parent's duty to nourish, love, and support a child doesn't start at age eighteen—it begins at parenthood, no matter how old you are. Some states require the parents of a teen mother or father to help out financially with their grandchild until the parents are adults.

As a parent, all decisions regarding your child's care are yours. This includes clothing, diet, childcare, and medical care and treatment. Make sure your child's shots are current, and take your child to a doctor when needed. If your child is neglected or abused, the state may remove him or her from your custody.[20]

If you're a single parent or you get divorced while you're a teenager, you have the right to seek custody of your child. If you're unable to reach an agreement with the child's other parent, a court will decide where the child will live, along with determining visitation and support issues. (Visitation is referred to as *parenting time* in some jurisdictions.) Most teen parents in this situation find it best for the child to remain with the mother, with liberal visitation rights given to the father. Shared or joint custody is rare with

---

[20] See chapter 5.

teen parents because of job, school, and transportation restrictions. The best interests of the child are considered first and foremost in deciding these issues.

Several programs to assist teen fathers are in place around the country. To promote responsible fatherhood as well as visitation and support by noncustodial fathers, communities are directing attention to young fathers.

You also have the right to place your child with the state or an agency if you're unable or unwilling to continue parenting. If you find the stress and pressure of being a parent overwhelming, ask for help. You can voluntarily place your child in a foster home or nursery while you work on solving whatever problems you have. This doesn't mean you're giving up your child permanently. It's only a temporary placement while you get help.

If you decide not to keep your child, you also have the right to sign a consent for adoption. Each state has specific requirements regarding adoption consents. Check first with an adoption agency, counselor, or lawyer. Be very careful about what you sign. Make sure you're fully informed about the law and the consequences of signing adoption papers. In many states, once you sign, it's final. Unless you can prove fraud or undue influence when you signed the consent, you can't get your child back if you later change your mind.

In addition, US states have "safe haven" laws for newborn infants. These laws vary from state to state. In general, however, they allow a parent, including teenagers, to leave a newborn of a certain age (for example, less than three days old or up to a month old) at a designated place such as a hospital, fire station, church, or with an emergency medical technician (EMT). The parent does not have to identify himself or herself or answer any questions. The safe haven provider is responsible for telling the local child welfare department about the child, and that department then takes custody of the baby.

Other assistance available to teen parents includes food stamps, financial aid from the government through Temporary Assistance for Needy Families, or TANF (formerly Aid to

Families with Dependent Children, or AFDC), and the Women, Infants, and Children program (WIC) for low-income pregnant mothers. Some welfare measures limit benefits. There is a five-year lifetime limit on all benefits, leaving the seventeen-year-old mother, for example, without TANF, food stamps, or WIC after she's twenty-two. Check with your local benefits office for specific information.

• The Responsible Teen Parent Program in Tennessee allows teen parents to defer or adjust child support obligations if they participate in approved activities including school, job training, and parenting skills classes.
• The Teenage Parent Program (TAPP) in Tucson, Arizona, offers childcare, training, and education.

My Girlfriend's Pregnant! A Teen's Guide to Becoming a Dad by Chloe Shantz-Hilkes (Annick Press,

2015). Covering issues ranging from child support to bonding with your child, this book shows young dads that they are not alone and that there are positive ways of dealing with the difficult choices that lie ahead.

Teen Dads: Rights, Responsibilities & Joys by Jeanne Warren Lindsay (Morning Glory Press, 2008). Straightforward information for young fathers about what to expect from their new role.

Teen Mom: You're Stronger Than You Think by Tricia Goyer (Zondervan, 2015). This frank and friendly book offers support, advice, and encouragement to young moms.

Your Pregnancy and Newborn Journey: A Guide for Pregnant Teens by Jeanne Warren Lindsay and Jean Brunelli (Morning Glory Press, 2004). Helpful advice and medical information from experts as well as from teens who've been there.

Bureau for At-Risk Youth
1-800-99-YOUTH (1-800-999-6884)
at-risk.com

Help and advice for raising happy, healthy children.

Many community and religious organizations conduct parenting classes. Call Child Protective Services (CPS), an adoption agency, or a family counseling center for a specific referral.

"DO TRAFFIC LAWS APPLY TO ME?"

Many of the rules of the motor vehicle code apply to you, whether or not you have a learner's permit or a driver's license. Traffic laws exist for the benefit and safety of passengers and pedestrians, as well as the person behind the wheel.

For example, crossing the street anywhere but in a crosswalk or at a traffic signal (jaywalking) may be against the law in your city or state. The same is true for hitchhiking. You may be fined or given community service hours for such offenses.

Your local traffic laws may also apply to bicycle riders. One law, for example, requires that you ride only on a regular and permanent seat, and only one person per seat. In some places, if a passenger is under four years of age or under forty pounds, he or she must wear a helmet. Wearing a personal stereo headset while bicycling may also be illegal. Holding onto a moving car while on a bike, inline skates, or a skateboard is both dangerous and against the law.

> - In 2015, 91 people age 20 or younger died in bicycle-car accidents.
> - In 2014, more than 240,000 people under age 20 were seen in emergency rooms for bike-related injuries.
> - That same year, an estimated 84,000 people under age 20 had injuries related to skateboarding.
>
> **Sources:** Safekids.org (2016); Governor's Highway Safety Association

Bike paths are to be used whenever and wherever they're available, and all riders should keep at least one hand on the handlebars at all times. Bike riding while under the influence of drugs or alcohol is illegal.

If you're bicycling at night, your bike should have a white or yellow reflector on the front and a red one on the back. Your town may also have special laws regarding the use of skateboards, inline skates, hoverboards, and so on.

If you break a traffic law, the judge may do one or more of the following:
- talk to you about the incident and the driving laws of your state
- ask the county or district attorney to look at the case and consider filing a charge against you
- take your license or permit away for a period of time or restrict your driving
- order you to go to traffic school
- order you to pay a fine, which could be hundreds of dollars
- order you to be supervised by a probation officer for a period of time
- require you to fix your car so it meets the minimum requirements of the law

- order you to complete a specified number of community service hours

The bottom line is to know what the laws are where you live, follow them, and use common sense and caution regarding all traffic situations.

"WHEN CAN I DRIVE THE FAMILY CAR?"

In many states, you may obtain a learner's permit before getting your license. It's illegal to drive without either a permit or license. States differ on the exact age requirements for permits and licenses. Some states have a graduated driver's license program restricting activities such as night driving for the first six to twelve months. If you're a student and taking a driving course, you may apply for a student permit and, once you're fifteen or sixteen, apply for a driver's license. A parent must sign the application with you, and they're responsible for your driving. If you're in foster care, you may have to wait until you're eighteen unless your foster parents are authorized and willing to sign the application.

Under special circumstances, your state may issue a junior permit so you can drive at a younger age. This is possible in some rural areas where transportation to and from school is limited. There are also exceptions for driving farm equipment; some states don't require you to be licensed. Check first before you operate any vehicle. When driving with a learner's permit, you must be accompanied by a responsible licensed driver.

If you hit someone or damage someone's property while driving, you and your parents are responsible for the hospital or repair bills. It's illegal and extremely dangerous to drive under the influence of alcohol or drugs. You must be twenty-one to drink in the first place, so you're committing two violations if you're under twenty-one and drinking and driving. If you've been drinking or using drugs, make arrangements to ride with a sober designated driver.

Once you're issued a driver's license, you automatically agree to take a test given by a police officer if you're suspected of drinking and driving. This test measures the amount of alcohol in your body, and it may be used as evidence in court. If the amount is over the legal limit, you're considered either under the influence of alcohol or intoxicated. You may be required to attend counseling or an alcohol education program.

Some states offer a Youthful Drunk Driver Visitation Program, in which you visit an alcohol recovery center, a hospital emergency room to witness persons injured in drunk-driving accidents, and/or the county morgue to view victims of drunk drivers. You may also be placed on probation or have your license suspended for a period of time. In some states, jail time is mandatory even for a first offense.

"WHAT HAPPENS IF I TALK ON MY PHONE OR TEXT WHILE DRIVING (TWD)?"

If you have a bucket list of things you want to do in the future, you might consider throwing it away if you text or use your cell phone while driving. The number of deaths due to distracted driving increases every year. In 2016, distracted driving reportedly played a role in crashes that killed an estimated 3,450 people. Some studies estimate that nearly 60 percent of moderate to severe crashes involving teen drivers are due to distracted driving. Another report found that approximately 9 percent of all drivers ages fifteen to nineteen are involved in fatal crashes related to distracted driving.

Almost all US states—plus the District of Columbia, Guam, Puerto Rico, and the Virgin Islands—have banned TWD for all drivers. Penalties include fines, jail, and loss of driving privileges. In Utah, a death caused by a texting driver is, by law, an inherently reckless act. Offenders face up to fifteen years in prison and a $10,000 fine. Cities have also passed laws banning TWD. In Phoenix, Arizona, for example, texting while driving could result in a fine of up to $400.

Other cell phone use while driving also plays a role in distracted driving.

Over a dozen states (as well as District of Columbia, Guam, Puerto Rico, and the Virgin Islands) prohibit all drivers from using handheld phones in any way while driving. In addition, more than three dozen states ban cell phone use by novice or teen drivers.

> In 2011, 17-year-old Aaron Deveau of Ohio was texting while driving. He crossed the center line of a street and hit a truck head-on. The crash killed the driver of the truck, 55-year-old father of three Donald Bowley, and seriously injured his girlfriend. Phone records showed that Aaron had sent nearly 200 text messages that day, with one being sent just two minutes before police said the crash took place. Aaron was convicted of negligent operation of a vehicle and motor vehicle homicide. He was sentenced to 2.5 years in prison and the loss of his driver's license for 15 years.

- Using a cell phone while driving delays a driver's reactions as much

as having a blood alcohol concentration of .08% (the legal limit).
- The American Medical Association claims that texting while driving is a public health risk. One study found that TWD could increase the amount of time drivers spend with their eyes off the road by 400%.
- Drivers who use handheld cell phones are four times as likely to get into crashes serious enough to injure themselves as drivers who don't.

Sources: Governor's Highway Safety Association; US Department of Transportation; Students Against Destructive Decisions; National Highway Traffic Safety Administration; American Medical Association; World Health Organization; TeenSafe.com

"WHAT ARE THE PENALTIES FOR DRINKING AND DRIVING?"

Automobile accidents are the top killer of teens in the United States, killing six teenagers between sixteen and nineteen years old every day in the US. Estimates show that more than 20 percent of these fatal accidents are due to alcohol. Two different kinds of tickets may be issued in an alcohol-related incident: one for *driving while intoxicated* (DWI) and another for *driving under the influence* (DUI). If you're stopped by the police, you may be asked to take a test to check the alcohol level in your blood. Remember that when you apply for a driver's license, you automatically agree to being tested upon request for your blood-alcohol level. If you refuse to take the test, your license may be suspended.

You may be given a field sobriety test involving physical exercises at the scene to determine your physical state—picking up a coin while standing on one foot, touching your nose, and so on. The officer may also check your eyes for dilation or rapid movements. Or you may be asked to take a breath or blood test, which will give a reading indicating your level of sobriety.

Legal blood-alcohol limits for driving are set by each state, but most states set the limit at .08 percent. However, in 2017, Utah lowered its legal limit to .05 percent, making it the lowest in the nation.

If your blood-alcohol level is under the state's legal limit, you may be cited for driving under the influence. If your level is at or over the limit, you'll receive a ticket for driving while intoxicated.

The penalties for either offense are serious. Loss of your driver's license for a period of time is common practice, while substantial jail time is imposed for second and subsequent offenses. You'll also notice a significant increase in your car insurance. A DUI or DWI stays on your record for years. Your insurance agent can give you the specifics under your state's laws.

Related offenses include having an open can of beer or bottle of alcohol in your car, soliciting someone to buy alcohol for you, and buying alcohol for a minor. All actions carry stiff penalties with far-reaching effects.

Teenagers and Alcohol: A Tale of Teenage Drinking and Driving by C.D. Shelton (Choice PH, 2012). In this self-published book, real facts and statistics are woven into an engaging fictional story of two teens faced with the pressure and consequences of making difficult decisions about alcohol and driving.

Frequently Asked Questions About Drinking and Driving by Holly Cefrey (Rosen Publishing Group, 2009). Helpful questions and answers for teens struggling with peer pressure and concerns about drinking and driving.

SADD (Students Against Destructive Decisions)
(508) 481-3568
sadd.org
SADD's mission is to empower young people to successfully confront the risks and pressures that challenge them in their daily lives.

MADD (Mothers Against Drunk Driving)
1-800-665-6233
madd.org and madd.ca

MADD specializes in programming for elementary school, middle school, and high school students to educate them about the dangers of mixing alcohol and/or drugs with driving. Consider signing the MADD "Contract for Life" with your parents. You'll find a copy of the contract on following pages, and at madd.ca/media/docs/contract_for_life.pdf.

TeenDriving.com

teendriving.com

Tips, information, common-sense advice, and links for new drivers.

- An estimated 6,480 juveniles were arrested in 2016 for driving under the influence. Of those arrested, 108 were under age 15.
- In 2015, an average of six teenagers from ages 16 to 19 died every day from car crashes, with more than 235,000 treated in emergency rooms for injuries related to car accidents. This age group is nearly three times more likely than older drivers to be in a fatal crash.

- In 2016, a total of 818 drivers and 569 passengers between the ages of 15 and 18 died in vehicles driven by teens. Among those passengers, 58 percent were not wearing seat belts when the crash happened.

Sources: Centers for Disease Control and Prevention; Office of Juvenile Justice and Delinquency Prevention; FBI.gov; National Highway Traffic Safety Administration

"DO I HAVE TO WEAR A HELMET WHEN I RIDE A MOTORCYCLE?"

Would you skydive for the first time without receiving landing instructions? How about suiting up without pads for Friday night's football game against your rival school? It's common sense to wear a helmet when riding a motorcycle, although some states don't require you to wear one. In other states, however, anyone under eighteen is required to wear a helmet while on a motorcycle (whether driving or riding as a passenger). Check the laws in your state, and remember that wearing a motorcycle helmet could save your life.

The same goes for riding bicycles. Twenty-one states, the District of Columbia, and many communities currently require children to wear a helmet while biking. Inexpensive helmets, education about bike safety, and legislation have helped increase the number of US children who wear bike helmets.

> ## Contract for Life
>
> *Help your friends and family stay alive—*
>
> *don't let them drink or use drugs and drive!*
>
> A reality check between friends and family members...
>
> I understand the dangers involved in operating a motor vehicle while impaired.
>
> I WILL NOT DRIVE if I have been drinking or using drugs. If I am placed in a situation where a person driving is impaired, I PROMISE to call you to ask for advice or a ride,

regardless of the hour or circumstances.

---------(NAME)---------

Because I care about you and others, when you contact me I PROMISE to do my best to help you through any situation in a nonjudgmental way, either by suggesting possible solutions, or by volunteering to provide or find alternative transportation, no matter what the hour or circumstances.

---------(NAME)---------

HOW THIS CONTRACT WORKS

• Both parties must read, discuss, and reach an agreement on the terms.

• This agreement provides an arrangement that has proven to be effective for many.

• Both parties may choose to attach terms to this contract, to better suit their situation. (Use the reverse side of this form.)

• This contract is also designed to be used as a forum for discussion between individuals.

- It can be a practical step in dealing with the realities of situations that involve impaired driving.
- This contract can be made between family members, friends, and others.

Plan a sober ride home before setting out, designate a sober driver, call home, take a taxi, walk with a friend, arrange to stay over with friends or family, or take local transit.

"WHAT IS JOYRIDING?"

Joyriding is defined as borrowing someone's car, bicycle, boat, or motorcycle without permission, with the intention of using it for just a while. Although joyriding isn't considered theft, it's still illegal because the owner's permission wasn't given.

It doesn't make any difference how long you keep the vehicle before returning it, or if you were only a passenger. If you know that the vehicle has been taken without the owner's consent, and you ride around in it (or on it), you're still held responsible. You don't have to be the one who took it or drove it to be considered accountable. Any damage to the vehicle may also become all or part of your responsibility. The exact circumstances surrounding the incident will be considered in determining the consequences.

In most jurisdictions, joyriding is a misdemeanor. Penalties for first-time offenders include diversion (counseling and community service hours) or a short probation period (possibly six months). If you're caught again, additional probation or intensive probation is possible as well as house arrest (being confined to your home except to attend school) or detention. If you have a driver's license or permit, it may be taken away temporarily.

> Car-surfing—also called ghost-riding—is an extremely dangerous practice. Consider the following stories.
> • When Florida resident Michael A. Smith was 23, he was at the wheel while his 18-year-old friend Cameron

Bieberle sat in a shopping cart and held on to Michael's SUV. Cameron hit a bump and flew out of the cart. He landed on his head and later died. Michael was convicted of vehicular homicide and sentenced to four years in prison, plus the permanent loss of his driver's license.

- In 2017, 18-year-old Sidney Jahn of Washington State was hanging out of his friend's car when the vehicle hit a highway guardrail. Sidney was thrown out of the car, hit his head, and died. The 18-year-old driver left the scene. He was later arrested and charged with felony hit-and-run.
- In 2015, Tsofia Mesica of California was holding on to the side of a moving car. She fell off and hit her head, and may also have been hit by another vehicle. Tsofia—who was 15 years old—later died of her injuries.

Think About It, Talk About It

1. A girl you dated a few months ago just told you she's pregnant and thinks you're the father. You're sixteen, an average student, not working, and you've never been in any trouble.

You don't want to get married, but you want to do the right thing if the baby is yours. Where do you go from here?

2. You and your friend are seventeen and talking about getting an apartment. Your parents approve, as long as you're responsible for all your bills—and stay out of trouble!

You don't want to have to call your parents for every little thing. How do you and your friend prepare for your new place and independence?

3. Your next-door neighbor has a tendency to "borrow" her uncle's car when he's out of town. One night she offers you a ride in the car.

What do you say to her?

4. You wind up at a friend's house on the other side of town, there are no adults around (they're on vacation), everyone has partied too much, and you're offered a ride home by a very tipsy friend.

You're not sure whether to accept the ride—you've also had a bit too much to drink. What's next?

CHAPTER 7

You and Other Important Rights

> **"Injustice anywhere is a threat to justice everywhere."**
> —Martin Luther King Jr., American civil rights leader and Nobel Prize winner

Laws regulate many aspects of your life—from how late you can stay out at night to whether you can sign a contract or cross the border into Mexico or Canada. This chapter addresses these and many other types of rights, including the rights of lesbian, gay, bisexual, and transgender teens. You'll even read about a fifteen-year-old whose lack of telephone etiquette took him to the US Supreme Court and changed the way juveniles across the nation are treated in the criminal justice system.

"CAN I SIGN A CONTRACT?"

Most transactions today are put into writing, from lengthy legal contracts to the fine print on ticket stubs to store receipts. Putting an agreement in writing—between two people, two companies, or a person and a place of business—provides a record of the agreement. Everyone feels safer this way, particularly if one side doesn't follow through. But not all contracts need to be in writing to be valid. Some jobs may be done on an "as-needed" basis, and no formal contract is involved. Once the work is done, payment is due. The law recognizes this type of informal agreement. Yard work, babysitting, and neighborhood car washes are examples.

A *contract* is defined as an agreement to do something for someone in exchange for something else. It may be between individuals, businesses, or governments. If one side fails to fulfill its part of the agreement, it's known as breaking the contract, or *breach of contract.* Generally, as a teenager, you may sue another person or business if you've been harmed or injured. Most states require that a parent, guardian, or other adult join in the lawsuit with you. Breaking a contract is a civil wrong, meaning that your case is filed in a civil, not criminal, court. The amount of money involved, whether $10 or $1,000,000, dictates the court where you'll file your lawsuit.

> Before you sign any document, read it carefully. Make sure you understand the terms—should you later decide you want out, the fact that you're a minor may not excuse you entirely from having to comply with the contract.

As a teenager, you may be able to enter into certain types of contracts. Your local laws tell you what kinds and under what circumstances. You may need to have a parent cosign the contract with you. A cosigner is fully responsible if you back out of the contract or are unable to fulfill the terms.

If you're married and therefore emancipated, you may be eligible to enter into other contracts—for example, the sale or purchase of a car or house. You can also obtain medical care and treatment for yourself and for your spouse. That may require your signature on a medical agreement, which is a type of contract.

"CAN I GET OUT OF A CONTRACT?"

The laws about contracts and minors aren't the same in every state. Because of your age and lack of business experience, you may in some cases be allowed to get out of a contract you sign. This is called *disaffirming a contract,* and it means you may refuse to honor its terms. The law recognizes that some businesses engage in unfair practices. Teenagers and young adults, in particular, are frequent targets of scam artists and aggressive marketing campaigns.

To learn what legal protection you have, refer to your state's laws. Ask your librarian for help, look online, or call your district attorney or attorney general's office and talk to a member of their consumer protection staff. The office may have a pamphlet to send you regarding your rights as a consumer.

In the United States, there's a "Cooling-Off Rule," also called the "Door-to-Door Sales Rule." Under certain circumstances, if you buy something at your home that costs more than twenty-five dollars, you have three business days to cancel the purchase. The sale must take place in your home or away from the seller's regular place of business—for example, at a home party, at a restaurant, or in a rented room. The rule doesn't cover mail or telephone orders, car sales, or sales at arts and crafts fairs. Contact the Federal Trade Commission (FTC) for specifics on how to cancel a sale and deal with any problems.

If you sign a contract with an adult cosigner, you may be able to disaffirm the contract, but the cosigner remains responsible. Not all contracts you enter into may be disaffirmed. If you've obtained products or services and fail to pay for them, the provider may take you to court and might involve your parents. This includes purchases involving food, clothing, lodging, and medical care. Other large-ticket items that you've contracted for—a car, sports equipment, or a sound system—may or may not be disaffirmed. You may be able to return the item without any payment to the store, or you may be required to pay for its use or any damage.

A note of caution: Before you make any out-of-the-ordinary purchase or enter into a purchase agreement, take some time to think it through. Discuss your plans with an adult, and carefully read the contract before you sign it. If you don't understand something in the contract, ask for clarification. If the salesperson is uncooperative or acts confused, walk away from the situation. If the offer seems too good to be true, it probably is. Finally, always get a copy of any contract you sign.

Federal Trade Commission
Consumer Response Center
600 Pennsylvania Avenue NW

Washington, DC 20580
1-877-FTC-HELP (1-877-382-4357)
ftc.gov

Call or write to request the "Cooling-Off Rule" information sheet, or do a search for it at the FTC website.

"CAN I GET A CREDIT CARD?"

Chances are you've talked with family or friends about credit cards and monthly bills. Questions or issues you might have talked about with others could include how they keep their spending under control, how they avoid debt, and how they establish good credit (and why it's important). From what you've observed, do you think having a credit card is a good idea?

Generally speaking, you need a parent or guardian to cosign in order to obtain a credit card if you're under twenty-one. The cosigner must have a good credit history. If, however, you can prove that you're independent and have sufficient income to cover the credit card debt you incur, then a cosigner isn't necessary.

A federal law called the Credit Card Accountability, Responsibility, and Disclosure Act was passed in 2009. The act was the result of Congress's concern over young adults with mounting debt. The act is designed to prevent credit card companies from targeting college students with "plastic" (credit cards and the accompanying responsibility, interest charges, and possible debt) before they enter the workforce. The act also prohibits excessive fees, raising interest rates without warning, and penalizing customers who pay their bills on time.

A 2016 report found that 85 percent of college students ages eighteen to twenty-four had a debit card. In addition, 56 percent had at least one credit card, with an average current balance of $1,076. Of the students with credit cards, 63 percent paid off the full balance due each month.[21]

---

[21] Source: Sallie Mae/Ipsos, "Majoring in Money," 2016

Search online for the Credit Card Accountability, Responsibility, and Disclosure Act of 2009 to read it in full and know what your rights and responsibilities are as a credit card holder.

"WHAT IF I'M DISCRIMINATED AGAINST BASED ON MY AGE, GENDER, RACE, RELIGION, OR SEXUAL ORIENTATION?"

Discrimination is defined as treating someone differently based on something other than merit, such as race, gender, or sexual orientation. You might know what it feels like to be singled out or treated differently. Maybe you've had an experience at school or work. Is discrimination legal? If it isn't, what can you do about it?

A.A. was in elementary school in Texas. He was a member of the Lipan Apache Indian Tribe and wore his hair in long braids as a symbol of his ancestry and religious beliefs. This hairstyle violated the school's dress code. A federal court overruled the school in favor of A.A.'s right to express his religious views.

Citation: *A.A. v. Needville Independent School District,* 611 F.3d 248 (Texas 2010)

It's true that teenagers can be and are discriminated against—legally. It happens every day in many ways. You can't drive until you reach a certain age; you have to go to school between certain ages;[22] you can't get married or hold certain jobs until you meet the age requirements; and so on. These are lawful age-based restrictions. Certain age restrictions are still allowed in the workplace (both for underage minors and the elderly). Also, employers may

---

22 See the chart in section entitled "Compulsory School Attendance".

pay employees different wages based on job performance and length of employment.

Whether at school, at work, or in the community, age discrimination against teenagers and other minors is legal if it's for a legitimate purpose.

At school, most gender-based discrimination has been eliminated. Classes, clubs, and organizations are integrated, with the exception of some gym classes. Team sports have also opened up over the years to include both genders, with some ongoing debate about contact sports such as wrestling and football.

Federal and state laws prohibit discrimination in the workplace based on race, religion, gender, and disability. Historically, there have been some exceptions. For instance, the US military once restricted most combat positions to men. However, in 2015, the military opened all combat roles to women.

While some state laws also ban workplace discrimination based on sexual orientation or gender identity, federal law does not yet offer this protection. However, the Supreme Court has held that employment decisions motivated by gender stereotyping are unlawful (*Price Waterhouse v. Hopkins*, 490 US 228, 1989).

Title VII of the Civil Rights Act states that sex, race, religion, and national origin are not relevant to the selection, evaluation, or compensation of employees. It is therefore unlawful for an employer to discriminate against any individual based on these factors. The Equal Employment Opportunity Commission interprets the act as prohibiting discrimination against employees on the basis of sexual orientation and gender identity. Federal courts have split on the interpretation of Title VII as applied to lesbian, gay, bisexual, and transgender (LGBT) people. In one recent case, however, the Second Circuit Court of Appeals in New York ruled that "sexual orientation discrimination—which is motivated by an employer's opposition to romantic association between particular sexes—is discrimination based on the employee's own sex." The court went on to state, "We now hold that sexual orientation discrimination constitutes a form of discrimination ... in violation of Title VII" (*Zarda v. Altitude Express*, 883 F.3d 100, 2018).

Additionally, over the past six decades, discrimination based on race has been declared illegal in all aspects of society. The landmark Supreme Court decision in *Brown v. Board of Education* (74 S.Ct. 686, 1954) declared the "separate but equal" doctrine unconstitutional. This ruling abolished separate schools for white and African American children. It's also illegal to discriminate on the basis of race regarding housing, public healthcare, public welfare services, and the military.

Equal Opportunities by Fiona MacDonald (Walrus Books, 2006). Written for teens, this book explores the treatment of minority groups in the United States and around the world.

If you feel that you've been unlawfully discriminated against, talk with your parents. Your rights are important—no one should be allowed to violate them. Your state attorney general's office may have a civil rights division. Give them a call for information and assistance.

"WHAT IS SEXUAL HARASSMENT?"

You've probably heard the term *sexual harassment* before. But people are often unsure of what it really means. For example, did you know that boys and men are sometimes the victims of sexual harassment? Or maybe you think that sexual harassment is limited to the workplace. But in fact, it is also a problem at school.

> **"A sexually abusive environment inhibits, if not prevents, the harassed student from developing her full intellectual potential and receiving the most from the academic program."**
> —11th Circuit Court of Appeals, *Davis v. Monroe County Board of Education* (1996)

The truth is, sexual harassment can happen anywhere, at any time, to anyone. Like rape,[23] it's significantly underreported, but it can't be ignored. You and your friends have rights regarding your feelings, and you have the responsibility to assert those rights.

In 1992, the US Supreme Court decided that students can sue for sexual harassment and collect money damages if their suit is successful. In 1996, a California jury awarded $500,000 to 14-year-old Tianna Ugarte in her sexual harassment lawsuit against a school district, with $6,000 coming specifically from Tianna's school principal at the time of the harassment. When she was 11 years old, her complaints about a 6th-grade boy harassing her were ignored by her school. The boy subjected Tianna to insults, vulgarities, and threats to beat her up. The jury concluded that schools must work to prevent sexually hostile learning environments.

---

[23] See chapter 5.

Citations: *Franklin v. Gwinnett County Public Schools,* 112 S.Ct. 1028 (1992); *Ugarte v. Antioch Unified School District* (1996)

FYI

Hey, Shorty! A Guide to Combating Sexual Harassment and Violence in Public Schools and on the Streets by Joanne N. Smith, Mandy Van Deven, and Meghan Huppuch (Feminist Press, 2011). This book from the nonprofit organization Girls for Gender Equity presents a model for teens to teach one another about sexual harassment, build awareness, and create change in their communities.

Equal Employment Opportunity Commission (EEOC)
 1-800-669-4000
 eeoc.gov
 Call the EEOC's toll-free hotline for information about filing a discrimination complaint.

Broadly speaking, sexual harassment is composed of unwelcome sexual advances. As Justice Potter Stewart once said about obscenity, "I may not be able to define it ... I know it when I see it." You may not always be able to say *why* you feel uncomfortable or threatened, but the harasser's tone, facial expression, and body language can all make you a victim of sexual harassment. It's an offense of perception—if you feel the act or comment goes beyond the usual teasing or flirting, or it's more than just a compliment, let the offender know.

> The #MeToo hashtag campaign gained global attention in 2017 following publicity surrounding alleged sexual misconduct by numerous celebrities. However, the movement had been created a decade earlier. In 2006, Tarana Burke started it as a grassroots effort to reach sexual assault survivors in underprivileged communities. As a survivor of sexual violence herself, Tarana used the phrase "me too" as a way to connect with other survivors, especially young

> women of color. The message to others is that they are not alone and that support is out there.

In part because sexual harassment often involves treating someone differently because of his or her gender, it's discrimination and against the law. Girls and women are more likely than males to be victims. Harassment can happen anywhere—at school, on the job, or in the community.

If you're a victim of unwanted sexual comments or actions, do something about it. You may choose to confront the harasser or write him or her a message, text, or email. Or you can report the incident to a school official, your boss, or a business owner. A formal complaint or legal action are other possible courses of action.

"WHAT ARE MY RIGHTS AS A LESBIAN, GAY, BISEXUAL,

OR TRANSGENDER TEENAGER?"

The law doesn't distinguish between lesbian, gay, bisexual, transgender, and heterosexual (straight) teenagers. The rights and protections provided are equally applicable to all groups, whether at home, school, or work. A violation of your rights due to sexual orientation is discrimination.

Regarding your education, your rights begin with the basic right to attend public school. You may not be excluded from enrolling or attending school because you're lesbian, gay, bisexual, or transgender. You have the right, as all students do, to be treated fairly. Your constitutional freedoms of expression and association are protected while at school.

Freedom of association means you're free to socialize with whomever you choose or date whomever you like. *Freedom of expression* means you're free to write for the school paper, distribute leaflets, wear buttons, or demonstrate—just as any other student is able to do. You may join or start school clubs and attend social functions, including dances. The law forbids any discrimination by extracurricular clubs or organizations. Displays of affection on campus may be restricted, but such restrictions must be applicable to all students, gay and straight alike. Under the *Tinker* test,[24] your activities at school may be restricted only if they disrupt the normal routine of the school or violate others' rights.

In recent years, LGBT students have challenged school rules about one of high school's biggest events: prom night. Federal law makes it clear that public schools cannot legally discriminate against LGBT students who want to bring same-sex dates to school dances. In 2009, Cynthia Stewart challenged her Alabama school's denial of her request to take her girlfriend to the prom. She succeeded. The following year, a Mississippi high school canceled its prom rather than allow Constance McMillen to wear a tuxedo and bring her girlfriend

---

[24] See chapter 2.

to the dance. She took the issue to court and won, with the school agreeing to pay Constance $35,000 and to adopt an anti-discrimination policy. And in 2011, Andii Viveros was crowned prom queen at a Florida high school. Andii is believed to be the first trans student to earn the title at a public high school in the United States.

> • In 1980, a federal court in Rhode Island ruled that school officials could not forbid a high school senior from attending his prom with a male date (*Fricke v. Lynch,* 491 F.Supp. 381, Rhode Island 1980).
> • In 2013, 16-year-old transgender student Cassidy Lynn Campbell was elected homecoming queen at her high school in California.
> • High school junior Aniya Wolf of Pennsylvania is a lesbian and doesn't like to wear clothes she considers "girly." In 2016, she was turned away at the door of her private school's prom because she wore a three-piece suit and a bow tie, which the school said violated the dance's dress code. William Penn High School (located in

> a different Pennsylvania town) then invited Aniya to its prom. She accepted. Aniya explains, "I've just always been like this, ever since I was little."

Another gender-related issue that has gained media attention regards the use of school bathrooms. Many schools currently have the policy that the gender listed on students' birth certificates dictates which bathroom they can use. State and federal courts have come down on both sides of the issue. A federal appeals court ruled in 2017 that seventeen-year-old Ashton Whitaker could use the boy's bathroom—which matched his gender identity—at his Wisconsin school. The judge wrote, "A policy that requires an individual to use a bathroom that does not conform with his or her gender identity punishes that individual for his or her gender nonconformance, which in turn violates" federal nondiscrimination laws. Ashton's lawsuit against the school was settled in 2018 when the district agreed to pay Ashton $800,000 to compensate for the pain and suffering he endured and to cover his legal fees (*Whitaker v. Kenosha Unified School District*, 858 F.3d 1034, Wisconsin, 2017). In a case from Maine, the court ruled in favor of a transgender student who had been denied access to the girls' restroom at her school, saying that the school's actions violated Maine's human rights laws. The court stated that in cases "where it has been clearly established that a student's psychological well-being and educational success depend upon being permitted to use the communal bathroom consistent with her gender identity, denying access to the appropriate bathroom constitutes sexual orientation discrimination" (*Doe v. Regional School Unit 26*, 86 A.3d 600, Maine, 2014).

On the other hand, in the case of R.M.A., the court's ruling went against the student. R.M.A., a female-to-male transgender freshman at a Missouri high school, lived as a male, changed his legal name to a traditionally male name, had his birth certificate changed to designate him as male, and presented himself as male to faculty, staff, and his fellow students. The school allowed him to play boys' football and track. However, the school did *not* permit R.M.A. to use the boys' bathroom or locker room. Consequently, he sued the school district for discrimination. The trial court dismissed the case, arguing that the state's anti-discrimination law provided "no existing, clear, unconditional legal right which allows ... R.M.A. to access restrooms or locker rooms consistent with R.M.A.'s gender identity" (*R.M.A. v. Blue Springs R-IV School District,* 2017 WL 3026757, Missouri, 2017).

- In 1993, Massachusetts became the first state to ban discrimination against gay and lesbian students in public schools. Students may initiate lawsuits against a school that discriminates or subjects them to harassment.
- In 2017, the Boy Scouts of America began accepting members based on the gender listed on their application, not what's stated on the applicant's birth certificate. The following year, the Boy Scouts began

accepting girls as Cub Scouts, with plans to accept older girls beginning in 2019.

• The Student Non-Discrimination Act of 2018 is pending in Congress. The bill seeks to prohibit any school program or activity that receives federal money from discriminating against any public school student on the basis of actual or perceived sexual orientation or gender identity.

• In 2017, journalist Danica Roem became the first openly transgender person to be elected to a state legislature in the United States. She defeated a 25-year incumbent to take a seat in Virginia's House of Delegates.

F Y I

Being Jazz: My Life as a (Transgender) Teen by Jazz Jennings (Crown, 2016). From a very early age, Jazz knew she had a girl's brain in a boy's body. At the age of 5, Jazz transitioned to life as a girl, with the support of her parents. Since then she has become a spokesperson for trans kids everywhere. Jazz shares her story in this memoir.

The Inexplicable Logic of My Life by Benjamin Alire Sáenz (Clarion Books, 2017). As a senior in high school, Sal is suddenly questioning everything. Adopted and raised by a gay man, he faces difficult issues of social responsibility, death, and redemption in this poetic exploration of family, friendship, love, and loss.

LGBTQ: The Survival Guide for Lesbian, Gay, Bisexual, Transgender, and Questioning Teens by Kelly Huegel Madrone (Free Spirit Publishing, 2018). This book is a helpful, honest resource for LGBTQ young people as well as for their friends and families.

GLSEN (Gay, Lesbian & Straight Education Network)
(212) 727-0135
glsen.org

GLSEN works to ensure safe schools for all students, regardless of sexual orientation or gender identity.

Contact GLSEN for information on ways to support this mission, such as creating a gay-straight alliance in your school.

Lambda Legal
(212) 809-8585
lambdalegal.org

Lambda Legal works to protect the civil rights of people who are LGBT. Their site provides information and referrals regarding issues related to sexuality and gender.

PFLAG
(202) 467-8180
pflag.org

PFLAG's website offers information supporting LGBT people and their families, including referrals to affiliated support groups and resources around the country. (PFLAG originally stood for Parents and Friends of Lesbians and Gays, but it now has a broader mission that includes all LBGT people and all members of their families.)

At home, your parents' obligation to provide for you doesn't change or end because of your sexual orientation.

Legally, they can't throw you out of the house or declare you emancipated because you're gay. Their authority over you continues, just as your responsibility to obey them continues. If you and your parents are unable to agree on or discuss these issues of sexuality, family counseling should be considered.

Your rights at work may also be protected under state employment laws. Although no specific federal law prohibits employment discrimination based on sexual orientation or gender identity, you may assert your due process, equal protection, and First Amendment rights. In 2014, a US Department of Justice (DOJ) memo stated that Title VII of the Civil Rights Act covered protection for transgender people against discrimination in the workplace. However, the DOJ issued a new memo on the subject in 2017. This reversed the earlier memo, arguing that the Civil Rights Act does *not* prohibit discrimination based on gender identity. This topic will likely continue to be debated in classrooms, courtrooms, and beyond in years to come.

If you're a straight teenager, here are a few things to keep in mind:

• Be careful about assuming that someone is gay or lesbian because he or she "looks" gay or lesbian. Ask yourself: "What does that mean, anyway? Where do I get my ideas about how LGBT people look?" Similarly, don't assume that someone *isn't* lesbian, gay, bisexual, or transgender because he or she doesn't "look" it.

• Just because you have warm feelings about a same-sex friend doesn't mean you're lesbian, gay, or bisexual. And just because an LGBT friend has warm feelings toward you doesn't mean they want or expect anything more than friendship.

• Some people seem to think that all gay men are attracted to all men and all lesbians are attracted to all women. Ask yourself: "Are all straight women attracted to all men, and vice versa?"

• Don't assume that someone who's lesbian, gay, bisexual, or transgender wants to "recruit" or "convert" others to also be LGBT. Like you, LGBT teens are just being themselves.

- According to a 2015 study, transgender and gender-nonconforming college students are at a higher risk for sexual violence than non-transgender (cisgender) students. The study found that 21% of trans students were assaulted compared with 18% of cisgender women and 4% of cisgender men.

The debate about sexual orientation also continues in the military. Many lesbian, gay, bisexual, and transgender individuals serve their country in the armed forces. Until recently, they had to keep their orientation a secret. Beginning in 1993, a policy called "Don't Ask, Don't Tell" (DADT) removed questions about sexual orientation from the enlistment form for new recruits. However, if the military found out that someone was gay, that person was likely to be discharged. In 2010, following intense debate, Congress officially overturned DADT.

> In 2011, California passed a law requiring all children in the state's public schools to study the contributions of lesbian, gay, bisexual, and transgender Americans to the development of California and of the United States. The goal of this law was, in part, to counter anti-LGBT stereotypes, prejudice, and bullying, and to reduce suicides among LGBT people.
> **Citation:** Calif. Educ. 51204.5

"WHAT ARE MY RIGHTS AS AN UNDOCUMENTED TEEN?"

Are you a Dreamer?

A Dreamer is a person who was brought to live in the United States as a child and who is without official documentation. Under the proposed DREAM Act (Development, Relief, and Education for Alien Minors Act)—which has been introduced to Congress multiple times but has not passed—and the DACA program that began in 2012 (but which has an uncertain future), Dreamers could remain in the country for two-year periods while awaiting a path to citizenship.

If you *are* a Dreamer, federal and state laws may affect what you can and can't do at home, at work, in the community, and at school. It is important to be aware of your rights and responsibilities as an undocumented teenager. The following questions are just a few you may ask about your status and your rights, especially as you get older.

- Can I be **deported?**
- Can I **travel** outside the United States?
- Can I **legally work** in the United States?
- Do I have to pay **taxes?**
- Can I get a **Social Security number?**
- Can I receive **public benefits** such as Medicaid, family planning services, financial assistance, healthcare, shelter, and food assistance?
- Can I open a **bank account?**
- Can I get a **driver's license?**

- What are my rights if I'm a **refugee?**
- What should I do if I'm contacted by the **police or by immigration authorities?** Should I cooperate with any questioning or ask for a lawyer before talking?

The answers to most of these questions depend on both federal law and individual state laws regarding the specific issues. For further information, search online for the phrase "undocumented student legal rights" and look for specific details regarding your rights and the laws in your state.

"WHAT IS DACA AND DOES IT APPLY TO ME?"

DACA—or Deferred Action for Childhood Arrivals—is a federal program that began in 2012. It allows individuals who came to the United States as undocumented children and who meet certain qualifications to request deferred action against removal from the United States. Once approved, DACA recipients are provided a work permit good for two years and can later apply for two-year extensions. Many of these young people came to the United States when they were infants or young children, brought by their parents. Close to 1 million individuals are enrolled in or eligible for the program.

In 2017, however, President Donald Trump said he would end DACA. While the program was still active in mid-2018, and lawmakers, activists, and others continue to push for DACA (or a similar program) to continue, its future remains uncertain. Without such a program, no path to citizenship or any permanent protections would exist for the young people who were once eligible for the program.

Under DACA, you can apply for deferred action if you meet the following qualifications:

1. Were under the age of thirty-one as of June 15, 2012
2. Came to the United States before reaching your sixteenth birthday
3. Have continuously resided in the United States since June 15, 2007, up to the time of application

4. Were physically present in the United States on June 15, 2012, and at the time of making your request for consideration of deferred action with US Citizenship and Immigration Services
5. Had no lawful status on June 15, 2012
6. Are currently in school, had graduated or obtained a certificate of completion from high school, had obtained a general education development (GED) certificate, or were an honorably discharged veteran of the Coast Guard or Armed Forces of the United States
7. Have not been convicted of a felony, significant misdemeanor, or three or more other misdemeanors, and did not otherwise pose a threat to national security or public safety

For more information about the program, go to uscis.gov (US Citizenship and Immigration Services) and search for DACA.

FYI

Dreams and Nightmares: I Fled Alone to the United States When I Was Fourteen by Liliana Velásquez (Parlor Press, 2017). Liliana fled Guatemala and traveled 2,000 miles alone to get to the United States. She shares her experiences and perseverance in search of a safe harbor to spend her teen years.

"HOW LATE CAN I STAY OUT?"

Depending on your age, there are certain times when you must be in at night. These are called curfews—state or local laws that require you to be off the street by certain hours. For example, your curfew may be 10:00 on school nights and midnight on weekends or in the summer.

Curfew is usually set by your city or town. Some communities have no curfew. Others, sometimes in response to juvenile crime—much of it taking place at night—have established curfews for minors. In Chicago, if you're under seventeen, you must be in by 11:00 on Friday and Saturday and by 10:00 the rest of the week. In Hawaii, your curfew is 10:00 every night, unless you're at least sixteen. Ask your parents, local police department, or librarian for the curfew where you live.

Some curfews have been tested in court and have been upheld as constitutional. Courts weigh three factors in determining if the law being challenged is legal when it applies only to minors: the particular vulnerability of children; their inability to make critical decisions in an informed, mature manner; and the importance of the parental role in raising children. All three factors have been found adequate to justify curfew laws.

If you have your parents' permission to be out after curfew, or if you're with an adult, you haven't violated the law. For example, your mother may send you to the store, or you may go out with friends and family after a football game, movie, or concert. If you violate a curfew, it may mean a fine or completing some community service hours. Some police departments will give you a ticket. Others may give you a warning and take you home or call your parents to come pick you up. In a number of cities (including Phoenix, New Orleans, and Chicago), parents are being held responsible if their kids continue to violate curfew. The resulting punishment may include fines and community service hours for the parents.

If you disagree with any ticket issued to you, you have the right to plead not guilty. If you go to trial and are found guilty, the penalty cannot be increased just because you exercised your right to fight the ticket.

"WHAT IF I SEE SOMEONE ABUSING AN ANIMAL?"

Most states have laws requiring the safe and humane treatment of animals. These laws include pets that have been brought to school, so don't forget about them when school is out or during weekends and vacations. The only exception to these protection laws is the lawful hunting of game in season, when the hunter is properly licensed.

Studies have shown that animal abuse can be a symptom of a deeply disturbed person. Findings support a relationship between child abuse, animal abuse, and domestic violence. Research in this area continues, while efforts are underway to cross-train child welfare and animal welfare professionals.

A person found guilty of animal abuse may be sent to jail or heavily fined. If you see someone abusing an animal, tell a responsible adult what happened. You may then decide to report the incident to the police, the local humane society, or an animal control office.

- Hitting and causing great bodily harm to a police horse in Minnesota is punishable by two years in jail or a $4,000 fine. (MSA 609.597)
- Dognapping and catnapping are illegal in Wisconsin. (Wis. Laws 951.03)
- In Vermont, dyeing or coloring baby chicks is against the law. (VT 5-62-121)

FYI

American Society for the Prevention of Cruelty to Animals (ASPCA)

(212) 876-7700

aspca.org

The ASPCA, which dates back to 1866, works to prevent the abuse of animals in the United States. Its website offers tips for helping protect animals in your community.

Humane Society of the United States

(866) 720-2676

humanesociety.org

Contact your local humane society or the national organization for information about pet adoption and ways to help abused, abandoned, or neglected animals.

"CAN I GO ACROSS THE BORDER WITH MY FRIENDS?"

You may be allowed to cross national borders without your parents. During the summer, winter vacation, or spring break, many students take school trips across the border to Mexico or Canada without their parents along.

Whether you're on a school trip or visiting a border town for a day, you'll need a passport or another accepted official document to verify that you're an American citizen. For information on passport requirements, visit dhs.gov (Department of Homeland Security). If you're under eighteen, take along a written statement from your parents authorizing emergency medical care. This is called a *power of attorney,* and it may save you from additional pain and aggravation. It might possibly save your life. (See below for an example of a basic form.)

Power of Attorney

I, _____, the _____ of _____,
    (name)   (mother/father)   (name of minor)

date of birth _____, do hereby authorize _____
                                                                       (name of custodian)

to obtain and sign for necessary medical care and treatment for
_____
        (name of minor)

You may add any particulars that apply to the situation, for example: location, length of stay, and date of return:

_____

_____

_____

Signature: _____ Date: _____

Notary: _____

NOTE: This is an example of a basic power-of-attorney form—it's not an official form. State laws differ regarding the specifics. Consult an attorney or a librarian, or search online for the name of your state and the phrase "power of attorney" to find the appropriate form where you live.

When traveling abroad, remember that the laws of the United States no longer apply. Make sure you know what's allowed and what isn't before you go. The penalties for violating the law may be far more severe than you'd expect in the United States. For example, in 1994, an American student traveling in Singapore was caught spray-painting cars. Authorities in Singapore punished him by caning his rear end.

Before your trip, make sure you know the curfew hours, legal drinking age, and traffic laws (including insurance requirements) of the nation you're visiting. Also be aware of whom you should contact and procedures you should follow in case of an emergency.

"CAN I GET INTO TROUBLE FOR SWEARING?"

Depending on the circumstances, using profanity or offensive hand gestures may cause serious problems for you. In some parts of the country, you could be charged with disturbing the peace or violating a local profanity law. At school, you could be suspended or disciplined with after-school detention or additional homework. In addition, your parents may be called and told about the incident.

For example, Victoria Mullins was a seventeen-year-old high school senior in Texas. While in speech class, another student was getting on her nerves. Victoria reportedly yelled at the student, "You're trying to start [expletive]!" The teacher sent Victoria to the principal's office, where she was given lunch detention and a warning to watch her language. Later in the day, the school resource officer gave her a ticket for disorderly conduct and abusive language. The original fine was $340. Then Victoria missed a hearing, which added $100. In 2011, an arrest warrant was issued (cost: $50) plus collection expenses of $147. Victoria's parents refused to pay the fine for her, so she took a waitressing job to pay off the total of $637.

> **"It is a highly appropriate function of public school education to prohibit the use of vulgar and offensive terms in public discourse."**
> —US Supreme Court, *Bethel School District v. Fraser*, 106 S.Ct. 3159 (1986)

- When paying a speeding ticket by mail in Liberty Town Court in New York, 22-year-old William Barboza crossed out "Liberty" and wrote "tyranny." He also wrote "F*** your sh***y town b****es" on the ticket. He was charged with aggravated harassment. However, a judge ruled that his complaints about the government did not constitute a threat and were in fact protected speech.

- Valerie Perez was 23 when she went to court for a traffic ticket. Upset at a delay in the proceedings, she used the "f-word" in the hallway, where a bailiff overheard her. Although it was not directed at the judge or said in her presence, Perez was found in contempt of court and sentenced to eight days in jail. After serving four days, the conviction was reversed and she was released. An appeals court later ruled that what she said did not constitute indirect criminal contempt of court and reversed the judgment.

Citations: *Barboza v. D'Agata,* 151 F.Supp.3d 363 (New York 2015); *People v. Perez,* 18 N.E.3d 981 (Illinois 2014)

"CAN I GET INTO TROUBLE BY USING THE TELEPHONE?"

When Gerald Gault was fifteen years old, he made an obscene telephone call. The call was traced to Gerald's house in Globe, Arizona. He was taken into custody, prosecuted, and placed in the state's school for boys. This is an extreme but true example of the consequences for telephone harassment. This case ended up in the US Supreme Court and led to a 1967 decision that changed the rights of all minors.

Before the now-famous *Gault* (87 S.Ct. 1428) decision, juveniles who got into trouble with the police had very few rights. They were treated more like property belonging to their parents. As a result of *Gault,* the Supreme Court stated that children enjoy identical rights in the criminal system as adults. This includes the right to remain silent, the right to a lawyer even if you can't pay for one, the right to receive a notice of the charges filed against you, and the right to face your accuser in a court of law. (For more information, see "*Miranda* warnings" in the Glossary.)

Laws regarding telephone use haven't changed since Gerald's call. Using a telephone to harass, annoy, scare, threaten, or swear at someone is, in most states, against the law. If caught, you'll be explaining yourself to a judge.

If you're a victim of telephone harassment, tell your parents. Write down the date and time of the call, and what was said. By taking immediate action, you can put an end to the harassment and assist in identifying the caller. The police and telephone company may get involved if the calls continue.

Although the case involving Gerald Gault arose from a telephone call, the Supreme Court's ruling affects juveniles arrested for any reason. For example, D.L.H. was 9 years old when police questioned him about the murder of his 14-month-old brother. A detective told D.L.H. that what happened had been an accident, that no one was going to jail, and that he wouldn't be taken away from his father. The court ruled that it had been deceptive and coercive to make these comments to a vulnerable child, and that D.L.H.'s responses were therefore inadmissible as evidence against him.

In another case, IMM, a 12-year-old boy who was in special education classes, was being questioned at the police station about alleged sexual contact with his 6-year-old cousin. His mother was present, but she remained outside the interrogation room. After 55 minutes, during which the officer made misleading statements, the boy confessed. The court ruled that IMM's confession could not be used against him since he wasn't read his *Miranda* rights, and because a "reasonable person" in the boy's position would not feel that he was free to end the interrogation and leave the police station.

Citations: *In re D.L.H., Jr.*, 32 N.E.3d 1075 (Illinois 2015); *US v. IMM*, 747 F.3d 754 (Arizona 2014)

"CAN I BUY AND USE FIREWORKS?"

When used carelessly or by people under the influence of alcohol or drugs, fireworks can quickly turn a celebration into a disaster. In 2017, an estimated 12,900 people visited emergency rooms with fireworks-related injuries. Of these patients, 36 percent were younger than fifteen years old.[25]

Before handling or buying fireworks, find out what's legal in your city or town. The police or fire department can give you specific information. In most states, fireworks are subject to restrictions. In California, for example, you must be eighteen to use or possess dangerous fireworks, including firecrackers, skyrockets, ground spinners, roman candles, sparklers longer than ten inches, any exploding device, and many others. "Safe and sane" fireworks (which include anything not classified as "dangerous") may be

---

[25] Source: Consumer Products Safety Commission

used in California if you're sixteen or older and can only be bought between June 28 and July 6 each year. Similar laws exist in many other states.

"DO I HAVE A RIGHT TO A CLEAN ENVIRONMENT?"

That right is what twenty-one young people from across the United States are arguing for in court after filing a lawsuit against the federal government in 2015. In *Juliana v. US*, the plaintiffs allege that the government has knowingly contributed to dangerous levels of carbon dioxide emissions and other aspects of climate change, and that young people's fundamental rights to life, liberty, and property have therefore been violated.

A 2018 report by the National Oceanic and Atmospheric Administration (NOAA), with the help of scientists from more than 60 nations, found that 2017 had been one of the three warmest years since record-keeping began in the 1800s. Global average sea level was also the highest on record since 1993, when satellite records began. Additionally, the levels of greenhouse gases (including carbon dioxide) were the highest ever recorded. NOAA concluded that "the major indicators of climate change continued to reflect trends consistent with a warming planet."

The young plaintiffs, who in 2018 ranged in age from eleven to twenty-two, are asking for a court order requiring the federal government to adhere to more ecologically responsible practices, as well as implement a climate recovery program reducing emissions to a safe level by the year 2100.

In ruling on a pre-trial motion, the federal judge assigned to the case stated, "I have no doubt that the right to a climate system capable of sustaining human life is fundamental to a free and ordered society."

Victoria Barrett is one of the plaintiffs in the case. She commented, "I didn't know I had the power and the ability to sue the federal government. This lawsuit is about showing that youths are the ones that are going to be making the change." Co-plaintiff Jaime Butler said, "I want everyone to understand that little kids can do these big things to help our environment." She adds, "How can people completely ignore what we're doing to the planet?"

> If you're interested in helping planet Earth, find out whether your school has an environmental club. If so, join! If not, you can start a club yourself to inspire others and gain support to help protect the planet. All you need is a few of your fellow students and a teacher or an adult sponsor to get the club up and running. Once you've done that, you'll have a huge variety of opportunities to spread the word and get others interested in taking care of the environment. You can find more help and tips online for starting an environmental club at your school.
>
> What are other ways you can get involved with environmental justice? One great step is to become informed

and educated on the issues so you can have intelligent conversations and help educate others. Additionally, social media is a great way to inspire others to care about something you're passionate about. Also look into reducing your carbon footprint by shopping responsibly and buying eco-friendly and local products, and check out nonprofit organizations like iMatter (iMatterYouth.org) that are looking for young activists and volunteers.

Think About It, Talk About It

1. While your parents are out, a teenager comes to your door selling magazine subscriptions. Some of the magazines look interesting, and forty-five dollars for a year's subscription to three magazines seems too good to pass up. You sign a form agreeing to the deal. Later, when you tell your parents, they insist you get out of the agreement.

Now what do you do?

2. It's 11:55 on a Friday night. Curfew is midnight, and you and your friends are walking home—another fifteen minutes away. You're stopped by the police, who question you about your age and what you're doing. It's now after midnight, and you're given a curfew ticket.

What do you think? Did you violate curfew? Do you think you'll be able to convince a judge that you would have been home by midnight? How would you prevent this from happening again?

3. Tiffany was fifteen when she started her freshman year at a high school in Kansas. In eighth grade, she had been a member of her junior high wrestling team with a record of five wins and three losses. She wanted to try out for her high school wrestling team but was prohibited because she was a girl. The school explained that there were concerns about her safety, potential disruption to the school setting, possible sexual harassment issues, and inconvenience to the wrestling program. Tiffany and her mother sued the principal, the coach, and the school district, charging them with violating her right to equal protection of the law. In 1996, a federal court agreed with Tiffany. The school was ordered to let her try out and participate if she made the wrestling team. The school's concerns were determined minimal compared with the personal loss of opportunity for Tiffany.

Do you agree with the decision? Why or why not? Should gender be a consideration in sports at school?

4. LGBT individuals frequently face bullying. Other times, students who are simply perceived to be LGBT are bullied. Consider the case of Jacobe Taras, a New York middle school student. Taunted at school and on the bus, Jacobe finally wrote, "Dear Mom and Dad. I'm sorry but I can not live anymore. I just can't deal with all the bullies, being called gay ... being told to go kill myself. I'm also done with being pushed, punched, tripped. I LOVE YOU." Jacobe killed himself with his father's shotgun. He was thirteen years old.

Some states have passed legislation requiring school officials to notify parents when their child is bullied on campus or at a school event (or when the student is bullying others). After Jacobe's death, his parents began working to put a similar law in place in New York. Known as "Jacobe's Law" (S1355B), it is pending before the New York state legislature. It would amend the state's Dignity for All Students Act (which addresses bullying) and require schools to notify parents if their child is being bullied or harassed for any reason.

But what if a student is not out (open about his or her sexuality or gender identity) in the community or at home? Some students fear that parents and families will reject or punish them for being LGBT. In that case, how does a school official notify the parents in this situation? Should the school put the student's privacy above a parent's right to know about his or her child being bullied?

5. During your junior year in high school, you learn that a friend is an undocumented immigrant. She is applying for some of the same grants and scholarships you are. Do you know if Dreamers are eligible for financial assistance with college tuition and expenses? Do you think they should be? What if the awarding of a scholarship came down to you and your friend? How would you feel and why?

CHAPTER 8

Crimes and Punishments

"When in doubt, tell the truth."
—Mark Twain, American author and humorist

Now that you know your rights and responsibilities, you might want to know the consequences of breaking the law. In the next two chapters, you'll learn about your involvement with the legal system—from the point of being charged with a criminal offense to your rights following a conviction and sentence.

> - In 2016, an estimated 856,130 people under 18 were arrested—7% fewer than had been arrested in the previous year. Of those arrested, 71% were boys and 29% were girls. Most of these arrests were for drug offenses, thefts, and assaults.

- In 2016, juveniles made up about 7% of all known murder offenders.
- Between 1980 and 2015, juveniles accounted for about 20% of all violent crime offenses.
- In 2016, females accounted for 41% of all juvenile arrests for larceny-theft, 37% of juvenile arrests for simple assault, and 36% of juvenile arrests for disorderly conduct.
- People under the age of 15 made up about 57% of all juvenile arrests for arson in 2016, and about one-third of juvenile arrests for aggravated assault and weapons violations.
- The FBI reported a 4% decrease between 2013 and 2014 in arrests of juveniles for violent crimes (murder, rape, robbery, and aggravated assault).

Sources: National Center for Juvenile Justice (2017); FBI Crime in the US report (2015); Office of Juvenile Justice and Delinquency Prevention, OJJDP.gov (2017)

Most young people are law-abiding citizens, but the few violent offenders have focused the nation's attention on all teens. You don't need to look too far for another story about a gang killing, drive-by shooting, drug bust, or sexual assault involving a teen offender.

It's important for you to know the terminology and consequences of illegal behavior. Criminal law, once applicable only to adults, now applies to you; there's only one set of criminal laws in each state, and they pertain to teens and adults alike. The language and procedures may differ between the adult and juvenile systems, but the basic criminal law is the same.

Do you know the difference between a felony and a misdemeanor? Do you know the difference between being charged as a delinquent and an incorrigible child? What about the laws regarding fighting at home or school, or joining a gang? You're probably familiar with the restrictions on alcohol and drugs, but did you know that having a juvenile record for substance abuse may follow you around as an adult?

"WHAT'S THE DIFFERENCE BETWEEN A FELONY AND A MISDEMEANOR?"

"High crimes and misdemeanors," "petty and status offenses," "city ordinances," "felonies," "infractions"—you've probably heard many, if not all, of these terms. Through TV, the movies, or personal experience, you've come across these references to crime. But what exactly are they, and what do they mean to you?

Crime is divided into categories: *felonies, misdemeanors,* and *petty offenses.* If a crime is committed by a minor, it's referred to as a *delinquent act.* The seriousness of the act determines its classification and the resulting penalty.

A *felony* is the most serious crime. Felonies include murder, assault, residential burglary, kidnapping, and other violent offenses. The penalty for conviction of a felony may include jail in excess of one year, probation, prison, a life sentence, or death (for adult offenders).

A *misdemeanor* isn't as serious as a felony. Conviction may result in a jail term, usually up to one year. You may also be placed on probation with specific terms such as counseling, restitution, drug tests, or community service hours. Misdemeanor offenses include shoplifting, trespassing, criminal damage under a certain dollar amount, and disorderly conduct.

To find out more about teen crime and its consequences, consider inviting a police officer, prosecutor, defense attorney, probation officer, or judge to speak at your school. He or she could discuss the laws that apply to you as well as the philosophy of criminal justice in America. Many police departments, prosecutors, and public defender offices have a community relations person you can contact to arrange for a speaker.

A *petty offense* or *infraction* is any violation of the law that isn't designated a misdemeanor or a felony. These are lesser offenses such as underage smoking, seat belt violations, or littering. They usually result in a small fine. A *status offense* is any act committed by an underage person that wouldn't be an offense if committed by an adult. Runaway incidents, curfew violations, possession of alcohol or tobacco, and truancy are all examples of status offenses. These acts are against the law only because you're a minor.

"WHAT IS A JUVENILE DELINQUENT?"

Words and phrases differ between the juvenile and adult justice systems. A long-standing philosophy is that children who break the law are to be nurtured and rehabilitated, not punished as criminals. Consequently, the language isn't as harsh when referring to juvenile offenders. Here's how the two "languages" compare:

In the juvenile system...	In the adult system...
juvenile	defendant
adjudication hearing	trial
disposition hearing	sentencing
detention	jail
department of juvenile corrections	prison
delinquent act	crime
delinquent	criminal

Only one set of criminal laws exists in each state, and it applies to everyone. However, when a child breaks one of these laws, he or she is dealt with in the juvenile justice system.

Another term closely associated with delinquency is *incorrigibility.* This applies only to minors—anyone under the age of majority (eighteen in most states). Any minor found guilty of a status offense is considered an incorrigible child.

If you've been truant, run away, been disobedient, violated curfew, or used or possessed alcohol or tobacco products, you may be declared by the court to be incorrigible. If this happens, you may be placed on probation for a period of time, usually six to twelve months. Whatever the problems and issues are, services will be provided to help you change things. If you're ever in this situation, work with the counselors and probation officers so you can get on with your life.

Many states expect parents to exercise control over their children and have put this expectation into law. Parental responsibility laws carry civil and criminal penalties for violation.

> **Can You Name These Well-Known Youthful Offenders?**
>
> **1.** This computer whiz was arrested for driving without a license and speeding in 1975 when he was 20 years old and again for driving without a license in 1977.
>
> **2.** This former professional basketball player started dealing drugs at age 12. He was arrested more than a dozen times before he was 15 years old. While being held at a youth detention center, he discovered his love for basketball.
>
> **3.** Not only does this person have a degree in criminology, he also has a criminal record. He was arrested multiple times between the ages of 14 and 17 for violations including theft

> and fighting. He grew up to become a professional wrestler, which led to an acting career.
>
> **Answers:** 1. Bill Gates, cofounder of Microsoft; 2. Caron Butler, two-time NBA All-Star; 3. Dwayne Johnson (also known as The Rock), former champion wrestler and now an actor in films including *Moana* and *Jumanji: Welcome to the Jungle.*

"AM I IN TROUBLE WITH THE LAW IF I DISOBEY MY PARENTS?"

Behavior that at one time was considered fun and mischievous—or just part of growing up—is now reason for you and your parents to appear in court. A sleepover with a friend that turns into several days may be viewed as a runaway act, a night out on the town may land you a curfew violation, and senior "ditch day" is considered truancy. These are examples of status offenses, and they can only be committed by someone under eighteen.

Your parents are required to provide for your care and upbringing. You, in turn, are required to obey them and follow their rules. The law gives parents a lot of freedom in raising families, but that freedom is not unlimited. If the rules of the house are reasonable under the law—even if they don't seem reasonable to you—they must be followed. If the rules place you in danger of being neglected or abused, however, you need to report what's going on and get help for yourself and your brothers and sisters.[26]

Parents who've tried punishments (such as grounding or loss of privileges) and have failed to improve their child's behavior can file an incorrigibility charge against their child. A judge will then decide what to do, from putting the child on probation to ordering counseling or detaining the child for a period of time if state law allows incarceration for incorrigible acts.

Disorderly conduct is another act that's against the law. It's sometimes

---

[26] See chapter 5, for more information on abuse and neglect.

called disturbing the peace, and it happens when you act in a way that upsets someone else. Examples include fighting, making loud noise, cursing, disruptive behavior in public, or refusing to obey an order from a police officer, firefighter, or school official. It's also possible to disturb the peace at home. If you're disruptive and your parents' peace is upset, you may end up in court.

Approximately 1 million children run away from home each year. One in seven juveniles between the ages of ten and eighteen leaves home each year. About three-fourths of these runaways are girls. In 2017, 4,789 unaccompanied people under the age of eighteen were living on the streets without supervision, caregiving, or regular help from a parent or responsible adult. Many more young people are homeless along with their families. Altogether, an estimated 2.5 million children experience homelessness in the United States. If you need help or someone to talk to in a difficult situation—or if you have a friend who does—call the operator or 911 for immediate assistance, or call a hotline for counseling or referrals in your community.

- Experts estimate that 6% to 22% of homeless girls are pregnant.
- Among runaway and homeless young people, 46% report being physically abused, 38% emotionally abused, and 17% sexually abused by a family or household member.
- Between 20% and 40% of homeless young people identify as LGBT.

Sources: Office of Juvenile Justice and Delinquency Prevention, OJJDP.gov; National Conference of State Legislatures (2016)

National Runaway Safeline
1-800-RUNAWAY (1-800-786-2929)
1800runaway.org
A referral service for teens in personal crisis.
Boys Town National Hotline
1-800-448-3000
www.yourlifeyourvoice.org

A 24-7 hotline—including options to text, chat, and email—for teens and families in crisis.

"WHAT WILL HAPPEN TO ME IF I GET CAUGHT SHOPLIFTING?"

***Scene One:** After school, Julie, Colin, and Matt stop at the local store for a snack and something to drink. Julie is by herself for a few seconds, and she slips a pack of gum into her pocket, knowing she doesn't have enough money to pay for all the items she wants. She pays for her chips and drink and leaves the store with her friends.*

***Scene Two:** Julie, Colin, and Matt have only three dollars between them. They stop at the store, and while Matt keeps the car running, Julie and Colin enter the store. While Colin distracts the clerk, Julie puts a six-pack of beer in her backpack. They leave the* *store and begin to party at a nearby park.*

Shoplifting is defined as taking property that's displayed for sale without paying for it. It's a crime with both civil and criminal consequences. It's also a crime that requires intent. If you were shopping and put something in your pocket, continued shopping, went to the checkout, and paid for everything but the item in your pocket, you could be questioned about your intentions. If it turned out that you had the money to pay for the item and didn't act or look suspicious during the incident, you would probably be allowed to leave. Otherwise, you could be held for further questioning or for the police.

Scene One above presents a different picture. Julie knew she didn't have enough money for everything she wanted, so she stole the gum and paid for the rest. This is shoplifting, and since her friends didn't know or play any part in the incident, they would be free to go if caught by the store owner.

Scene Two is a classic "beer run," where each person involved knows exactly what's happening and what his or her role is. Just because Julie took the beer doesn't mean the others won't be prosecuted if caught. Under the law, anyone aiding a crime shares full responsibility as if he or she had actually committed the act. Julie, Colin, and Matt could all be charged with shoplifting and possession of alcohol.

In many jurisdictions, a store can collect a civil penalty, plus the cost of the item taken, from the shoplifter or his or her parents. For example, the civil penalty for the stolen six-pack could be $100, plus the retail cost of the beer.

In Washington State, if you don't pay your restaurant bill, your parents may be responsible for up to $1,425. (WA 4.24.230)

If you shoplift, the police may send their report to the local prosecutor, who decides whether to file charges. If charges are filed, you'll be in court facing possible detention or probation. Underage first-time shoplifters usually go through a diversion program, which includes counseling, community service hours, and restitution. If you're caught a second time, probation may be considered, with specific terms set by the court. If you continue to steal, it's possible you'll receive detention or placement with the state Department of Juvenile Corrections. Some states determine whether shoplifting is a felony based on the value of the goods taken or based on whether the incident is or is not a first-time offense. A second or subsequent shoplifting conviction may carry harsher penalties.

"IS IT AGAINST THE LAW TO FIGHT?"

An everyday spat between siblings or friends isn't against the law. But if the argument escalates and someone is injured, the law has been broken. Fighting is referred to by different names, depending on the incident and whether injuries occur. *Assault, disorderly conduct,* and *disturbing the peace* are terms often used to describe an exchange of words or blows with another person.

Let's say you're at home after school, and your sister walks in wearing your new shoes. She didn't ask to borrow them, and now they're scuffed up. You start yelling at each other, and you get angrier when she argues that *you* do the same thing with *her* clothes. You throw the TV remote control, and it hits her on the head.

This is an example of a verbal fight that turned into an assault. You weren't threatened by your sister, so you can't claim self-defense. If you're the aggressor and made the first contact, you may be charged with assault.

Assume that this confrontation lasts for a while or goes on all night. Your father is home, he's unable to control the two of you, and he becomes increasingly upset over the situation. Your acts have disturbed your father's peace and quiet. Both you and your sister could be charged with disorderly conduct.

You're a victim of disorderly conduct if someone near you disrupts your peace by fighting, exhibiting violent behavior, swearing, or making loud noise. Or you could get involved in an after-school fight behind the gym or under the bleachers. *Mutual combat*—in which you and another person or persons agree to fight—may be disorderly conduct or a violation of a local law. It's clearly against school policy, requiring you to face disciplinary action by the school. If you're trained in boxing or the martial arts, your level of proficiency may be considered by the court and could increase any consequences imposed, depending on the circumstances of the case.

- In 2016, 23.6% of students in grades 9–12 reported being in a physical fight in the previous 12 months.
- That same year, 19% of high schoolers reported being bullied on school property, and 6.7% said they stayed home from school at least once in the previous 30 days because they felt unsafe at school or on the way to or from school.
- Also, 6% reported being threatened or injured with a weapon at school.

> **Source:** National Center for Injury Prevention and Control

Random fighting takes place on school grounds from elementary school through the twelfth grade. Kids often resort to violence when faced with a challenge. A wrong look or comment, certain colors or styles of clothing, or unintentional contact with someone in the hall may spark a confrontation.

Many schools and communities offer classes in conflict resolution. If your school doesn't have this kind of program, see if you can help set up something. Trained professionals are available in most communities and may be willing to speak to students and teachers. Check with your local police department or domestic violence shelters for more information.

"WHAT IS TRESPASSING?"

"Do Not Enter," "Private Property," "No Trespassing." You've probably seen these signs on vacant lots, in wooded areas, on abandoned houses, or near factories. *Trespass* is defined as entering or remaining on someone's property without permission. If a sign is posted (whether you see it or not), or if you've been told by the owner not to be on the property, this is considered adequate notice. Disregarding these rules can result in a charge of trespass, which is a misdemeanor.

Similarly, if a property owner or security officer tells you to leave the property and not return, that's also considered notice. If you *do* return, you're trespassing. If you shoplift or are disruptive at a mall and a security guard tells you to leave and not return, you must comply. As long as you're not excluded based on race, gender, religion, or disability, the restriction placed on you is valid.

Other places that are off-limits include mines, railroad cars and tracks, and fenced commercial yards. If a property is fenced, it's a good indication that you need permission to be there. This includes fenced property in rural areas where you might want to hunt or target practice. Places that aren't as obvious include your neighbor's yard or pool, school grounds when school is out, or church property and parks when they're closed. Someone's car and/or garage are off limits, unless you have permission. If you're ever in doubt about whether you're trespassing, keep your eyes open for posted signs or ask for permission from the property owner.

Harold Hodge was a college student when he stood in the US Supreme Court's plaza wearing a sign around his neck criticizing the Court's decisions regarding police misconduct and discrimination against minorities. A police officer told him he was violating the law, and after three additional warnings, Hodge was arrested and charged with violating the federal Display Clause. This 1949 law prohibits certain types of speech at the Supreme Court, such as "display[ing] in the Building and grounds a flag, banner, or device designed or adapted to bring into public notice a party, organization, or movement." Hodge agreed to stay away from the Court's grounds for six months, in exchange for the charge being dismissed.

Citation: *Hodge v. Talkin*, 799 F.3d 1145 (District of Columbia 2015)

"WHAT IF I START A FIRE THAT GETS OUT OF CONTROL?"

Most fires are either accidental or acts of nature: defective wiring or appliances, campfires, explosions, or lightning. A number of fires, though, are intentionally set. Depending on the amount of damage and the exact cause, these fires constitute crimes called *arson* or *reckless burning.*

Arson is defined as unlawfully and knowingly damaging property by causing a fire or explosion. Reckless burning is recklessly causing a fire or explosion that results in property damage. You may not have intended to damage anything, but your behavior was careless and reckless. For example, making a firebomb or any explosive device is dangerous and illegal. Whether a fire was intentional or not, you and your parents may have to pay for all or part of the damage you caused.

If you find yourself in a fire situation and are unsure what to do, get help immediately by dialing the operator or 911, or contact your fire department.

> When A.B. was 15, he was hanging out with friends when he threw two fireworks into a canyon in Oregon's Colombia River Gorge. His actions started the Eagle Creek wildfire, which burned 75 square miles of forest and other land before it was contained. It damaged homes, caused a shutdown of a major highway, and required many evacuations. A.B. pleaded guilty to reckless burning of public and private property and other related charges. When he was sentenced in 2018, he was given five years of probation and ordered to complete community service with the US Forest Service. A.B. was also ordered to pay restitution of $36.6 million to cover the costs of firefighting, property damage, and repair and restoration to the gorge itself. He has 10 years to pay the fee,

> which may be reduced if he follows the rest of the court's orders.
> **Citation:** *In the Matter of A.B.* (Hood River County Juvenile Department, signed order of May 18, 2018)

"WHAT IF I DAMAGE SOMEONE ELSE'S PROPERTY?"

If you damage property, it makes little difference whether it was a car, home, school, or business. The issue is one of accountability and restitution. If the act is intentional or malicious, it's called *vandalism,* which is a misdemeanor or a felony, depending on the amount of damage. Otherwise, it's called *criminal damage.*

In 2016, an estimated 39,120 juveniles were arrested for vandalism. But most cases of property damage are accidental or careless. Some states set a limit on how much your parents have to pay for your acts of property damage, but it may be as high as

$10,000. Other states have no limit, which means you and your parents are responsible for paying for *all* damages.

- In Arizona, a 16-year-old who spray-painted 32 homes, a half-dozen cars, and various garage doors and fences was tried as an adult and sentenced to two months in jail and three years of probation.
- Two teenagers in New Jersey were charged in federal court with spray-painting swastikas on headstones in a Jewish cemetery. They both pleaded guilty to the vandalism. Kevin, age 18, was sentenced to 15 months in prison, and Christopher, age 19, was sentenced to 12 months in prison.

Defacing property means marking, scratching, painting, or tagging property that doesn't belong to you and without the owner's permission. For example, if you paint graffiti on your neighbor's car or fence, you've broken the law and are responsible for the repairs. Some cities put taggers to work removing or painting over graffiti.

States with major graffiti problems have passed laws enforcing serious penalties. In California, if the damage is less than $400, the tagger may be fined up to $1,000 or placed on probation for up to three years. If the tagger causes over $400 in damage, the offense is a felony with fines up to $10,000 and possible jail time. The tagger's driver's license could also be suspended for one year. If the offender is a juvenile and is unable to pay the fine, his or her parents are responsible. Rhode Island limits the use and possession of spray paint to those over eighteen, unless approved by the parents. Graffiti artists in Florida may lose their driver's license for up to one year.[27]

However, if you attain a certain status in the art world as a graffiti artist, your work *may* be protected under the law. The federal Visual Arts Rights Act of 1990 (VARA) grants artists certain rights, including some protections

---

[27] Sources: California Penal Code 594; Rhode Island Statute 11-9-19.1; Florida Statute 806.13

against modifications to or destruction of their work. In a lawsuit filed in New York (*Cohen v. G&M Realty LP,* 320 F.Supp.3d 421, 2018), a federal judge determined that VARA applies to graffiti and graffiti artists. In that case, a building owner whitewashed forty-nine murals created by twenty-one artists on the walls of his warehouse. The court found a violation of VARA and the artists were awarded $6.7 million in damages.

"CAN I GAMBLE? WHAT IF I WIN THE LOTTERY?"

"You wanna bet?" "Put your money where your mouth is." "I'll bet you $5 I'm right." Everyone has said something like this at one time or another. Most of the time, you're kidding. However, if you're serious and you expect to collect on a bet or pay it off if you lose, you may have broken the law.

In most states, minors may not bet, gamble, or be in a bar, saloon, or casino where gambling occurs. This includes betting at a horse or dog track, buying a lottery ticket, or any type of gambling (with dice, cards, or other games of chance). These rules generally apply, even in some states with legalized gambling. The exchange of money or property involved in gambling is unlawful when it comes to minors.

In 2016, 260 people under the age of 18 were arrested for gambling. Of those arrested, 88% were male, and 11% were under the age of 15.
Source: Office of Juvenile Justice and Delinquency Prevention (2016)

Although you must be an adult to gamble, you can receive lottery tickets as a gift. If you win, you may be allowed to keep part of the prize, depending on the amount. States vary on this—some give you a percent of the total amount, while others require that the money be paid to your parents or guardians.

If you or a friend has developed a habit of gambling and the situation is getting out of hand, contact Gamblers Anonymous. Some groups have programs specifically for teens. Some

of the symptoms of becoming a compulsive gambler include:
- a growing preoccupation with gambling
- gambling greater amounts of money over a longer period of time
- increased restlessness when not gambling
- gambling more to win back your losses
- missing school or work to gamble
- growing debt

National Council on Problem Gambling
1-800-522-4700
ncpgambling.org
A hotline offering support, information, and referrals to a Gamblers Anonymous or Gam-Anon (loved ones of gambling addicts) group in your area.

Gamblers Anonymous
(626) 960-3500
gamblersanonymous.org
Find information and help for a gambling addiction.

"WHAT IF I USE A FAKE ID?"

This identification card shows the real cardholder—but the statistics are false. Peter's birthdate is wrong as well as his address. When Peter bought this for five dollars at a park-'n'-swap, he was only seventeen years old. Using this ID, he successfully passed himself off as twenty-one and was able to buy beer on several occasions. Then one night a liquor store clerk asked Peter for additional ID, which he didn't have. Peter was caught.

Using a fake ID is against the law and is either a misdemeanor or petty offense. It doesn't make any difference why you're using it or where. You may be trying to get into an age-restricted club, movie, or pool hall, or even enlist in the armed forces.

If you're caught using a fake ID and don't admit to your acts, an additional charge of false reporting may be filed. Any attempt to mislead a police officer to avoid getting into trouble usually backfires. Law enforcement and the courts take into consideration your statements when first contacted by the police. If you break the law, you're better off being honest and straightforward when questioned.

Think About It, Talk About It

1. You may have told yourself, "What's the big deal about shoplifting? It's so easy to do, especially in a crowded store. I've never been caught, plus the store makes so much money—what I take doesn't hurt them." Why do you think the penalties for shoplifting are so stiff?

2. You're at a party at your friend's house while her parents are away for the weekend. After a few beers, you somehow manage to break her mom's favorite vase.

You feel guilty and want to do the right thing, but you don't want to get your friend in trouble for having the party. What should you do?

3. A friend of yours has a fake ID. When you confront him about it, he says, "It's fun to have, and sometimes it works. I'm not hurting anyone by using it."

Do you think he's right?

CHAPTER 9

You and the Legal System

> "The language of the law must not be foreign to the ears of those who are to obey it."
> —Learned Hand, American federal court judge who ruled in almost 3,000 cases

At some point in your life, you may be involved in a lawsuit or have to appear in court. You may get sued, be a defendant in a criminal trial, or get called to court as a witness or a juror. Or maybe you'll study to become a paralegal, an attorney, or one of the many other professional members of the legal community. Whatever the case, you'll need a basic knowledge of the legal system. This chapter will give you a head start.

If you've followed any high-profile court case in the news, you already have some familiarity with the legal system. At first glance, it may appear complicated, but you'll see that it's logical and largely based on common sense. Even the mysteries that surround Latin terms and legal theories aren't difficult to solve.

This chapter will give you an understanding of the court system, the nature of a lawsuit, and the function of a jury. You'll see the distinctions between juvenile and adult courts, as well as the purpose for transferring some teenagers under age eighteen to the adult criminal system. You'll also learn about the ultimate consequence of breaking the law as a teenager: a life sentence. Did you know that, in a homicide case, a teenager can be sentenced to life in prison without parole?

"WHAT IS A LAWSUIT?"

Have you ever worked for someone, babysat, or done yard work and not been paid? Was your first car a lemon and the seller refused to do anything about it?

> Everyone has the right to go to court to ask for help in resolving a dispute. However, when this right is abused, the court may limit its access. For example, an inmate in West Virginia, serving a life sentence for murder, filed five lawsuits seeking hundreds of thousands of dollars in damages. He claimed injury for such incidents as glass in his yogurt, an exploding television, and an exploding can of shaving cream! All of his lawsuits were thrown out of court as frivolous, and restrictions were placed on his use of typewriters and computers.

If your answer to either of these questions is yes, you may have a lawsuit on your hands. A *civil lawsuit* is a disagreement with someone about property, personal behavior, injury, or any activity that affects your rights. A *criminal lawsuit* can only be filed by the government—by a prosecutor. This isn't a private suit, with one person against another or against a company. A criminal suit pits the government (city, state, and such) against an individual.

In your dispute, if all attempts to resolve the issue fail, you may ask a court to settle it through a lawsuit. With the help of your parents, a guardian, or an attorney, you may be able to sue the person or company that violated your rights. Generally, until you're an adult, you can't file a lawsuit by yourself. An adult, usually a parent—called a *next friend*—must file the suit on your behalf.

Once the lawsuit is filed, the court—with or without a jury—decides the case after considering the evidence, the laws relevant to the case, and the arguments of both attorneys. You and your opponent are required to follow the court's decision.

Millions of lawsuits are filed in the United States each year. Some take years to settle or get to trial. *Alternative dispute resolution* (ADR) is a process of settling many of these lawsuits without waiting for your day in court. The trend in litigation, with the exception of criminal prosecution, includes some form of ADR.

A similar practice, called *plea bargaining*, exists in criminal cases. This takes place when the prosecutor offers to reduce the charge against you if you agree to admit to the reduced charge. Let's say you're caught breaking into someone's house and stealing fifty dollars. The prosecutor files two charges against you—burglary and theft. The "bargain" offered is your admission to one of the charges in return for dismissal of the other. This is a common and necessary practice in criminal and juvenile delinquency cases. There are too many cases filed for each to go to trial, and the offender's rehabilitation and treatment can begin sooner if a plea bargain is accepted.

Mediation and *arbitration* are two methods of dispute resolution that have become increasingly popular around the nation. You may have experienced similar methods at school in settling disputes with other students. Mediation involves a neutral third person who assists the parties in the lawsuit to reach a compromise. Suggestions and proposals regarding settlement are made. If an agreement can't be reached, the parties may agree to take the next step—arbitration—or go to trial.

In arbitration, the parties to the lawsuit agree in advance to let a third person consider the case and decide the issues. You and your attorney meet with the arbitrator and your opponents. The case is discussed, both sides present their evidence and arguments, and the arbitrator reaches a decision. The arbitrator is usually someone who has knowledge and experience in the area concerning the lawsuit. He or she is generally trained in arbitration skills. Hundreds of cases are settled this way, saving time, money, and aggravation for everyone involved.

In 1964, three civil rights workers were murdered in Mississippi. Andrew Goodman, age 20, James Chaney, age 21, and Michael Schwerner, age 24, were attacked by Ku Klux Klan members while registering black voters. In 2005—41 years later—80-year-old Edgar Ray Killen was convicted of three counts of manslaughter and sentenced to 60 years in prison.

If all attempts at resolution fail and you're considering filing a lawsuit, make sure the time limit hasn't expired. A *statute of limitations* requires that lawsuits be filed within a specified time (two years, for example). If you go past the deadline, you won't be able to pursue your rights. This law applies to both civil and criminal cases, with a few exceptions in criminal law. Murder and treason, for example, have no statute of limitations. These crimes may be charged at any time, even decades after the incident.

"WHY ARE THERE SO MANY DIFFERENT COURTS?"

Throughout the United States, different courts have different responsibilities. The courts derive their authority from state and federal constitutions and from laws passed by state legislatures and Congress. Each court has the authority to hear specific cases. This authority is referred to as a court's *jurisdiction*. For example, a justice or municipal court may deal only with misdemeanor violations of city laws or small-dollar civil lawsuits, not felonies or high-dollar cases. Higher courts *(appellate courts)* review lower court decisions.

There are basically two court systems in the United States: *federal* and *state.* Each is divided into three levels. The lowest is the *trial court,* and the second and third levels are *appellate courts.* Various lower courts exist, such as the *municipal court, justice court,* and *police court.* Each of these has specific subject matter jurisdiction. Only those cases that the law designates may be heard in each court. *Tribal courts* have exclusive jurisdiction over matters involving each sovereign nation of Native Americans in the US.

The basic structure of the court system remains stable—trial courts with one or two levels of appellate courts. However, with a growing population and an increase in the number of lawsuits filed, more judges and courts are needed at all levels.

Under a law called the Federal Juvenile Delinquency Act (18 United States Code 5031 to 5042, 1938), juveniles may be charged in federal district court in some circumstances. It applies to persons under twenty-one who allegedly violated a federal law before the age of eighteen. The goal of the act is to give young people who have been charged with serious, federal crimes an opportunity to engage in rehabilitation or treatment as opposed to solely being punished. The act is also intended to give these young offenders certain due process rights and to protect them from incarceration with adults.

In trial courts and lower courts, juries are called to hear the evidence and decide the case. At the trial court level, witnesses testify, exhibits are introduced, and the attorneys argue the case. Once the case is concluded, either the judge or the jury decides what the facts are and applies the law to the facts. The losing side may appeal the decision to a higher court.

A fairly recent phenomenon is the presence of television cameras in the courtroom. In the interest of public education, an open society, and the "right to know," some courts have opened their doors to the public and allowed the proceedings to be broadcast on TV. It's a judge's decision on a case-by-case basis whether to allow media coverage. Adoption, mental health, and child protection cases are usually closed hearings.

Each level of court has its own judges and its own qualifications to become a judge. Depending on where you live, you'll either have to run for office or seek to be appointed. Generally, a higher degree of education is required for judges in courts responsible for higher-dollar lawsuits. Many judgeships require a minimum of law school, state bar admission to practice, and three to five years of legal practice. Others don't require you to be a lawyer.

> In 2016–2017, the following numbers of cases were filed in US federal courts:
> - 59,788 criminal cases
> - about 21,000 cases related to immigration offenses
> - approximately 25,000 drug-related cases
> - about 11,600 property offense cases

- about 274,000 civil cases
- just over 40,000 personal injury cases

Source: uscourts.gov

"WHAT IS A JURY?"

A jury has been described as a random slice of the community chosen to decide a lawsuit. After you turn eighteen, you may receive a notice in the mail requiring you to appear for jury duty in your state of residence. Your name is randomly selected from a list that has been compiled from a variety of sources, such as the motor vehicle or voter registration lists.

The process of a jury weighing the evidence and deciding the facts of a case began in Greece around 500 BC. Juries of 500 people would hear and decide cases and impose penalties. American juries have been scaled down to twelve or fewer members. Juries decide the facts of a case by considering the evidence presented by both sides. The evidence may be *physical* (a gun, X-rays), *demonstrative* (charts or diagrams), and *testimonial* (witnesses who take the stand and testify). Once the jury determines what happened, its only duty is to apply the law to those facts. The judge tells the jury what the laws are regarding the case. A verdict is reached by applying the law to the facts of the case.

You may be one of six to twelve members sworn in to decide a civil or criminal case. If you have a good reason not to serve, you may be excused. For example, the nature of your work or a family emergency may keep you from serving. If you're excused, you may be called for jury duty at a later date. The length of the trial is also taken into consideration. Additional jurors may be sworn in as alternate jurors in lengthy trials. If a juror becomes ill or a family emergency calls him or her away, an alternate replaces that juror.

- While serving jury duty in Oregon, Grant Faber, 25, decided not to return to court after the lunch break. The judge issued a warrant for Faber's arrest. When police located

Faber at home and arrested him for contempt of court, he commented that he left because he was "extremely bored" and "just couldn't take it" anymore.

- Susan Cole of Denver, Colorado, responded to a jury summons by appearing in court looking somewhat disheveled. She smeared her makeup, wore mismatched shoes and reindeer socks (in June), and had curlers in her hair. She also claimed to have mental health challenges including post-traumatic stress disorder (PTSD). She was dismissed from jury duty but found herself back before the same judge after bragging on a radio talk show about how she'd gotten out of jury duty. She pleaded guilty to perjury and was given two years of probation and required to complete 40 hours of community service.

Beware of Jury Scams

Most courts contact potential jurors by snail mail—*not* by phone, email, or text. If your local state or federal court summons you to serve on a jury, you'll receive an official notice in the mail. You'll also be given a contact number for the court. And even if you haven't been summoned, you can research the process. Most courts have websites where you can log on for information about how jury service works in your area.

However, some scammers make personal calls telling people they have failed to show up for jury duty and ask for information including Social Security numbers and birthdates. With this information, they can steal people's identity and access their bank accounts. They may also ask for credit card numbers. But courts don't charge fees for serving on a jury, so a real representative of the courts would not need someone's credit card number. If you ever receive a call like this that seems suspicious, do not give out any personal information.

- Forty-five percent of Americans who are sent jury notices show up at

the courthouse. (Some notices aren't received, some are ignored, and some people get excused before their date of appearance.)
- Of those who appear, almost two-thirds do not end up serving on juries due to work, personal conflicts, illness, or a lawyer's challenge.
- President George W. Bush was called for jury duty in 2006, and President Barack Obama was called to serve in 2010 and 2017.

Source: National Center for State Courts (2016)

In choosing a jury, any form of discrimination is prohibited. You can't be excluded solely because of your race, gender, sexual orientation, religion, or ethnicity. Once you're called to the courthouse as part of a pool to be interviewed, you may be excused for various reasons, but not for purely discriminatory ones.

You may be paid a fee for each day you serve as well as for travel expenses. These vary around the country. Depending on the type of case, you may be *sequestered* during all or part of the trial. The purpose of sequestering is to protect or insulate you from outside influences. Once sequestered, the jury stays together until it reaches a verdict. The court makes arrangements for your meals and overnight stays in a hotel. The court bailiff is your contact with the outside world and is responsible for seeing that your needs are met. There may be restrictions on which newspapers, magazines, social media, and TV or radio programs are available to you while you're sequestered. You may also be ordered to limit your use of electronic devices and the internet or ordered not to use them at all.

In most states, juvenile courts don't have juries. In those states, the judge acts as both the jury (in deciding the facts) and the judge (in applying the law to the facts). However, if you have a youth court in your community, you may also be able to participate in a fellow student's case as a juror. (To learn more about this kind of court and how you could be on a jury, see the box about teen courts on the following pages in section entitled, "WHAT DOES DIVERSION MEAN?".) If a juvenile is transferred to adult court, a jury may be used to decide the case.

Here are a few other jury terms you may be wondering about:
- *Foreman.* The juror designated to speak for the jury, selected by the jury at the beginning of their deliberations.
- *Deliberation.* Once the formal presentation of evidence during the trial ends, the juvenile court judge decides the case. In adult or juvenile cases with juries, the jury's duty is to decide the facts of the case, apply the law given to them by the judge to the facts as they find them, and reach a decision. To *deliberate,* as applied to a jury, means to consider and weigh the facts as a group.
- *Instructions.* These are the laws about the subject matter of the case (such as what negligence is in a car accident case or what the legal definition of shoplifting is). The judge reads the instructions to the jury. Some courts allow the jury to

keep a copy of the instructions during deliberations.
- *Verdict.* The formal finding or decision of the jury. A criminal case requires a unanimous verdict. The majority vote decides a civil case. The verdict is decided in secret, with only the jury members present, and then reported to the court.
- *Hung jury.* A jury that is deadlocked or unable to reach a verdict after a reasonable time of deliberation. This results in a *mistrial.* The case may be retried or possibly settled by the parties without a trial.
- *Jury view.* A jury is taken to an accident scene to view where the event took place. For example, in 1995, the jury in the O.J. Simpson murder trial was taken to both the defendant's home and the scene of the crime. Jury views are rare.
- *Grand jury.* A group of men and women who are sworn in to consider evidence presented to them by the prosecutor. Their job is to determine whether there's reason to believe *(probable cause)* that a crime has been committed and who

committed it. The grand jury doesn't determine guilt or innocence. In deciding that a crime has been committed, the grand jury votes for charging the person responsible, which results in an *indictment.* The person charged pleads either guilty or not guilty. If the plea is "not guilty," the person may go to trial before a regular jury of six to twelve people.

Rent or stream a movie to learn more about our legal system. Here are 10 films that offer insights into the roles of jurors, judges, and lawyers:

• ***12 Angry Men*** (1957). Jury deliberations in a murder trial.

• ***Anatomy of a Murder*** (1959). The story of a murder trial in rural Michigan.

• ***The Caine Mutiny*** (1954). This action film about World War II in the Pacific features the court-martial of a naval officer.

- ***Criminal Justice*** (1990). A robbery and assault followed by a rigged lineup exposes the pressures on everyone involved in the criminal justice system.
- ***A Few Good Men*** (1992). A military lawyer defends marines accused of murder. (NOTE: Rated R for language.)
- ***My Cousin Vinny*** (1992). Two college students are accused of murder in rural Alabama. One's cousin—an inexperienced, loudmouthed New York City lawyer—defends them. (NOTE: Rated R for language.)
- ***The Ox-Bow Incident*** (1943). The trial of an accused horse thief by other cowboys gives a chilling view of frontier justice.
- ***To Kill a Mockingbird*** (1962). A white lawyer confronts prejudice in the Depression-era Deep South to defend a black man against an undeserved rape charge.
- ***Loving*** (2016). The story of a young couple who were arrested for interracial marriage in Virginia. Their legal battle led to the 1967 Supreme

Court decision that struck down laws against interracial marriage (also called anti-miscegenation laws) in the US.

• ***RBG*** (2018). Supreme Court justice Ruth Bader Ginsburg—who is sometimes called "the Notorious RBG"—has become a pop culture icon. This documentary follows her life, including her journey through law school, her career as an accomplished civil rights attorney fighting for gender equality, and her appointment to the Supreme Court in 1993—making her only the second female justice to serve on the Court.

"IS EVERY COURT DECISION FINAL?"

Once a decision is made by a judge or jury at the trial court level, either side can ask a higher court to review the case. The right to appeal, however, isn't available in every type of case. Check your state's rules about the appeal process. Also check the time requirements and deadlines so you don't miss one.

At the appellate court level, none of the excitement or drama of a trial occurs. The job of a court of appeals or your state's highest court is to review what took place during the trial and examine any mistakes that were made.

Oral arguments in appellate courts are open to the public. See if you can arrange for your civics or social studies class to attend one. Write or call the court in advance to find out what cases are scheduled. Then your class may select one of particular interest to observe.

There is no jury in an appeal, nor any witness testimony. Appeals focus on written arguments, called *briefs*, about the issues raised by the lawyers on each side of the case. Sometimes the appellate court allows the attorneys to orally argue their position—which also gives the court the opportunity to question the attorneys about certain points of law or facts of the case.

There's no such thing as a perfect trial. Mistakes are made by attorneys, witnesses, and the court. The appellate court looks at the errors pointed out by the attorneys in their briefs and decides whether they are serious enough to merit action. If what took place at trial amounts to what's referred to as *harmless error,* the trial court's decision will remain in place. If, however, *fundamental error* occurred that affected one of the party's rights, the trial court decision may be reversed or modified.

If you lose a case because of an attorney's error or negligence, you may consider filing a malpractice lawsuit against the attorney. There's a difference between gross error or negligence and an attorney's theory of a case and trial strategy. Judges have immunity from such a lawsuit, even if what they did was clearly wrong. In order for judges to competently review and judge the many matters before them without fear of being sued, the law grants them protection. (This protection is limited to official court business and doesn't cover unrelated acts in the judge's private life.)

In a criminal case, a reversal may mean a new trial for the accused. In a civil case, it may also mean a new trial or a settlement of the case, as opposed to the time and expense of a new trial. If you had a free lawyer representing you at trial, he or she may be appointed to continue representing you on appeal.

Generally, in criminal or delinquency cases, teenagers are appointed a lawyer (public defender). This is also true in abuse, neglect, and abandonment cases. In other types of cases, such as emancipation or change of name, free legal representation may not be available. However, through community legal services or similar organizations, advice and/or assistance may be available for sliding-scale fees.

In the sense that there is no higher court to appeal to, US Supreme Court decisions are final. However, the justices can consider an issue that has already been ruled on and reverse the decision. In addition, it can sometimes take years for all states or jurisdictions to comply with a Supreme Court ruling. That compliance requires follow-through and enforcement, which may be slow to come. Consider these two examples:

- In 1940, the Supreme Court ruled that schools could discipline a student for refusing to salute the US flag.[28] But in 1943, the Court changed its mind, stating that such a rule violates students' free speech rights.[29]
- In 1952, the Supreme Court began considering the issue of segregation of students in public schools when *Brown v. Board of Education* first came before the Court. Another round of arguments was heard in 1953. In 1954, a unanimous decision (9-0) was announced outlawing segregated public schools in the US and declaring the practice unconstitutional.[30] However, it took

---

[28] Minersville School District v. Gobitis, 60 S.Ct. 1010 (Pennsylvania 1940)

[29] West Virginia State Board of Education v. Barnette, 63 S.Ct. 1178 (West Virginia 1943)

[30] Brown v. Board of Education (Kansas 1954)

years for schools to actually become less segregated. Three years after the case's decision, federal troops were needed to escort nine black students into Central High School in Little Rock, Arkansas, and many schools remained heavily segregated in practice.

In fact, even today, the desegregation of all public schools in the country has never been fully accomplished. Due to economic and social factors, an issue called "resegregation" has developed in recent decades. Some school districts have made efforts to reverse this trend. In a 2007 case *(Parents Involved in Community Schools v. Seattle School District,* 127 S.Ct. 2738), the US Supreme Court ruled that public schools could use race as one factor in public school admission as a way to achieve greater diversity in school populations.

"HOW SHOULD I DRESS FOR COURT?"

Most people who have to go to court are nervous about what to expect. Walking into a courtroom can be an intimidating experience to begin with. You don't want to be reprimanded or turned away because of something you're wearing. First impressions are largely based on appearance—if you're dressed inappropriately for court, it will be noticed.

A general rule of thumb is to dress as if you were going to a nice restaurant or event. You don't have to go overboard—it's not a formal occasion, so a suit or a fancy dress is not required. Many lawyers advise their clients in advance about proper attire for court. Even if you don't have a lawyer, following a few simple do's and don'ts will make your experience less stressful.

Before you enter the courthouse, leave your gum and cigarettes outside. (If you're under eighteen, you shouldn't be smoking anyway, but that's another matter.) Dress appropriately for the weather—the judge and staff will have done so, and they will expect you to do the same. But even if your court date is on the hottest day of the year, don't forget that you are visiting a place where serious business is conducted. Don't wear flip-flops or go barefoot, and do not wear tank tops or muscle shirts or go shirtless. Miniskirts should be left at home, as should midriff-baring shirts and strapless outfits. Many courts keep large T-shirts at the front desk to hand out to visitors who are showing too much skin. Most courts also discourage wearing baggy or sagging jeans and other pants, especially those that expose undergarments. Overall, a good guideline is to dress conservatively, modestly, and in clean, neat clothes, such as a button-up shirt and jeans without holes.

Community Legal Services (Legal Aid) is a federally funded program that provides free legal assistance to low-income individuals. There are residential and financial requirements for Legal Aid eligibility. Legal Aid

> attorneys handle domestic relations and domestic violence (orders of protection) cases, as well as issues regarding housing, homelessness, migrant children, education, bankruptcy, consumer rights, and health. Generally, representation isn't available for criminal, abortion, or immigration matters.

Remove your hat as well as headphones or any other electronic devices. If you're allowed to keep your cell phone with you, make sure it's turned off. You may have to go through metal detectors and security when entering the building. The security guards may give you additional advice or instructions about your conduct and appearance. Don't bring any food or drink into the courtroom. Gang colors and insignias are usually prohibited due to security and in the interest of witness protection. You can always call the court in advance and ask about the details of its dress code.

"WHAT HAPPENS IN JUVENILE COURT?"

Some people may call it "juvy," "children's court," "juvenile court," or "juvenile hall." The names change from state to state, but the court's job and authority over you are the same. Your age determines whether you'll appear in juvenile or adult court. In most states, juvenile court jurisdiction ends at age eighteen. In a few states, you may remain under the authority of the juvenile court until you're twenty-one.

Juvenile courts deal with a range of legal issues pertaining to children and teenagers. For example, juvenile courts handle cases involving child abuse and neglect, abandonment by parents, termination of parents' rights, and adoption. All delinquency and incorrigibility[31] cases are also handled in juvenile court. Miscellaneous other hearings covering name changes, mental health issues, and abortion may be conducted in the juvenile court.

---

[31] See chapter 8.

Once you're involved with the juvenile court system, you have many of the same rights as an adult. You may be appointed an attorney to represent you or a guardian to speak about what's in your best interests.

In a delinquency case (where you're charged with breaking the law), you may remain silent, plead guilty or not guilty, and go to trial if you choose. In some states, you may be entitled to a jury trial. You may also have the right to appeal a decision you disagree with.

The trials or hearings in juvenile court aren't as formal as those in adult court or the cases you see on TV. In general, the philosophy of juvenile justice is to focus on treatment and rehabilitation, not punishment. If you're not locked up for a period of time or sent to the Department of Corrections, you may be placed on probation, which could last until you turn eighteen or twenty-one. You may be released early if you follow all the terms of your probation and you don't break any more laws.

Terms of probation may include performing a certain number of community service hours, attending a class or counseling program, paying the victim restitution, paying court fees and fines, and having restricted access to social media.

Your probation officer meets with you on a regular basis and stays in touch with your parents and teachers. If you violate your probation, you'll find yourself back in court facing more serious consequences.

Probation terms and terms of restitution in juvenile cases can vary widely, and courts sometimes go to significant lengths to bring justice to victims through these terms. For example, A.B. was fifteen when he committed a home burglary, damaging the victim's property and stealing her truck. At his sentencing, A.B. was ordered to pay the victim $13,000 in restitution. Part of the victim's claim included the cost of installing a security system in her home. The court concluded that A.B. had "shattered [the victim's] sense of personal safety" and that her request for restitution was not unreasonable, since it was "a direct consequence of [A.B.]'s decision to violate her privacy" (*In re A.B.,* 2016 WL 7156477, Arizona, 2016).

In another case, a juvenile admitted to possession of cell-phone video and photos of sexual activity he engaged in with an underage girl. After they broke up, he blackmailed her into paying him to keep the videos and photos private. The court placed him on probation and required him to submit to warrantless searches of all electronic devices and to give his probation officer the passwords for access to his accounts. On appeal, the court upheld these probation terms (*In re Q.R.,* 7 Cal. App. 5th 1231, California, 2017).

In the noncriminal cases in juvenile court (abuse, neglect, and adoption), you may be involved as a witness. These are considered civil cases, meaning you won't receive any time in detention or with the Department of Corrections. You may be placed by the court in a foster home or residential treatment center until the problems that brought you to court are worked out.

"WHAT DOES DIVERSION MEAN?"

If you've been charged with a minor crime—usually a low misdemeanor or petty offense—you may be eligible for what's called a *diversion program.* This is common practice in both juvenile and adult courts nationwide. Diversion is usually not available for felonies.

Diversion means that your charge is handled in a way that "diverts" the case—moves it away—from the criminal or juvenile justice system. If you complete the terms of a diversion program, you have a chance to avoid trial and a criminal record.

Every jurisdiction is different as to what qualifies for participation in diversion. Shoplifting clothes worth $250 may qualify for diversion in one state but not another. Overall, if you're a first-time offender and your crime is considered a minor infraction, you may be eligible for diversion.

At the first hearing on the charge, you'll meet with a probation officer who will explain the process to you. He or she will tell you about diversion and whether it's available to you. If it is, and if you admit to the charge, then you can participate in the program. It usually calls for you to complete a specified number of community service hours, pay a fine, make payment to the victim, and/or attend educational classes or counseling for drugs or other issues, if appropriate.

Teen courts or peer juries are voluntary, alternative programs that help first-time offenders avoid going to juvenile court and establishing criminal records. These programs are a form of diversion and may be run by juvenile courts, juvenile probation departments, or school districts. A teen court is staffed by teenagers who are volunteers from the community. They act as the jury, prosecutor, defense attorney, and bailiff. Usually an adult (such as a local attorney or judge) acts as the judge.

Teen courts only deal with status offenses or low-level misdemeanors such as shoplifting, traffic violations, and alcohol and tobacco offenses. If the teen offender admits to the charge, the teen jury decides the appropriate penalty. That may include community service, a class about the alleged crime and consequences in the juvenile justice system, an order to serve on a teen court jury, or other penalties. Completion of all penalties results in the case's dismissal. However, if the teen fails to comply with the chosen consequences, the case can then be referred to a local prosecutor to file formal charges.

The United States has more than 1,050 youth court programs. For information about finding or starting one in your area, visit youthcourt.net.

Source: National Association of Youth Courts, youthcourt.net

Once you complete all the diversion program's terms, the case is closed. You don't have to appear before a judge and you don't have a public criminal record. Some jurisdictions refer to this process as "deferred judgment" or "deferred prosecution." When you complete the diversion terms, a judgment is not entered into the court's record. Instead, a dismissal of the charge is entered. The court will maintain its own record showing that you completed diversion in case you return on another offense. Diversion is usually not available a second time.

If you maintain your innocence, which is your right, the case will be set for trial. You will not be participating in diversion, since it calls for an admission of the crime.

"WHAT IF I'M TRIED IN ADULT COURT?"

Depending on your age, if the crime is serious, a prosecutor may file charges against you in adult court or ask the juvenile court to transfer you to adult court. All states have a procedure that allows juveniles to be tried as adults. Some states have adopted an automatic transfer rule, which means you go directly to adult court for certain crimes. Some have also authorized "reverse transfer," allowing a minor to be returned to the juvenile system from adult court. For example, consider a fifteen-year-old who is charged with a home burglary and, under state law, finds himself in adult criminal court. The judge may send the offender to juvenile court if this is his first offense, he played a minor role in the crime, and a psychological evaluation shows him to be a good candidate for rehabilitation.

> The federal government, District of Columbia, and most US states set the age of adult criminal responsibility at 18. Nine states set the age at 17, while North Carolina sets the age at 16.

In the 1990s, drastic changes took place in the juvenile justice system. Due to a high rate of juvenile crime, a get-tough attitude swept the United States. Most states changed their laws to put more teenagers in the adult system. The philosophy of treatment and rehabilitation gave way to longer sentences and fewer services for minors. Then, as juvenile crime subsided and adult prison for minors proved unsuccessful, the pendulum swung back toward the center and a focus on rehabilitation.

Some important rules affecting teens in the adult legal system have their origins in a 1966 court case. Sixteen-year-old Morris Kent was on probation when he was charged with rape and robbery. He confessed to the charges and was transferred to adult court. No investigation was done before the transfer, and the court didn't state the reasons for sending Morris to the adult system. He was found guilty and sentenced to thirty to ninety years in prison. The US Supreme Court reversed the transfer, stating that Morris, although a juvenile, was entitled to full due process—which meant a hearing, investigation, and a written statement of the court's decision and reasons.

Since Morris's case, all juveniles who are charged with a crime are entitled to full due process. This includes minors who face the possibility of transfer to adult court. As a teenage defendant, you are appointed a lawyer to represent you. It's the prosecutor's job to present evidence to the court regarding the seriousness of the charge and why you should be tried as an adult rather than a juvenile. Your lawyer will argue in favor of you staying in the juvenile system for treatment and rehabilitation.

- In 2014, approximately 4,200 juvenile cases were transferred to adult courts. The majority of juveniles transferred were 16-and 17-year-old males.
- In 2015, 31,487 juveniles who were ruled to be delinquent were committed to secure juvenile facilities. In 2016, 4,656 juveniles were held in adult jails and prisons across the country.

Sources: Equal Justice Initiative, eji.org; TheSentencingProject.org (June 2018)

The court must determine not only what's best *for* you but also how to protect the community *from* you until rehabilitation occurs. Community safety is a priority. Some of the factors the court considers include your age and level of maturity, the time remaining to work with you in the juvenile system, the seriousness of the crime, your criminal history, family support, and whether services have been offered to you in the past. If, for example, you have completed a substance abuse program but you continue to break the law, the court would consider those facts in determining if the juvenile system has anything else to offer you or if you should be transferred to adult court.

If you're not transferred to adult court, your case will proceed as a juvenile court matter, where jurisdiction ends at age eighteen or twenty-one. If you're transferred to adult court, you'll be afforded all the rights of an adult criminal defendant. This also means that the penalties usually reserved for adults now apply to you—including a number of years in prison, and in some cases, a life sentence with or without the possibility of parole.

The Supreme Court has determined that a person who commits a crime while a minor (under eighteen) cannot *automatically* be sentenced to life in prison without the possibility of earning parole. In *Miller v. Alabama* (132 S.Ct. 2455, 2012), the Court stated that "youth matters" in determining penalties. The Court also commented that "the distinctive attributes of youth diminish the ... justifications for imposing the harshest sentences on juvenile offenders, even when they commit terrible crimes." The Court did not exclude the possibility of life without parole for a juvenile offender but stated this should be the outcome only after a hearing to consider specific details and circumstances of the case. Justice Elena Kagan commented, "We think appropriate occasions for sentencing juveniles this harshest possible penalty will be uncommon."

During a sleepover in 2014, two 12-year-old girls from Wisconsin lured another 12-year-old into the woods. They later said they planned to kill her to prevent an internet horror character called Slender Man from hurting their families. One of the girls—Morgan Geyser—stabbed the victim 19 times, while the other girl—Anissa Weier—encouraged her. The victim survived, and both of her attackers were arrested and charged with attempted murder.

The court ruled that the girls would stand trial as adults. Anissa pleaded guilty by reason of mental disease and, in 2017, was found by a jury to be mentally ill. She was sentenced to 25 years in a state mental hospital. Morgan pleaded guilty to attempted murder and was committed in 2018 to 40 years in a mental hospital. The victim now attends high school.

"CAN I BE PUT IN JAIL?"

Yes. If you're locked up, against your will and away from your home, you're in jail. It may be referred to as *detention, lock-up, secure care,* or some other less harsh term than *jail,* but your freedom is still restricted.

At the point you first become involved with the police, you may experience a stay in detention. If you're arrested, you can be taken into custody and held for approximately forty-eight hours. If formal charges aren't filed within that period, you'll be released. If charges are filed, you'll appear in court within a day or two, and the judge will decide if you'll be detained further or released to a responsible person.

If you're a danger to yourself or others, you may be held until the next hearing. This could be several weeks. Then, if you're found not guilty, you'll be released. If you're found guilty by the court or you plead guilty, you may be detained until sentencing takes place. At that point, you may receive additional time in a locked facility, or you may be placed on probation with a designated number of days in detention as a consequence of the crime you committed.

There are any number of scenarios in which you could be locked up once you're in the juvenile system. If you're placed on probation and you violate your terms, you're sure to spend time in detention. If you're sent to the Department of Corrections, you could remain there until you're eighteen, until you complete your sentence, or until the department releases you on parole.

States differ on the maximum length of stay for juveniles in locked facilities.

Teenagers determined by the court to be incorrigible[32] may also be locked up. This often happens with teenagers who are chronic runaways or who are out of control at home. Courts are reluctant to release teens knowing they'll be on the streets that night.

In some states, the law requires that detained teens be kept separate from adult prisoners. Many facilities around the country have separate buildings so no contact with adults is possible. Teenagers who are tried as adults and sentenced to jail or prison may also be kept separate until they turn eighteen. Then they join the general adult prison population. A scary thought!

"IF I'M CONVICTED OF A SEX CRIME, DO I HAVE TO

---

[32] See chapter 8.

REGISTER AS A SEX OFFENDER?"

Sex offender registration is not limited to adults convicted of sex crimes. Many states require juveniles to register with law enforcement if found delinquent for certain offenses. Laws differ from state to state, as does the length of time you're required to remain in the registry. However, your sentence applies even if you move to a different state.

Sex offender registration is referred to as Megan's Law, named after seven-year-old Megan Kanka. In 1994, Megan was raped and murdered in New Jersey. The federal law has been adopted (and sometimes modified) by individual states. Because of Megan's Law, registered sex offenders must notify their community of their conviction, and convicted juveniles and adults must provide DNA samples. Before being released, adult sex offenders are screened and entered into a national database.

Lester Packingham of North Carolina was 21 years old when he was convicted of taking "indecent liberties" (meaning engaging in inappropriate sexual behavior with a minor). As a convicted sex offender, he was banned by state law from using social media sites that could be used by minors, including Facebook and Twitter. Several years later, in 2010, Packingham received a traffic ticket that ended up being dismissed, and he posted on Facebook to celebrate the dismissal. He was arrested and convicted for violating the ban on using social media.

However, in 2017, the Supreme Court ruled to reverse Packingham's conviction and critiqued North Carolina's social media ban as too broad. In the 8-0 ruling, Justice Kennedy wrote:

"With one broad stroke, North Carolina bars access to what for many are the principal sources for knowing current events, checking ads for employment, speaking and listening in the modern public square, and

> otherwise exploring the vast realms of human thought and knowledge. Foreclosing access to social media altogether thus prevents users from engaging in the legitimate exercise of First Amendment rights."
>
> **Citation:** *Packingham v. North Carolina,* 137 S.Ct. 1730 (2017)

These registration laws are not limited to the most serious sex offenses, such as sexual assault, rape, and sexual conduct with a minor. Some states also require registration for sexting (the practice of taking nude or semi-nude pictures of yourself and texting them to someone else). Whether done as a joke, to flirt, or to bully, sexting involving minors has been criminalized in a number of states.

"DOES THE DEATH PENALTY APPLY TO ME?"

When Billy was fifteen years old, he and his brother and two friends murdered Billy's brother-in-law. Billy kicked and shot the victim in the head, slit his throat, and dragged his body, chained to a concrete block, to a river, where it remained for almost four weeks.

Billy was transferred to adult court, tried by a jury, and sentenced to death for first-degree murder. Billy appealed his case, which was eventually heard by the US Supreme Court. In 1988, the court stated that the execution of any person who was under sixteen at the time of his or her offense would "offend civilized standards of decency." The court decision went on, "[M]inors often lack the experience, perspective, and judgment expected of adults.... The normal fifteen-year-old is not prepared to assume the full responsibilities of an adult." Billy's death sentence was set aside, and he was resentenced to life in prison.

In 2005, the US Supreme Court extended its view to all minors including those who were sixteen and seventeen years old at the time of the crime. In the case of *Roper v. Simmons* (125 S.Ct. 1183), the court commented that juveniles are more vulnerable or susceptible than adults to negative influences and outside pressures, including peer pressure. Justice Anthony Kennedy wrote: "When a juvenile offender commits a heinous crime, the State can exact forfeiture of some of the most basic liberties, but the State cannot extinguish his life and his potential to attain a mature understanding of his own humanity." He went on to say: "The age of eighteen is the point where society draws the line for many purposes between childhood and adulthood. It is, we conclude, the age at which the line for death eligibility ought to rest."

Juveniles on death row across the country were resentenced to reflect this change to the law.

A Matter of Life and Death

• The first execution of a juvenile offender in the United States was in 1642. Sixteen-year-old Thomas Graunger of the Plymouth Colony was hanged for bestiality with a cow and a horse.

• Between 1900 and 1950, approximately 20 teenagers under the age of 16 were executed in the United

States. Before 1900, two 10-year-olds were executed, as well as an 11-year-old and five 12-year-olds. Since 1973, 226 juveniles have been sentenced to the death penalty. Twenty-two of them were executed; one was 16 and the others 17 at the time of their crimes. The remainder of the 226 benefited from the 2005 abolishment of the death penalty for juvenile crimes. Their sentences were changed, in many cases, to life in prison.

• The last execution in the US for crimes committed while a minor was in 2003 in Oklahoma. Scott Allen Hain was 17 when he and an accomplice carjacked a vehicle being used by Laura Sanders and Michael Houghton, ages 22 and 27. Hain and his partner eventually robbed Sanders and Houghton, locked them in the trunk of the car, and set the vehicle on fire, killing both of them. Hain was executed when he was 32.

• Capital punishment for juveniles is prohibited under international law. However, three countries currently maintain the death penalty for juveniles: Iran, Saudi Arabia, and Sudan.

Sources: Victor L. Streib, *Death Penalty for Juveniles* (Indiana University Press, 1987); Sherri Jackson, "Too Young to Die: Juveniles and the Death Penalty," *New England Journal on Criminal and Civil Confinement,* Spring 1996; Death Penalty Information Center (2017)

"CAN MY JUVENILE RECORD BE DESTROYED?"

Adults of all ages return to court asking for their juvenile records to be destroyed. The reasons vary: a new job, continuing education, a credit application, or military service. You don't necessarily have to have a specific reason. You may just want to clear the record because you believe that what you did as a juvenile shouldn't adversely affect the rest of your life.

Having a record means that your name, charge, and other vital statistics have been entered into a local and/or national computer system. Once you're charged with a crime or delinquent act and found guilty, you have a record. In some jurisdictions, the fact that you were arrested, whether convicted of a charge or not, may result in a record. So it's worth knowing in advance what the law is in your state.

Most states have a procedure whereby juvenile records may be destroyed. The decision is usually *discretionary*—destruction isn't automatic upon request. You may be required to appear in court to discuss your request with the judge. It's usually not necessary to have a lawyer.

The court will want to know why you want your record destroyed. They'll ask what you're doing now (school, job, family, and so on), and whether you've had any problems with the law since becoming an adult. If you can show the court that you've been rehabilitated, your request will probably be granted. On the other hand, if you've continued to have brushes with the law, are on probation as an adult, or have outstanding traffic tickets, your request may be denied. You can always renew your request at a later date, when a period of time has passed without incident.

The court also takes into consideration what your juvenile offenses were, your age at the time of the offenses, and whether you've successfully completed the terms of your sentencing. If you still owe work hours or restitution, for example, it's unlikely that your juvenile record will be destroyed. Make sure you come to court in the best possible position.

A twenty-two-year-old once asked a court to destroy his juvenile record, including a number of burglaries and shoplifting charges. When asked why, he stated that he was scheduled to be sentenced the following week in adult court for armed robbery. He didn't want the judge to know about his juvenile history, which would justify a harsher penalty. Do you think the judge had to think long and hard about this request?

Visit these websites to find out more about teens and the law:

Center on Juvenile and Criminal Justice

cjcj.org

This nonprofit organization works to understand and reduce juvenile incarceration.

LawFun at Duhaime's Encyclopedia of Law

duhaime.org/LawFun.aspx

This fun and fascinating site includes a timetable of world legal history, information on the history of Canadian law, links to a legal dictionary, as well as a list of the dumbest things ever said in court.

Think About It, Talk About It

1. A four-year-old girl sleeping on her living-room couch was killed by a stray bullet in a drive-by shooting. A sixteen-year-old boy was arrested and transferred to adult court for her murder. You're eighteen and have been called to serve on the jury. The prosecutor is going to ask for a life sentence if the defendant is found guilty.

What do you think about this case? Could you be an impartial juror? If asked, could you vote for a life sentence with or without parole? What do you think about eighteen- and nineteen-year-olds serving on juries for cases in which other teenagers are on trial?

2. Bobby is seventeen years and eleven months old. The juvenile court in Bobby's state has jurisdiction over minors until they turn eighteen. Bobby has a clean record, goes to school, and works part time. Just before his eighteenth birthday, Bobby's caught transporting sixty pounds of marijuana. He was going to be paid $500 cash to take a suitcase to the airport and check it on a certain flight. But an airport drug-sniffing dog caught him in the act. Because of the large amount of marijuana, Bobby was charged with possession for sale and transportation. The state wants him transferred to adult court.

What do you think should be done? With only one month remaining before Bobby turns eighteen, is there time for rehabilitation? Does the quantity of drugs make the crime more serious? If he's not transferred and instead is handled in the juvenile system for one month, isn't that just a slap on the wrist?

3. Christian R. was eight years old when he shot and killed his father and a family friend in 2008. Under Arizona law, he could have been tried as an adult.

What do you think should be done for and with this child? Should he be tried as an adult because of the seriousness of his acts? Should he be tried at all? What do you think about prison for young offenders? How long should they stay? Should they receive counseling, schooling, and/or special treatment?

Appendix

Custody Factors

If your parents get a divorce, will the court listen to your wishes about who will get custody of you and how the custody arrangements will work? Will the court appoint an attorney or guardian to advocate for you? That depends on which state you live in. Here's a state-by-state chart that answers these questions. An "X" means yes.

State	Children's Wishes	Attorney or Guardian Appointed
Alabama	X	—
Alaska	X	X
Arizona	X	X
Arkansas	X	X
California	X	X
Colorado	X	X
Connecticut	X	X
Delaware	X	X
District of Columbia	X	X
Florida	X	X
Georgia	X	X
Hawaii	X	X
Idaho	X	X
Illinois	X	X
Indiana	X	X
Iowa	X	X
Kansas	X	X
Kentucky	X	—
Louisiana	X	X
Maine	X	X
Maryland	X	X
Massachusetts	—	X
Michigan	X	X

Custody Factors continued

State	Children's Wishes	Attorney or Guardian Appointed
Minnesota	X	X
Mississippi	X	X
Missouri	X	X
Montana	X	X
Nebraska	X	X
Nevada	X	—
New Hampshire	X	X
New Jersey	X	X
New Mexico	X	X
New York	X	X
North Carolina	X	—
North Dakota	X	X
Ohio	X	X
Oklahoma	X	X
Oregon	X	X
Pennsylvania	X	X
Rhode Island	X	X
South Carolina	X	X
South Dakota	X	X
Tennessee	X	X
Texas	X	X
Utah	X	X
Vermont	X	X
Virginia	X	X
Washington	X	X
West Virginia	X	X
Wisconsin	X	X
Wyoming	X	—
CANADA	X	X

Source: 51 *Family Law Quarterly* No.4 (Winter 2018)

Compulsory School Attendance

At what ages do you have to go to school? Here's a state-by-state chart showing the ages of compulsory school attendance. If you have questions about exceptions or specific requirements, check the laws in your state or province

State	Ages of Compulsory School Attendance	State	Ages of Compulsory School Attendance
Alabama	6–17	Montana	7–16
Alaska	7–16	Nebraska	6–18
Arizona	6–16	Nevada	7–18
Arkansas	5–18	New Hampshire	6–18
California	6–18	New Jersey	6–16
Colorado	6–17	New Mexico	5–18
Connecticut	5–18	New York	6–16
Delaware	5–16	North Carolina	7–16
District of Columbia	5–18	North Dakota	7–16
Florida	6–16	Ohio	6–18
Georgia	6–16	Oklahoma	5–18
Hawaii	5–18	Oregon	6–18
Idaho	7–16	Pennsylvania	8–17
Illinois	6–17	Rhode Island	5–18
Indiana	7–18	South Carolina	5–17
Iowa	6–16	South Dakota	6–18
Kansas	7–18	Tennessee	6–18
Kentucky	6–18	Texas	6–19
Louisiana	7–18	Utah	6–18
Maine	7–17	Vermont	6–16
Maryland	5–18	Virginia	5–18
Massachusetts	6–16	Washington	8–18
Michigan	6–18	West Virginia	6–17
Minnesota	7–17	Wisconsin	6–18
Mississippi	6–17	Wyoming	7–16
Missouri	7–17	**CANADA**	6–16

Source: National Center for Education Statistics (nces.ed.gov, 2017)

Compulsory Provision of Services for Special Education

All states are required to provide special education services for students who qualify for them. If you're between the ages listed for your state, and if you're in need of special education services, you're entitled to receive them from your school district. Be sure to check your state's laws for exceptions or specific requirements.

State	Ages of Compulsory Provision of Services for Special Education	State	Ages of Compulsory Provision of Services for Special Education
Alabama	6–21	Montana	3–18
Alaska	3–22	Nebraska	birth–20
Arizona	3–21	Nevada	birth–21
Arkansas	5–21	New Hampshire	3–21
California	birth–21	New Jersey	5–21
Colorado	3–21	New Mexico	3–21
Connecticut	3–21	New York	birth–20
Delaware	birth–20	North Carolina	5–20
District of Columbia	2–21	North Dakota	3–21
Florida	3–21	Ohio	3–21
Georgia	birth–21	Oklahoma	birth–21
Hawaii	birth–19	Oregon	3–20
Idaho	3–21	Pennsylvania	6–21
Illinois	3–21	Rhode Island	3–21
Indiana	3–22	South Carolina	3–21
Iowa	birth–21	South Dakota	birth–21
Kansas	3–21	Tennessee	3–21
Kentucky	birth–21	Texas	3–21
Louisiana	3–21	Utah	3–22
Maine	5–19	Vermont	3–21
Maryland	birth–21	Virginia	2–21
Massachusetts	3–21	Washington	3–21
Michigan	birth–25	West Virginia	5–21
Minnesota	birth–21	Wisconsin	3–21
Mississippi	birth–20	Wyoming	3–21
Missouri	birth–20	CANADA	Each province sets its own limits.

Source: Digest of Education Statistics (2015)

Glossary

Acceptable Use Policy (AUP). A written statement by a school declaring its policy of acceptable uses of the school's computers and personal digital devices (such as cell phones), as well as penalties for violations. The policy is usually found in a school's student handbook.

Adoptive home study. An investigation and report, usually by a social worker, of a single person or couple wishing to adopt a child. The study covers all aspects of the applicant's life including motivation to adopt; medical, criminal and social history; education and career; finances; marriages; and a fingerprint check. It also includes statements from relatives and references from nonrelatives.

Age of majority. In most states, eighteen is recognized as the age of adulthood, entitling you to make your own decisions and manage your personal affairs. It is also the age (in most states) at which, if you commit a crime, you are tried as an adult.

AIDS. Stands for *acquired immunodeficiency syndrome,* a breakdown of the body's defense system caused by *HIV,* which kills blood cells. Research continues for a cure. In the meantime, be aware of the dangers of unprotected sex and drug use (needles).

Alternative dispute resolution (ADR). A method of settling a disagreement without going to court. It's intended to save time, money, and aggravation. Two types of ADR are *arbitration* and *mediation.*

Appeal. The right to ask a higher court (called an *appellate court)* to review a decision made by a lower court. This is done by reading a transcript of what took place in the lower court, and listening to the oral arguments of the attorneys involved. The attorneys may also file written arguments about their case, called *briefs.*

Arbitration. A process in which both sides of a dispute agree to allow a third person (who is not involved) to settle their differences. You may choose the arbitrator yourself, or one will be chosen for you. The arbitrator's decision is binding on both sides.

Brief. A concise, written statement about a case, with arguments about issues raised by the lawyers. Briefs are read by the appellate court and help in making decisions about these issues.

Bullycide. Suicide stemming directly or indirectly from being bullied or cyberbullied—usually an act of depression and loneliness.

Bullying. Harmful behavior against another person, usually of a repetitive nature—it may include physical or psychological acts of aggression.

Capital punishment. The death penalty.

Censorship. The act of limiting access to material found objectionable; for example, books, movies, and music with explicit sexual content, violence, or profanity.

Child Protective Services (CPS). A government agency responsible for investigating reports of child abuse, neglect, and abandonment. A CPS caseworker may remove children from the home and is required to offer services to reunite the family.

Conscientious objector. A person who refuses to serve in the military or bear arms because of his or her moral or religious beliefs.

Contempt of court. "Direct contempt" occurs when a person does or says something in the judge's presence that is offensive or disruptive. "Indirect contempt" is when a person does something outside of the court's presence, such as violating a court order.

Corporal punishment. Physical discipline including swats, paddling, and spanking.

Custodial interference. Violation of or interference with a lawful custody order of the court, by the noncustodial parent or anyone else.

Cyberbullying. The use of electronic devices to convey intimidating or harassing messages (for instance, text or instant messages, graphic harassment, and email).

Damages. In the legal system, an amount of money awarded by a jury or judge to compensate a victim of a civil wrongdoing. Damages may be compensatory (intended to compensate victims for their losses) or punitive (intended to serve as an example to others, signaling that certain behavior is unacceptable).

Delinquent. A minor who violates a criminal law. If found guilty, he or she is called a *juvenile delinquent.*

Detention. Temporary confinement of a minor in a locked facility. This may be as a consequence of an action committed by the minor, or for the safety of the minor or the community between hearings.

Disaffirm. To get out of a contract without meeting all of its terms.

Discrimination. The act of treating an individual or a group differently than others because of race, gender, religion, nationality, sexual orientation, or disability. Not all discrimination is illegal. Teenagers are subject to legal age restrictions regarding employment, curfew, alcohol, and driving.

Diversion. If you receive a ticket or are charged with a low misdemeanor or status offense, you may be eligible for diversion. The program is usually for first-time offenders and may include community service, educational classes, or random drug testing. Once you finish the program, your case is dismissed and you don't have a criminal record. Diversion is sometimes called deferred prosecution or deferred judgment.

Double jeopardy. Going to trial a second time for the same offense. There are exceptions to this, but generally you're protected against the government trying you twice.

Due process. Also called *due process of law,* this is your right to enforce and protect your individual rights (life, liberty, and property) through notice of any action against you, and the right to be heard and confront the opposing side.

Emancipation. The process of becoming legally free from your parents or guardian. This may be the result of a court order, an act on your part (marriage, military enlistment), or other circumstances your state's laws allow. If you're emancipated, your parents lose their authority over you and are no longer responsible for you.

Felony. A classification of the criminal laws that carries the strictest penalties, usually a minimum of one year in jail. A felony is more serious than a misdemeanor or petty offense.

Foster care. When a child is removed from his or her home by Child Protective Services (CPS), the police, or court order, he or she is placed in a home until it is safe to return to the parents. Placement may be in a foster home, child crisis center, group home, or emergency receiving home. These homes are usually licensed and regulated by the government.

Grand jury. A group of citizens who decide whether there is enough evidence to charge someone with a crime. They listen to the government's evidence presented by a prosecutor behind closed doors. Unlike a criminal trial that is open to the public, grand jury proceedings are closed hearings. They usually deal with felonies, not misdemeanors or lesser crimes. If the grand jury finds sufficient evidence against the person, they issue a formal charge called an *indictment*.

Guardian. An individual with the lawful power and duty to take care of another person, including his or her property and financial affairs. The court may appoint a guardian for a minor if necessary, and sometimes the minor may select a guardian or object to the one being considered. A guardian may also be selected by your parents and named in their will.

HIV. Stands for the *human immunodeficiency virus,* which causes AIDS. The body's immune system is made up of white blood cells (T-cells), which protect the body from infection. The virus kills the T-cells, lowering the body's defenses against disease and infection.

Home detention. Once a defendant is charged with a crime, the judge may let him or her return home, but only on certain conditions. Also called "house arrest," this typically means that the defendant is allowed to leave the house only during certain windows of time, such as to go to school, work, or medical appointments. A violation may result in detention until the defendant's next hearing.

Hung jury. A jury that cannot agree on a decision in the case. This usually happens after hours or even days of considering the evidence and it means that the case may be retried.

Incorrigible child. A child (usually a teenager) who breaks rules or laws that don't apply to adults. Examples include missing school, running away, using alcohol or tobacco, and disobeying parents or guardians.

Indictment. A formal charge against a person for committing a crime, brought against him or her by a grand jury.

Jurisdiction. The legal right of a judge and a court to exercise its authority; the power to hear and determine a case. Specific rules exist regarding jurisdiction. Without it, a court is powerless to act.

Mediation. A way of settling a dispute that includes a third person, who is neutral and attempts to get both sides to reach an agreement. Mediation is used in family court, in juvenile court, and in some civil cases.

Minor. Someone who is not legally an adult. Generally, someone under age eighteen.

Miranda warnings. These are the rights suspects are read when in police custody. You have the right to remain silent; you have the right to have a lawyer appointed to represent you; if you cannot afford a lawyer, one will be appointed for you; and any statement you make may be used against you in a court of law. As a result of the *Gault* decision (see chapter 7), these rights belong to minors as well as adults.

Misdemeanor. A criminal offense less serious than a felony, with a jail sentence of one year or less.

No contest. A defendant who pleads "no contest" is agreeing with the state's case as outlined by the prosecutor in open court. The judge then decides if there's enough evidence to find the defendant guilty beyond a reasonable doubt (in criminal cases). If yes, sentencing follows. A "no contest" plea is not common in juvenile court.

Petty offense. A minor crime with a maximum penalty of (usually) a few months in jail or a fine (often set by law up to several hundred dollars).

Plea bargain. An agreement between the state and offender that, in return for a guilty plea, the charge or charges are reduced. Consequently, there is no trial and the court proceeds directly to sentencing. However, a judge is not required to accept the plea if he or she believes it goes against the interests of public safety or is unfair to the victim.

Power of attorney. A written document giving someone else the authority to act for you—to obtain medical care, for example, in the absence of your parents. See chapter 7, for a sample form.

Probable cause. Exists where the facts and circumstances within an officer's knowledge are sufficient in themselves to cause a person of reasonable caution to believe that an offense has been or is being committed.

Probation. A program in which you're supervised by the court or probation department for a period of time. Special terms of probation may include time in detention, community service hours, counseling, a fine, restitution, or random drug testing.

Restitution. The act of restoring a victim to the position the victim was in before suffering property damage or loss or personal injury. A minor placed on probation may be required to pay the victim for any loss that the minor caused. If the amount is great, payment may be spread out over months or years.

Search and seizure. The ability of a person in a position of authority (police or school teacher) to search you or your property (room, car, locker) and take anything unlawful or not legally in your possession.

Self-incrimination. Since you have the right to remain silent (see *Miranda warnings*), you aren't required to help the police build their case against you. You don't have to be a witness against yourself. This protection comes from the Fifth Amendment of the US Constitution.

Sequester. To sequester a jury means to isolate them or separate them from their families and the public until the case is decided. This is rarely done, and usually only in high-profile or sensational trials.

Sexting. Sending graphic images or sexually explicit photos or videos by way of text messages to friends.

Sexually transmitted disease (STD). A disease or infection contracted as a result of sexual activity. STDs require immediate medical treatment.

Shared custody. When the court gives both parents in a divorce the responsibility to share the care and control of their children. Sometimes called *joint custody*.

Social media. Interactive online environments where users share their profiles, blogs, photos, messages, and so on. Some popular sites and apps include Twitter, YouTube, and Instagram.

Sole custody. When one parent in a divorce receives custody of the child, and the other parent is given liberal visitation rights (for example, weekends, vacations, and summer).

Status offense. A crime that is lesser than a misdemeanor or felony, and which can only be committed by a minor (such as truancy). In other words, the same behavior by an adult would not qualify as a crime.

Statute of limitations. A time limit, set by statute, within which a plaintiff must file a civil lawsuit, or a prosecutor must file charges against someone. A few crimes, such as murder and treason, have no statute of limitations. In these cases, charges can be filed any time—even decades after the crime has taken place.

Statutory rape. Unlawful sexual relations with a person under the age of consent, which may be sixteen, seventeen, or eighteen, depending on your state. It's a crime even if the underage person consents.

Subpoena. An official document requiring a person to appear in court or at another legal proceeding (such as at a deposition), or requiring a person to produce specific documents, such as copies of Facebook or Instagram posts, text messages, or emails.

Termination of parental rights. A legal process by which the relationship between a child and his or her parents is ended. The biological parents are no longer the legal parents of the child, which frees the child for adoption. Some reasons for terminating a parent's rights include abuse or neglect of the child, abandonment, mental illness or criminal history of the parent, or severe alcohol or drug use.

Texting. Sending a message to someone over your cell phone.

Transfer. In juvenile law, this is the process by which a minor is charged with a crime and tried in adult court rather than juvenile court. Due to the seriousness of the charge and the juvenile's history, he or she may be treated as an adult, making the juvenile eligible for adult consequences including life imprisonment with or without the possibility of parole.

Truancy. The failure to go to school when required unless you're excused by the school for a good reason, such as illness, a doctor's appointment, or a family emergency. In some states, truancy is an offense that could land you in court.

Warrant. In the juvenile and criminal justice systems, two types of warrants exist: arrest warrants and search warrants. Both are court orders issued by a judge or magistrate based on probable cause that a crime has been committed and that the person named in the warrant committed it. A search warrant is limited in scope and names a place to be searched as well as the object of the search (drugs or weapons, for example).

Workers' compensation. A program for employees that covers your expenses for work-related injuries or illness. It's a no-fault program, which means you're paid even if the accident was your fault. Minors may receive workers' compensation.

YouTube. A video-sharing website where users can upload, view, and share clips of themselves or others.

Selected Bibliography

BOOKS AND JOURNALS

Ceglia, John T., "The Disappearing Schoolhouse Gate: Applying *Tinker* in the Internet Age," 39 *Pepperdine Law Review* 939, April 2012.

Ferrara, Christopher A., "Customizable 'Sexual Orientation Privacy' for Minor Schoolchildren: A Law School Invention in Search of a Constitutional Mandate," 43 *Journal of Law and Education* 65, Winter 2014.

Jackson, Sherri, "Too Young to Die: Juveniles and the Death Penalty: A Better Alternative to Killing Our Children: Youth Empowerment," *New England Journal on Criminal and Civil Confinement,* Spring 1996.

Jett, Mickey Lee, "The Reach of the Schoolhouse Gate: The Fate of *Tinker* in the Age of Digital Media," 61 *Catholic University Law Review* 895, Summer 2012.

King, Shani M., "Alone and Unrepresented: A Call to Congress to Provide Counsel for Unaccompanied

Minors," 50 *Harvard Journal on Legislation* 331, Summer 2013.

Kretz, Adam, "The Right to Sexual Orientation Privacy: Strengthening Protection for Minors Who Are 'Outed' in Schools," 42 *Journal of Law and Education* 381 (2013).

Rachmilovitz, Orly, "No Queer Child Left Behind," 51 *University of San Francisco Law Review* 203 (2017).

Rothstein, Jeremy H., "Track Me Maybe: The Fourth Amendment and the Use of Cell Phone Tracking to Facilitate Arrest," 81 *Fordham Law Review* 489, October 2012.

Seymore, Malinda L., "Sixteen and Pregnant: Minors' Consent in Abortion and Adoption," 25 *Yale Journal of Law & Feminism* 99 (2013).

Streib, Victor L., *Death Penalty for Juveniles* (Bloomington, IN: Indiana University Press, 1987).

White, Ryan, with Ann Marie Cunningham, *Ryan White: My Own Story* (New York: Dial Books, 1991).

Wilson, Jeffrey, and Mary Tomlinson, *Children and the Law* (Toronto: Butterworth Co., 1986).

OTHER SOURCES

American Lung Association
Center for Women Policy Studies
Centers for Disease Control and Prevention
Children's Defense Fund
Child Welfare League of America
Common Sense Media
Cyberbullying Research Center
Death Penalty Information Center
Federal Food and Drug Administration
Guttmacher Institute
Humane Society of the United States
National Campaign to Prevent Teen and Unplanned Pregnancy
National Center for Health Statistics
National Center for Juvenile Justice
National Center for State Courts
National Institute on Drug Abuse
National Safety Council
Office of Juvenile Justice and Delinquency Prevention
Rape, Abuse and Incest National Network
Substance Abuse and Mental Health Services Administration
Teenage Research Unlimited
US Bureau of Labor Statistics

US Census Bureau
US Consumer Product Safety Commission
US Department of Commerce
US Department of Education
US Department of Health and Human Services
US Department of Transportation

About the Author

Thomas A. Jacobs, J.D., was an Arizona assistant attorney general from 1972 to 1985, where he practiced criminal and child welfare law. He was appointed to the Maricopa County Superior Court in 1985, where he served as a judge pro tem and commissioner in the juvenile and family courts until his retirement in 2008. He also taught juvenile law for ten years as an adjunct professor at the Arizona State University School of Social Work. He continues to write for teens, lawyers, and judges.

Visit Judge Jacobs's website, AsktheJudge.info, for free interactive educational tools that provide current information regarding laws, court decisions, and national news affecting teens. It's the only site of its kind to provide legal questions and answers for teens and parents with the unique ability to interact with Judge Jacobs and his daughter, attorney Natalie Jacobs, as well as with other teens.

Other Great Resources from Free Spirit

They Broke the Law—You Be the Judge
True Cases of Teen Crime
by Thomas A. Jacobs, J.D.
For ages 12 & up. *224 pp.; PB; 6" x 9".*

Every Vote Matters
The Power of Your Voice, from Student Elections to the Supreme Court

by Thomas A. Jacobs, J.D., and Natalie C. Jacobs, J.D.

For ages 13 & up. *224 pp.; PB; 6" x 9".*

Available Online
Judge Tom Jacobs's interactive website AsktheJudge.info

Available Online for Free
Lesson Plan Guide and Leader's Guide
freespirit.com/leader

LGBTQ
The Survival Guide for Lesbian, Gay, Bisexual, Transgender, and Questioning Teens (Revised & Updated 3rd Edition)

by Kelly Huegel Madrone, foreword by Jillian Weiss

For ages 13 & up. *272 pp.; 2-color; PB; 6" x 9".*

Words Wound
Delete Cyberbullying and Make Kindness Go Viral

by Justin W. Patchin, Ph.D., and Sameer Hinduja, Ph.D.

For pricing information, to place an order, or to request a free catalog, contact:

For ages 13 & up. *200 pp.; 2-color; PB; 6" x 7 1/2".*

Interested in purchasing multiple quantities and receiving volume discounts?

Contact edsales@freespirit.com or call 1.800.735.7323 and ask for Education Sales.

Many Free Spirit authors are available for speaking engagements, workshops, and keynotes.

Contact speakers@freespirit.com or call 1.800.735.7323.

Free Spirit Publishing Inc.
6325 Sandburg Road • Suite 100 •
Minneapolis, MN 55427-3674
toll-free 800.735.7323 • local 612.338.2068 • fax 612.337.5050
help4kids@freespirit.com • www.freespirit.com

Index

A

Abortion, *160, 201, 203*
Abortion: Opposing Viewpoints Series (Haugen), *203*
Above the Influence (website), *226*
Abuse,
　See also Neglect,
　animal, *331, 334*
　cases of, *191*
　Child Protective Services (CPS) and, *191*
　definition, *34*
　fatalities, *11*
　religious beliefs and, *36*
　reporting, *189, 191, 193*
　resources on, *193*
　sexual, *189, 191, 193, 363*
　statistics on, *193*
　types of abuse, *189*

Acceptable Use Policy (AUP), *120*
ACLU, *70*
Adopted: The Ultimate Teen Guide (Slade), *9*
Adoption,
　abortion and, *203*
　Family Medical Leave Act (FMLA), *162*
　learning about biological parents, *7*
　name changes and, *249*
　out of foster care, *11*
　overview, *5*
　process, *5, 7*
　resources on, *9*
Adoption consent, by teen parents, *270, 271*
Adoption records, *7*

Adoptive home study, *7*
Adult court, teenagers tried in, *421, 423, 425*
Affirmative action, *95, 97*
Age,
  See also Eighteen, age, compulsory school attendance and, *53, 55*
  juvenile court and, *412, 415*
  marriage and, *265*
  requirements for driving, *278*
  restrictions on jobs and, *153, 155*
  running for public office and, *263*
Age discrimination, *304*
Age of majority, *245, 359*
Age restrictions, *304*
Aggravated rape, *205*
AIDS,
  diagnosis and counseling, *182*
  going to school with, *101, 103*
  resources on, *184, 187*
Aid to Families with Dependent Children (AFDC), *271*
Alabama, *253, 314*
Al-Anon, *230*
Alaska, *115, 169, 230*
Alateen, *230*
Alcoholics Anonymous, *230, 235*
Alcohol use,
  age to buy alcoholic beverages, *228*
  bike riding while under the influence of, *276*
  dangers of, *228, 230*
  drinking and driving, *228, 278, 280, 283, 285, 289*
  getting help for, *182, 235*

penalties for driving and, *283, 285* resources, *230*

All the Broken Pieces (Burg), *9*

Alpert, Phillip, *140, 142*

Alternative dispute resolution (ADR), *387*

American Academy of Pediatrics (AAP), *215*

American Association of Suicidology, *217*

American Cancer Society, *226*

American Lung Association, *226*

American Medical Association, *283*

American Red Cross, *187, 189*

American Society for the Prevention of Cruelty to Animals (ASPCA), *334*

Americans with Disabilities (Gold), *101*

Americans with Disabilities Act (ADA), *99, 155, 157*

Anatomy of Murder (film), *402*

Animal abuse, *331, 334*

Apartment, getting your own, *251*

Appeals, in trials, *405, 407*

Appellate courts, *27, 391*

Arbitration, *389*

Arizona, *27, 57, 59, 66, 75, 77, 124, 142, 153, 173, 221, 253, 271, 280, 377*

Arkansas, *27, 63, 86, 410*

Armed services, joining the, *263, 265*

Arrests,
  for drinking and driving, *287*
  Miranda warnings, *340, 342*

put on job applications, *164, 167*
statistics on, *352*
Arrest warrant, *337*
Arson, *372, 375*
Assault, *368*
　See also Sexual assault,
Athletes,
　drug testing, *80, 82*
　prohibiting gender-based discrimination in, *92*
Attire,
　See also Dress code,
　school, *66, 68*
　when going to court, *410, 412*
Attorneys,
　See Lawyers,
Automatic teller machine (ATM), *173*
Automobile accidents, *280, 283, 285, 287*

A Few Good Men (film), *402*
A Thin Line (website), *112*

B

Backpacks, school personnel searching, *73, 75, 77, 80*
Bad Apple (Ruby), *112*
Bank accounts, *171, 173, 176*
Bank It website, *173*
Barber, Harley, *88*
Barboza v. D'Agata (2015), *340*
Barboza, William, *340*
Barker, McKenzie, *133*
Barrett, Victoria, *346*
Bathrooms, transgender students in school, *316, 318*
Bean, Matthew, *124*
Beer, drinking, *228, 230*

Being Jazz: My Life as a (Transgender) Teen (Jennings), *321*
Bellotti v. Baird (1976), *201*
Bell, Ruth, *198*
Belvidere School District, New Jersey, *80*
Bicycle riders, *274, 276*
Bierberle, Cameron, *291*
Bill of Rights, *42, 45, 48, 265*
Biological parents, *7*
Birth control, *196, 198, 201*
Birth parents, *7*
Black armbands, wearing to school, *66, 68*
Blackmun, Harry, *201*
Blood-alcohol level, *283, 285*
Blood donation, *187*
Boaz, John, *88*
Bochner, Arthur, *176*
Bochner, Rose, *176*
Booker, Devin, *86*
Border (United States), traveling across the, *334, 337*
Bortell, Alexis, *233*
Bowley, Donald, *280*
Boy Meets Depression: Or Life Sucks and Then You Live (Breel), *217*
Boy Scouts of America, *318*
Boys Town National Hotline, *217, 363*
Branding, *221*
Braun, Eric, *176*
Breach of contract, *296*
Breathalyzer, *82*
Breel, Kevin, *217*
Briefs, *405*
Brown, Linda, *50*
Brown v. Board of Education (1954), *50, 306, 410*
Brunelli, Jean, *274*
Bullycides, *112, 115*
Bullying,

See also Cyberbullying,
Bureau for At-Risk Youth, *274*
Burg, Ann E., *9*
Bush, George W., *398*
Business, starting your own, *176*
Butler, Caron, *359*

C

Cadier, Florence, *18*
California, *34, 167, 230, 258, 291, 309, 316, 325, 344, 377*
Campbell, Cassidy Lynn, *316*
Canada,
　American children adopted in, *7*
　laws on electronic harassment, *115*
Capital punishment, See Death penalty,
Car crashes, *280, 283, 285, 287*
Cars,
　See Driving,

Car-surfing, *291*
Carter, Michelle, *133*
Cefrey, Holly, *285*
Cell phones,
　cheating during tests using, *136*
　sexting on, *140, 142*
　used while driving, *280, 283*
Center for Native American Youth, *219*
Center on Juvenile and Criminal Justice, *438*
Centers for Disease Control and Prevention (CDC), *184, 196, 215, 221, 223*
Chambers, Don, *173*
Chaney, James, *389*
Changing Bodies, Changing Lives (Bell), *198*
Charter school, *45*
Cheating at school, *136*
Checking accounts, *173*
Child abuse,

See Abuse,
hild custody,
See Custody,
Childhelp National Child Abuse Hotline, *193*
Child labor laws, *50, 151, 153, 160*
Child pornography, *140, 142*
Child Protective Services (CPS), *11, 32*
   guardians appointed by, *40*
   medical neglect and, *182*
   parenting class referral from, *274*
   role of, *191*
Children's Defense Fund, *256*
Child support, *25, 27, 29*
Child Welfare Information Gateway, *193*
Christen, Carol, *157*
Christian Scientists, *38*
Church-state separation, *91*
Civics Education Initiative, *59*
Civics test, *57, 59*
Civil lawsuit, *387, 391*
Civil penalty, *365*
Civil Rights Act (1964), *155, 160, 162*
Clementi, Tyler, *112*
Climate change, *344, 346*
Clothing,
   See Attire,
Cobain, Bev, *217*
Cocaine Anonymous, *235*
Cohen v. G&M Realty LP (2018), *377, 379*
Cole, Susan, *395*
College and college students,
   affirmative action and, *95, 97*
   credit and debit cards, *302*
   First Amendment rights and, *42*

College campuses, *42*
Colorado, *27, 57, 120, 138, 164, 230, 233*
Columbine school shooting, *120*
Community groups, *32*
Community Legal Services, *412*
Community service, *53, 55, 124, 131, 228, 274, 276, 331, 356, 368, 375, 415, 419*
Compulsory school attendance, *53, 55*
Computer(s),
   consequences at school for use on a home, *115, 117*
   law enforcement searching your, *80*
   school Acceptable Use Policy (AUP) and, *120*
   teachers monitoring students' use of a school, *120, 121*

Confidential Intermediary (CI) Program, *7*
Conflict resolution classes, *370*
Conscientious objectors, *265*
Contempt of court, *25, 129, 131, 340*
Contraception,
   See Birth control,
Contract for Life, *289*
Contracts,
   adult cosignor, *298, 300*
   breach of contract, *296*
   breaking a, *296, 298*
   cosignor, *298*
   definition, *296*
   getting out of, *298, 300*
   signing, *298*
Controlled Substances Act, *233*
Cooling-Off Rule, *298, 300*
Corinna, Heather, *198*

Corporal punishment, *34, 59, 61, 63*

Counseling,
  abortion and, *203*
  for alcohol or drug abuse, *182, 235*
  your parents' divorce and, *14, 16*

Court cases,
  See also Juvenile justice system; Lawsuits; Legal system; Supreme Court,
  on abuse and neglect, *191*
  on custody and visitation issues, *18*
  examples of intersection between online activity and the law, *133*
  judges, *393*
  judges in, *407*
  juries, *391, 393, 395, 398, 400, 402*
  number of (2016-2017), *393*
  on obscene telephone call, *340*
  on reckless burning, *375*
  on searches and seizures, *77*
  on telephone harassment, *340, 342*
  trial hearings open to the public in, *393*

Court orders,
  divorcing parents and, *29*
  emancipation and, *243*
  name changes and, *249*
  for visits from grandparents, *23*

Credit Card Accountability, Responsibility, and Disclosure Act (2009), *302*

Credit cards, *302*

Crime and criminal charges,
See also Juvenile justice system,
arson or reckless burning, *372, 375*
assault, *368*
disorderly conduct, *368, 370*
disturbing the peace, *368*
fake IDs, *380, 382*
felonies, *355*
fighting, *368, 370*
gambling, *379, 380*
juvenile vs. adult justice system, *356*
for marijuana use, *233*
misdemeanors, *355, 356*
mutual combat, *370*
property damage, *375, 377, 379*
reporting on job applications, *164, 167*
selling marijuana, *230, 233*
shoplifting, *363, 365, 368*
standing trial as adults, *421, 423, 425*
statistics, *352*
status offense, *356*
trespassing, *370, 372*
Criminal court cases, *407*
Criminal damage, *375, 377*
Criminal Justice (film), *402*
Criminal lawsuits, *387, 389*
Crisis Text Line, *219*
Cruel and unusual punishment, *34, 42*
Curfews, *329, 331*
Custodial interference, *21, 23*
Custody,
joint or shared, *16, 18*
modification of, *21, 23*
sole custody, *16*

speaking up about issues with, *18, 23*
teen parents, *270*
Cyberbullying,
  about, *108*
  criminal charges for, *131*
  examples of, *110, 133*
  going to prison for, *121, 124*
  punishment for, *110*
  resources on, *112*
  statistics on, *110*
Cyberbullying insurance, *121*
Cyberbullying suicide and, *112, 115*

D

DACA (Deferred Action for Childhood Arrivals), *327, 329*
Daly, Melissa, *18*
Damages, *377, 379*
D'Angelo, J., *184*
Date rape, *207*
Death of a parent, guardians and, *38, 40*
Death penalty, *432, 435*
Debit cards, *302*
Defacing property, *377*
Define the Line (website), *112*
Deliberation, during court trial, *400*
Delinquent acts, *355* See also Crime and criminal charges,
Demonstrative evidence in court cases, *395*
Department of Homeland Security, *334*
Depression, *212, 215, 217, 219*
Desk, school personnel searching your, *75*
Deveau, Aaron, *280*
Digital abuse,

See also Internet, the,
DiMeglio, Erin, *92*
Disabilities, children with, *97, 99, 155, 157*
Disability Resource Community, *101*
Disaffirming a contract, *298*
Discipline,
  See also Punishment(s),
  off-campus speech resulting in school, *115, 117*
  by parents, *32, 34*
  at school, *34, 59, 61, 99*
  who has the legal right to, *32*
Discrimination,
  age restrictions for teenagers and, *304*
  based on gender identity, *323*
  definition, *304*
  due to pregnancy, *210*
  employment, *155, 160, 162*
  gender-based, *92, 95, 212, 304, 306*
  LGBT people, *73, 306, 314, 316, 318*
  pregnancy, *210*
  school rules and, *70, 73*
  sexual harassment, *164*
  when choosing a jury, *398*
  of women of childbearing age, *212*
Disorderly conduct, *362, 368, 370*
Display Clause, *372*
Displays of affection, *314*
District of Columbia, *53, 77, 124, 230, 280, 287*
Disturbing the peace, *362, 368*
'Ditch day', *362*
Diversion program, *233, 368, 416, 419, 421*

Divorce,
  about, *14*
  among married teens, *267*
  child's 'best interests' and, *16*
  child support and, *25, 27, 29*
  counseling and, *14, 16*
  custodial interference and, *21, 23*
  custody and, *16, 18*
  grandparents' visitation rights, *23, 25*
  having your opinion heard about, *16*
  resources on, *18, 21*
  speaking up about custody issues, *18, 23*
  visitation and, *18, 23, 25*
Doctor(s),
  screening children for depression, *215, 217*
  visiting without your parent's permission, *179, 182, 184*
Doe v. Regional School Unit 26 (2014), *318*
Donating blood and organs, *187*
Donovan, Sandy, *176*
Don't Ask, Don't Tell (DADT) policy, *325*
Door-to-Door Sales Rule, *298, 300*
Double jeopardy, *59*
Dougherty, Terri, *88*
Draft, military, *263, 265*
DREAM Act, *325*
Dreamers, rights of, *325, 327*
Dreams and Nightmares (Velásquez), *329*

Dress code, *68, 160, 162, 316*
Drinking and driving, *228, 278, 280, 283, 285, 289*
Driver's license,
  blood-alcohol level tests and, *283*
  organ donation and, *187*
Driving,
  cell phone use while, *280, 283*
  Contract for Life, *289*
  deaths related to distracted, *280*
  drinking and, *283, 285, 287*
  joyriding, *291*
  learner's permit, *278*
  motorcycles, *287*
Driving under the influence (DUI), *228, 278, 280, 283, 285*
Driving while intoxicated (DWI), *283*

Dropping out of school, *53, 55*
Drug counseling, *182, 235*
Drug testing, *80, 82, 160*
  bike riding while under the influence of, *276*
  driving under the influence of, *278, 289*
  getting help for, *235*
  harm of, *233, 235*
  overdose deaths, *235*
  resources, *237, 238*
  on school property, *73, 75, 82*
Due process, *42, 59, 323, 391, 423*
DUI (driving under the influence), *228, 283, 285*

E

Eating disorders, *34*
E-cigarettes, *223, 235*
Education,

See also School(s),
  affirmative action and, *95, 97*
  on rape, *207*
Education for All Handicapped Children Act (1975), *97*
Education neglect, *45, 189*
E.E.O.C. v. Abercrombie & Fitch (2015), *162*
Eighteen, age,
  child support payments and, *29, 32*
  foster care and, *14*
  jobs you cannot have before, *153*
  legal adulthood at, *243*
  registering with Selective Service System, *263*
  tattoos and, *221*
Eighth Amendment, *34, 42, 48*

Elauf, Samantha, *162*
Emancipation,
  contracts and, *298*
  explained, *243, 245, 247*
  marriage as a teenager, *267*
  medical care and, *182*
  payment to blood donors and, *187*
Emergency medical care, *334*
Emotional abuse, *189*
Emotional neglect, *34, 189*
Employee-at-will, *155*
Employment (place of),
  age restrictions and, *153, 155*
  being fired and, *155*
  discrimination and, *155, 157, 160, 210, 212, 304, 306*
  gender-based discrimination, *212*

income taxes and, *169, 171*
job applications, *164, 167*
labor laws and, *151, 153*
LGBT rights at, *323*
minimum wage and, *167, 169*
resources on, *157*
restrictions on number of hours, *155*
saving earnings from, *171, 173, 176*
sexual harassment and, *164*
starting your own business, *176*
summer jobs, *153*
tattoos and, *221*
your rights at, *160, 162*

Environment, your right to a clean, *344, 346*

Environmental justice, *346*

Equal Access Act of, *84*

Equal Employment Opportunity Commission (EEOC), *157, 162, 306, 311*

Equal Opportunity in Education Act (1972), *95*

Equal Protection Clause, *97*

Establishment Clause, First Amendment, *91*

Evans, Katie, *126*

Every Vote Matters (Jacobs and Jacobs), *261*

Executive branch of government, *261*

Expulsion, school, *34, 55, 59, 124*

F

Faber, Grant, *395*

Facebook, *115, 117, 121, 124, 126, 129, 131, 133, 430*

Fair Labor Standards Act (1938), *153, 167*
Fake ID, *380, 382*
Family and Medical Leave Act (FMLA), *160, 162*
Faragher, Beth Ann, *164*
Faragher v. City of Boca Raton (1998), *164*
Farm equipment, driving, *278*
Fathers, teen, *270*
Federal courts, *391*
Federal Juvenile Delinquency Act (1938), *391*
Federal laws,
  child labor laws, *153*
  on children with disabilities, *97*
  on credit cards, *302*
  on discrimination, *155, 157*
  Dreamers and, *325, 327*
  on juveniles charged in federal district courts, *391*
  on marijuana use, *230, 233*
  on pregnancy discrimination, *210*
  on sex offender registration, *430*
  tax, *169*
Federal Trade Commission (FTC), *300*
Feinstein, Stephen, *198*
Felonies, *191, 355, 375*
Fenced property, *372*
Field sobriety test, *283*
Fifth Amendment, *42, 48, 75, 77*
Fights, *368, 370*
Firearms, *251, 253*
Firebombs, *375*
Fires, *372, 375*
Fireworks, *342, 344*

First Amendment, *36, 48*
  Establishment Clause, *91*
  extended to students, *42*
  freedom of expression and, *86*
  freedom of religion, *36*
  freedom of speech and expression, *42, 68*
  internet protected by, *108, 117*
  social media ban, *430*
  student protest and, *70*
  symbolic speech and, *68*
  #TakeAKnee protest and, *70*
Fischer, Susan, *9*
Fisher v. University of Texas at Austin (2013), *97*
Florida, *95, 126, 129, 133, 140, 153, 164, 169, 291, 316, 377*
  See also Parkland, Florida, school shooting,
Foreman, *400*
Foster care, *9, 11, 14*
  deciding against abortion and, *203*
  'permanency' for children and teens in, *29, 32*
  teen parents placing their child in, *270*
  unpaid leave from work and, *160*
FosterClub, *14*
Fourth Amendment, *42, 48, 73, 75, 138*
Fourteenth Amendment, *201*
Freedom of association, *314*
Freedom of expression and speech, *314*
  cyberbullying and, *126*
  First Amendment and, *42, 68*

hairstyles at school and, *70*
on the internet, *108*
limitations on, *84, 86*
meaning of, *314*
online, *108*
Pledge of Allegiance and, *86*
resources on, *88*
student profanity and, *86, 88*
#TakeAKnee movement, *70*
Tinker decision, *66, 68, 70, 108*
Freedom of Expression and the Internet (Dougherty), *88*
Freedom of religion, *36, 42*
Freedom of the press, *42*
Free Speech (Boaz), *88*
Frequently Asked Questions About Date Rape (Orr), *207*
Frequently Asked Questions About Drinking and Driving (Cefrey), *285*
Fricke v. Lynch (1980), *316*
Full due process, *423*
Fundamental error, *407*
FYI (For Your Information),
  on abortion, *203*
  on abuse and neglect, *193*
  on adoption, *9*
  on alcohol and drug abuse, *230*
  American Red Cross, *189*
  on bullying, *126*
  credit cards, *302*
  on depression and suicide, *217, 219*
  on divorce, *18, 21*
  on drinking and driving, *285*

on employment, *157*
on foster care, *14*
on freedom of speech and expression, *88*
on gambling, *380*
on gun violence, *256*
Internal Revenue Service, *171*
on internet safety and cyberbullying, *112*
on the legal system, *402, 405*
on legal system for teens, *438*
for LGBT people, *321*
on money and banking, *173*
on pregnancy, *212*
on pregnancy and teen parenting, *274*
on rape and sexual assault, *207*
on sex, birth control, and pregnancy, *198*
on smoking and tobacco use, *226, 228*
on starting your own business, *176*
on students with disabilities, *101*
for teen parents, *274*
for teens in crisis, *363*
on undocumented children, *329*
on voting, *261*

G

Galas, Judith C., *217*
Gamblers Anonymous, *379, 380*
Gambling, *379, 380*
Gang rape, *205*
Gates, Bill, *359*
Gault, Gerald, *340*
Gays and lesbians, See Lesbian, gay, bisexual, and

transgender (LGBT) people,
GED (general educational development) program, 53, 55, 59
Gender-based discrimination, 92, 95, 212, 304, 306
Gen Xers, 258
Georgia, 77
Geyser, Morgan, 425
Ghafoerkhan, Olivia, 207
Ghost-riding, 291
Ginsburg, Ruth Bader, 82
Girls for Gender Equity, 311
Givens, Jordan, 101
GLSEN (Gay, Lesbian & Straight Education Network), 321
Gold, Susan Dudley, 88, 101
Gonorrhea, 182
Goodman, Andrew, 389
Government, branches of, 261, 263
lawsuit against federal, 346, 348
restrictions on running for public office, 263
Goyer, Tricia, 274
Graffiti, 379
Graffiti artists, 377, 379
Grand jury, 402
Grandparents, number of US children living with, 5
visitation rights, 23, 25
Gravelle, Karen, 9
Greenbriar High School, Arkansas, 63
Greer, Wylie, 63
Griffith, Susan, 157
Group chats, 131
Grutter v. Bollinger (2003), 97
Guam, 280
Guardians, 38, 40
See also Parents,

Gun ownership, *251, 253*
Gun violence, *63, 256*
Gun Violence: Opposing Viewpoints Series (Merino), *256*

H

Hairstyles, *70, 160, 304*
Hamilton-Wilkes, Viola, *157*
Harmless error, *407*
Harritone Senior High School, Pennsylvania, *120*
Harvard University, *131*
Haugen, David M., *203*
Hazelwood School District v Kuhlmeier (1988), *84*
Headscarves, *162*
Head tax, *256*
Healthcare, See Medical care and treatment,
Helmets,
    worn while driving a motorcycle, *287*
    worn while riding a bicycle, *274, 276, 287*
Herpes, *182*
Hey, Shorty! (Smith, Van Deven, and Huppuch), *311*
Hickory High School, Pennsylvania, *117*
High school, See School(s),
High school dropouts, *53*
Hijab, *162*
Hinduja, Sameer, *112*
Hitchhiking, *276*
HIV,
    blood donation and, *189*
    diagnosis and counseling, *182, 184*
    going to school with, *101, 103*
    resources on, *184, 187*

young people diagnosed with (2016), *184*
HIV Positive! (website), *184*
Hodge, Harold, *372*
Hodge v. Talkin (2015), *372*
Holidays, religious, *91*
Homeless children, *50, 362, 363*
Home, rules at, *2, 5, 32, 34*
Homeschooling, *45*
Home study, adoptive, *7*
Houghton, Keeley, *121*
House arrest, *291*
Humane Society of the United States, *334*
Hung jury, *400*
Hunting, *334*
Huppuch, Meghan, *311*

I

iCivics.org, *261*
IEPs (Individualized Education Programs), *99*
Illinois, *221*
iMatter (organization), *346*
Immunizations, *50, 270*
Income (minimum wage), *167, 169*
Income taxes, *169, 171*
Incorrigible youth, *359, 362, 427*
Indiana, *101*
Indictment, *402*
Info for Teens (website), *198*
Infractions, *356*
In loco parentis, *34*
In re Caitlyn B. (2017), *245*
Instagram, *88, 115, 129*
Instructions (court cases), *400*
Insurance, cyberbullying, *121*

Internal Revenue Service (IRS), *169, 171*
Internet, the,
See also Cyberbullying; Social media,
criminal charges for comments made on, *131, 133, 136*
cyberstalking, *124*
First Amendment protection and, *108*
resources about, *112*
revenge porn on, *124*
school discipline for off-campus speech on, *115, 117*
Staying Safe Online Contract, *148*
used for cheating at school, *136*
Investments, *176*
Iowa, *34, 66*
Ireland, *7*
Isom, DeQuan, *263*
I Wanna Know! (website), *187*

J

Jackson, Justin Ray, *131*
Jacobs, Natalie, *261*
Jacobs, Tom, *261*
Jahn, Sidney, *291*
Jail, *427*
Jaywalking, *276*
Jennings, Jazz, *321*
Job applications, *164, 167*
Jobs,
See Employment (place of),
Johnson, Dwayne, *359*
Joint custody, *16, 18*
'Joke' awards, *99*
Jons, Hadley, *129, 131*
Joselow, Beth Baruch, *21*
Joselow, Thea, *21*
Joyriding, *291*
J.S. v. Bethlehem Area School District (2002), *110*

Judicial branch of government, *261, 263*
Judicial bypass procedure, *201, 203*
Juliana v. US (2015), *344*
Juliett, Leah, *124*
Juries, *391, 393, 395, 398, 400, 402*
Jurisdiction(s), *391, 407, 425*
Jury duty, *393, 395, 398*
Jury scams, *398*
Jury view, *402*
Justice court, *391*
Juvenile courts, *400*
   See also Juvenile justice system,
Juvenile crime,
   See Crime and criminal charges,
Juvenile justice system,
   adult system vs., *356*
   age and, *412, 415*
   being put in jail, *427*
   categories of crime, *355, 356*
   clearing your juvenile records, *435, 436*
   death penalty and, *432, 435*
   diversion program, *416, 419, 421*
   incorrigible youth, *359, 362, 427*
   parental responsibility and, *359, 362*
   probation and, *415, 416*
   types of cases handled in, *415*
   your rights in, *415*
Juvenile records, *435, 436*

K

K2 (synthetic cannabis or marijuana), *233, 235*
Kaepernick, Colin, *70*
Kanka, Megan, *430*

Kansas, *27, 50*
Kennedy, John F., *95*
Kent, Morris, *421, 423*
Kentucky, *59*
Kidnapping, *21, 23*
Kids Help Phone, *217*
Kids Voting USA, *261*
Killen, Edgar Ray, *389*

L

Labor laws, *151, 153, 160*
Lacks, Cecilia, *86*
Lambda Legal, *321*
LawFun at Duhaime's Encyclopedia of Law, *438*
Lawsuits,
  See also Court cases,
  on bathrooms for transgender students, *316, 318*
  breaking a contract and, *298*
  discrimination and, *162*
  explained, *387*
  against the federal government for a clean environment, *346, 348*
  filing within a specified time, *389, 391*
  on graffiti and graffiti artists, *377, 379*
  malpractice, against attorney, *407*
  on medical marijuana, *233*
  against school for invasion of privacy, *121*
  settling before your day in court, *387, 389*
  on sexual harassment in school, *309*

on social media posts and First Amendment rights, *126*

Lawyers,
  divorce of parents and, *16*
  divorcing your parents and, *29*
  errors in trials, *405, 407*
  judges and, *393*
  in juvenile court, *415*
  Miranda warnings and, *340*
  for teens in adult courts, *423*

Layshock v. Hermitage School District (2007), *117*

Learner's permit, *278*

Lee v. Weisman (1992), *91*

Legal Aid, *412*

Legal system, *384*
  See also Court cases; Juvenile justice system; Lawsuits,
  appeals in, *405, 407*
  court's jurisdiction, *391*
  death penalty, *432, 435*
  detention, *427*
  detention and prison time, *427*
  different types of courts, *391, 393*
  errors in trials, *405, 407*
  films on, *402, 405*
  how to dress for court, *410, 412*
  sex offender registration, *430, 432*
  teenagers tried as adults in, *421, 423, 425*
  types of courts, *391, 393*

Legislative branch of government, *261*

Lesbian, gay, bisexual, and transgender (LGBT) people,

adoption by, *5*
California schools studying contributions of, *325*
first elected to a state legislature, *318*
information for straight people on, *323*
in the military, *325*
resources for, *321*
rights at school, *314, 316, 318*
rights at work, *323*
school bathrooms and, *316, 318*
Title VII of the Civil Rights Act and, *306*
your parents and, *321, 323*
LGBTQ (Madrone), *321*
Liberty Town Court, New York, *340*
Life sentence without parole, *425*
Lindsay, Jeanne Warren, *274*
Lindsay, Victoria, *129*
Locker rooms, *318*
Locker, school personnel searching your, *73, 75, 80, 253*
Lock-up, *427*
Logan, Jessica, *140*
Logic (rapper), *215*
Lottery tickets, *379*
Loving (film), *405*
Lundman v. McKown (1995), *38*
Lyon, Maureen E., *184*

M

MADD (Mothers Against Drunk Driving), *285*
Maiden name, *247*
Maine, *201, 230, 316, 318*
Malpractice lawsuit, *407*
March Against Revenge Porn, *124*
March for Our Lives, *261*

Marijuana,
  laws on selling or using, *230, 233*
  medical, *230, 233*
  searches and, *73, 75, 77*
  statistics on use of, *237*
Marjory Stoneman Douglas High School, Parkland, Florida, *63, 256*
Marriage,
  age for, *265*
  emancipated teen, *267*
  name changes and, *247*
  same-sex, *267*
Maryland, *253*
Massachusetts, *153, 230, 267, 318*
Maternity leave, *160, 162, 210*
McMillen, Constance, *314, 316*
Mediation, *389*
Medical care and treatment,
  in foster care, *14*
  religious beliefs and, *36, 38*
  without parent's permission, *179, 182, 184*
Medical marijuana, *230, 233*
Medical neglect, *182*
Megan's Law, *430*
Meier, Megan, *112*
Mental disabilities, child support payments and, *27, 29*
MentalHelp.Net, *230*
Merino, Noel, *256*
Mesica, Tsofia, *291*
#MeToo movement, *311*
Michigan, *129*
Miklowitz, Gloria D., *207*
Military draft, *263, 265*
Military, LGBT individuals in, *325*
Military Selective Service Act, *263*
Millennials, *258*

Miller v. Alabama (2012), *425*
Minimum wage, *167, 169*
Minnesota, *38, 334*
Miranda warnings, *340*
Misdemeanors, *191, 291, 355, 356, 372, 375, 382, 391, 416*
Mississippi, *138, 314, 316, 389*
Missouri, *59, 86, 318*
Money,
   average annual income of teens, *177*
   savings, *171, 173, 176*
   spent by teens, *177*
   wages, *167, 169*
Money Basics for Young Adults (Chambers), *173*
Moore, Emily, *121*
Morgan, Nick, *68*
Motorcycles,
   wearing a helmet when riding, *287*
Motor vehicles,
   See Driving,
Mullins, Victoria, *337*
Municipal court, *391*
Mutual combat, *370*
My Cousin Vinny (film), *402*
My Girlfriend's Pregnant! (Shantz-Hilkes), *274*
My Life After Now (Verdi), *184*
My Parents Are Getting Divorced (Cadier and Daly), *21*

N

Name changes, *247, 249, 318*
Narcotics Anonymous, *235*
National and Community Service Act, *53, 55*
National borders, crossing, *334, 337*
National Campaign to Prevent Teen and

Unplanned Pregnancy, *212*
National Center for Health Statistics, *267*
National Center for Missing and Exploited Children, *112*
National Council on Problem Gambling, *380*
National Domestic Violence Hotline, *193*
National Guard, *53*
National Kidney Foundation, *189*
National Prevention Information Network, *187*
National Responsible Fatherhood Clearinghouse, *212*
National Runaway Safeline, *219, 363*
National Suicide Prevention Lifeline, *219*
Native Americans, *391*
Neglect,
  cases of, *191*
  Child Protective Services (CPS) and, *191*
  definition, *34*
  education, *45, 189*
  medical, *182*
  religious beliefs and, *36*
  reporting, *189, 191, 193*
  resources on, *193*
  statistics on, *193*
  teen parenting and, *270*
  types of neglect, *189*
Neighborhood Accountability Board, *133*
Nelson, Richard E., *217*
Netherlands, the, *7*
Nevada, *169, 230*

Newborn infants, 'safe haven' laws for, *271*
New Jersey, *80, 88, 377, 430*
New Jersey v. T.L.O, *73, 75*
Newspaper, school, *84, 86*
Newtown, Connecticut, school shooting, *256*
New York, *306, 340, 377*
Next friend, *387*
Nicotine Anonymous, *226*
Ninth Amendment, *48*
North Carolina, *120, 131, 164, 249, 430*
North Dakota, *59, 77*
NoTobacco.org, *228*
NSTeens, *112*
Nude photos, *124, 133, 140, 142, 432*
Nude search, *75*

O

Obama, Barack, *398*
Obergefell v. Hodges, *267*
Ohio, *68, 140, 171, 280*
Oklahoma, *162, 435*
Olff v. East Side Union High School District (1972), *70*
'1-800--273-8255' (song), *215*
Oregon, *82, 230, 375, 395*
Organ donation, *187*
Orr, Tamra B., *207*
Overtime pay, *169*

P

Packingham, Lester, *430*
Paddling, *34, 61*
Parental consent, abortion and, *201, 203*
    for getting birth control, *196*
    for joining the armed services, *265*
Parental kidnapping, *21, 23*

Parental responsibility laws, *359*
Parenting time, *270*
Parents,
  See also Divorce; Stepparent(s); Teen parents,
  adoptive, *5, 7*
  children 'divorcing' their, *29, 32*
  controlling your income, *176*
  cosigning contracts, *298*
  cosigning for credit card, *302*
  death of, *38, 40*
  discipline by, *32, 34*
  disobeying rules of, *362*
  divorced, *14, 16, 18*
  duties and decisions by, *32*
  duty to support a child, *25, 27, 29, 32, 34, 36, 38, 40, 42, 45, 48, 50, 53, 55, 57, 59, 61, 63, 66, 68, 70, 73, 75, 77, 80, 82, 84, 86, 88, 91, 92, 95, 97, 99, 101, 103, 105, 108, 110, 112, 115, 117, 120, 121, 124, 126, 129, 131, 133, 136, 138, 140, 142, 144, 146, 148, 151, 153, 155, 157, 160, 162, 164, 167, 169, 171, 173, 176, 177, 179, 182, 184, 187, 189, 191, 193, 196, 198, 201, 203, 205, 207, 210, 212, 215, 217, 219, 221, 223, 226, 228, 230, 233, 235, 237, 238, 241, 243, 245, 247, 249, 251, 253, 256, 258, 261, 263, 265, 267, 270, 271, 274, 276, 278, 280, 283, 285, 287, 289, 291, 293, 296, 298, 300, 302, 304, 306, 309, 311, 314, 316, 318, 321, 323, 325, 327, 329, 331, 334, 337, 340, 342, 344, 346, 348, 350, 352, 355, 356, 359, 362, 363, 365, 368, 370, 372, 375, 377, 379, 380, 382, 384, 387, 389, 391, 393, 395, 398, 400, 402, 405, 407, 410, 412, 415, 416, 419, 421, 423, 425, 427, 430, 432, 435, 436, 438, 439, 460, 462, 465*

emancipation from, (See Emancipation), going to the doctor without permission from, *179, 182, 184* guardians taking place of, *38, 40* neglect by, (See Neglect), overseeing money you have earned, *171, 173* religion and, *36, 38* responsibility for school attendance, *57* responsibility for violation of their child's curfew, *331* returning from foster care to, *11* your sexual orientation and, *321, 323*
Parents Involved in Community Schools v. Seattle School District (2007), *410*
Parkland, Florida, school shooting, *63, 256*
Passports, *334*
Past Forgiving (Miklowitz), *207*
Patchin, Justin W., *112*
Peer juries, *419*
Penalties,
    death penalty, *432, 435*
    for drinking and driving, *285, 287*
    drug violations, *233*
    for not registering with the Selective Service System, *263*
    felonies, *355*
    for graffiti, *377*
    for hitting a teacher, *61*
    for joyriding, *291*
    in other countries, *337*

related to
car-surfing, *291*
for shoplifting, *365, 368*
for swearing, *337*
for texting while driving, *280*
transfers to adult court and, *425*
Pennsylvania, *171*
Perez, Valerie, *340*
Permits, driving, *278*
Personal financial proficiency seal, *173*
Peters, Kim, *253*
Petty offenses, *355, 356, 382, 416*
Pew Research Center, *258*
PFLAG, *321*
Phillips, Will, *86*
Physical abuse, *189*
Physical disabilities, child support payments and, *27, 29*
Physical discipline, *59, 61*
Physical evidence in court cases, *395*

Physical neglect, *189*
Piercings, *221*
Plagiarism, *136*
Planned Parenthood, *196*
Planned Parenthood Locator Service, *203*
Plea bargain, *387, 389, 460*
Pledge of Allegiance, *86*
Police,
confiscating your phone, *142*
fake IDs and, *382*
Miranda rights, *340, 342*
search and seizures by, *80*
testing your blood-alcohol level, *283*
Police court, *391*
Poll tax, *256, 258*
Power of attorney, *334, 460*
Prayers, school, *91, 92*
Pregnancy,

abortion and, *201, 203*
birth control and, *196*
employment and, *160, 162*
medical care without parental consent and, *182*
resources, *198, 212, 274*
school newspaper article on teen, *84, 86*
statistics on teen, *196*
while in school, *53, 210*
WIC program and, *271*
your rights and, *210, 212*
Pregnancy Discrimination Act (1978), *210*
Presidency, running for the, *263*
Price Waterhouse v. Hopkins (1989), *306*
Prince, Phoebe, *112*
Prince v. Massachusetts (1944), *38*
Prison, *21, 121, 124, 129, 263, 280, 355, 377, 384, 423, 425*
Privacy,
  abortion and, *201, 203*
  adoption records and, *7*
  drug and alcohol treatment, *182*
  of minors in school settings, *82*
  monitoring students' use on a school computer and, *120, 121*
Private schools, *45, 70, 73*
Probable cause, *80, 142, 402, 460*
Probation, *124, 359, 362, 368, 415, 416, 460*
Probation officer, *415*
Profanity, *86, 88, 337*
Property,
  arson and, *375*

damage to someone else's, *375, 377*
damaging school, *63, 66*
defacing, *379*
search and seizure of, *73, 75, 77*
trespassing on someone else's, *370, 372*

Property damage, *375, 377, 379*

Protests,
black armbands, during Vietnam War, *66, 68*
following Parkland, Florida, school shooting, *63, 256*
at schools, *63, 66, 70*
#TakeAKnee movement, *70*

Public office, running for, *261, 263*

Puerto Rico, *53, 280*

Punishment(s),
See also Penalties,
abuse cases and, *191*
for animal abuse, *334*
cruel and unusual, *34, 42*
for cyberbullying, *110*
incorrigible acts, *362*
by parents, *32*
school, *59, 61*
for school damage, *63, 66*

R

Race-based quotas, *97*

Racial discrimination, *50, 155, 160, 162, 304, 306*

Racial segregation, *50, 410*

Racist rant, *88*

RAINN (Rape, Abuse and Incest National Network), *207*
Random drug testing, *80, 82*
Rankin, Kenrya, *176*
Rape, *205, 207, 210*
  aggravated, *205*
  date rape, *207*
  gang rape, *205*
  reporting, *207, 210*
  resources on, *207*
  statistics on, *205*
  statutory rape, *205*
RBG (film), *405*
'Reasonable suspicion' searches based on, *75*
Reckless burning, *375*
Redding, Savana, *75*
Regents of University of California v. Bakkes (1978), *97*
Registering to vote, *258*
Relatives, marrying, *265*
Religion,
  disagreeing with your parents about, *36, 38*
  discrimination based on, *155, 160, 162, 304, 306*
  dress code at work and, *162*
  in public schools, *91, 92*
Renting an apartment, *251*
Reporting rape and sexual assault, *207, 210*
Required reporter, *191*
Resegregation, *410*
Resources,
  See FYI (For Your Information),
Responsible Teen Parent Program, *271*
Restitution, *66, 356, 368, 375, 415, 416, 436, 460*
Revenge porn, *124*

Rhode Island, *91, 129, 316, 377*

Rights,
- of children with disabilities, *97, 99, 101*
- in juvenile court, *415*
- of LGBT students, *314, 316, 318, 321, 323, 325*
- student privilege vs. student, *80*
- of teen parents, *270, 271*
- at work, *160, 162, 323*

R.M.A. v. Blue Springs R-IV School District (2017), *318*

Robbins, Blake, *120, 121*

Rock the Vote, *261*

Roem, Danica, *318*

Roe v. Wade, *201*

Roy, Conrad III, *133*

Ruby, Laura, *112*

Rules,
- about dress and appearance, *66, 68, 70, 73*
- cell phone use, *136, 138*
- disobeying your parents', *362*
- disobeying your schools', *59, 61, 63*
- LGBT students challenging school, *314, 316*
- preventing school violence, *73*
- private school, *70, 73*
- set by your parents, *32, 362*
- in your house, *2, 5, 32, 34*

Runaway youth, *245, 362, 363, 365, 427*

Ryan White Comprehensive AIDS Resource Emergency Act (1990), *101*

S

SADD (Students Against Destructive Decisions), *285*

Sáenz, Benjamin Alire, *321*
'Safe haven' laws, *271*
Sales, canceling, *298, 300*
Same-sex marriage, *267*
Saving money, *171, 173, 176*
Scams, jury, *398*
Schab, Lisa M., *18*
School(s),
 Acceptable Use Policies (AUPs) at, *120*
 affirmative action and, *95, 97*
 age ranges for compulsory attendance, *53, 55*
 attendance laws, *45, 55*
 being served with a search warrant at, *80*
 the Bill of Rights and your rights at, *42, 45*
 breaking rules at, *59, 61, 63*
 cell phones and the internet used for cheating at, *136*
 civics test requirement for graduating from, *57, 59*
 damaging property of, *63, 66*
 discipline at, *34, 59, 61, 99*
 dropping out of, *53, 55*
 drug testing at, *80, 82*
 fights at, *370*
 freedom of expression at, *66, 68, 84, 86, 88, 91*
 gender-based discrimination in, *92, 95, 304*
 hairstyles worn at, *70*
 for homeless children, *50*

immunization requirements, *50*
LGBT rights at, *314, 316, 318*
minimum age at beginning, *45*
off-campus speech resulting in consequences at, *115, 117*
personnel confiscating phones and reading texts, *136, 138*
prayer at, *91, 92*
pregnancy and, *210*
private, *45, 70, 73*
racial segregation and, *50*
religion in, *91*
rights of students with disabilities in, *97, 99, 101*
standing for or reciting the Pledge of Allegiance at, *86*
swearing in, *337*
transgender students in bathrooms, *316, 318*
unreasonable searches and seizures at, *73, 75, 77*
violence in, *66, 73*
zero-tolerance policies on weapons, *253*

School newspaper, *84, 86*

School shootings, *63, 256*

Schwebel, Courtney Blair, *249*

Schwerner, Michael, *389*

Search and seizure, *42, 73, 75, 77, 160, 460*

Search warrants, *77, 80, 142*

Second Amendment, *48, 256*

Secondhand smoke, *223*

Secure care, *427*

Self-incrimination, *42, 460*
'Separate but equal' doctrine, *306*
Sequester, *398, 400, 460*
Service dogs, *101*
Seventh Amendment, *48*
Sex and sexual activity,
　See also Pregnancy; Rape,
　abortion and, *201, 203*
　birth control and, *196, 198*
　resources on, *198, 207*
　statistics on teen, *196*
Sex crimes, *430, 432*
Sex education classes, *198*
Sex, Etc. (website), *198*
Sex offender registration, *430, 432*
S.E.X. (Corinna), *198*
Sexting, *140, 142, 432, 460*
Sexual abuse, *189, 191, 193, 363*
Sexual assault, *182, 205, 207, 210, 323*
Sexual Assault: The Ultimate Teen Guide (Ghafoerkhan), *207*
Sexual harassment, *164, 309, 311, 314*
Sexuality and Teens (Feinstein), *198*
Sexually graphic images, *124, 133, 142*
Sexually transmitted diseases (STDs), *182, 184, 187, 460*
Sexual orientation, discrimination or exclusion based on, *73, 304, 306, 398*
　See also Lesbian, gay, bisexual, and transgender (LGBT) people,
Shantz-Hilkes, Chloe, *274*

Shared custody, *16, 18, 462*
Shelby County v. Holder (2013), *258*
Shelton, C.D., *285*
Shoplifting, *363, 365, 368*
Shorr, Kathy, *256*
SHOT: 101 Survivors of Gun Violence in America (Shorr), *256*
Singapore, *337*
Single parents, *270*
Sixth Amendment, *48, 131*
Slade, Suzanne Buckingham, *9*
Smith, Joanne N., *311*
Smith, Michael A., *291*
Smoking cigarettes, *221, 223, 226, 228*
Social media,
　average use of, *105*
　ban on using, for sex offender, *430*
　posts hurting you at a later time, *126, 129, 131*
Social Security number, *155, 176*
Social workers, *189, 191*
Sole custody, *16, 23, 462*
South Carolina, *59, 171*
South Dakota, *169, 253*
South Plantation High School, Florida, *92*
Spanking, *34*
Special education, *103, 342*
Spice (synthetic cannabis or marijuana), *233, 235*
Sports,
　drug tests for school, *80, 82*
　gender-based discrimination and, *304*
　#TakeAKnee movement, *70*

Title IX and, *92, 95*
Start It Up (Rankin), *176*
State courts, *391*
State laws,
  abuse and neglect defined by, *34*
  on ages at which minors can marry, *265*
  on businesses owned by minors, *176*
  on cyberbullying, *115*
  Dreamers and, *325, 327*
  emancipation, *243, 245*
  on emergency mental healthcare, *215*
  on fireworks, *344*
  foster care, *11*
  income tax, *169*
  on marijuana use, *230*
  on minimum age for starting school, *45*
  on name changes, *247*
  on parental consent for abortion, *201, 203*
  on revenge porn, *124*
  'safe haven', *271*
  school attendance laws, *55*
  on school damage, *66*
  on visitation rights for grandparents, *23, 25*
  on weapon ownership, *253*
State minimum wage, *167*
State v. Mortimer (2001), *120*
Status offense, *356, 359, 462*
Statute of limitations, *389, 391, 462*

Statutory rape, *205, 462*
Staying Safe Online Contract, *148*
Stealing school property, *63*
Stepparent(s),
   adoption by, *5*
   name changes and, *249*
   visitation rights of former, *25*
StopBullying.gov, *126*
Student Non-Discrimination Act (2018), *318*
Substance abuse, See Alcohol use; Drug use or abuse,
Suicide, *212, 215, 217*
   cyberbullying and, *112, 115*
   resources on, *217, 219*
Suicide Awareness Voices of Education (SAVE), *219*

Summer jobs, *153*
Summer Jobs Worldwide 2012 (Griffith), *157*
Supreme Court,
   on abortion, *201*
   on automatic sentence for life in prison without parole, *425*
   on church-state separation, *91*
   on cruel and unusual punishment, *34*
   on death penalty for minors, *432*
   on drug testing, *82*
   on First Amendment protection on the internet, *108*
   on freedom of speech or expression at schools, *84*
   on hairstyles worn at schools, *70*

on racial discrimination, *50, 306, 410*
on religious freedom, *38*
reversing decisions, *407, 410*
on saluting the US flag, *407*
on same-sex marriage, *267*
on school searches, *73, 75*
on sexual harassment, *164*
on student speech (Tinker case), *108*
on telephone harassment, *340*
Tinker v. Des Moines Independent Community School District, *66, 68, 70*
violating the federal Display Clause and, *372*
on voting, *258*
Suspension, school, *34, 55, 59, 66, 124, 131*
Swats, *59*
Swearing, *61, 337, 340*
Sycamore High School, Ohio, *140*
Symbolic speech, protection of, *68*
Syphilis, *182*
#TakeAKnee movement, *70*

T

The BADvertising Institute (website), *228*
The Caine Mutiny (film), *402*
The Divorce Workbook for Teens (Schab), *18*
The Inexplicable Logic of My Life (Sáenz), *321*
The New Totally Awesome Business Book for Kids (Bochner and Bochner), *176*

The Ox-Bow Incident (film), *402*
The Power to Prevent Suicide (Nelson and Galas), *217*
The Survival Guide for Money Smarts (Braun and Donovan), *176*
Talking to others,
   about abortion, *203*
   about cyberbullying, *115*
   about rules your parents set, *34, 36*
   about your parents' divorce, *18*
   about your religious beliefs, *38*
   when things are seriously wrong in your family, *32*
   when you are depressed, *217*
Tattoos, *160, 221*
Taxes, *169, 171*
Tax forms, *171*
Teacher(s),
   carrying guns while at work, *253*
   cyberbullying and harassing, *110, 126*
   failure to obey, *59*
   hitting a, *61*
   taking cells phones and reading text messages on, *136, 138*
Teenage Parent Program (TAPP), *271*
Teenagers and Alcohol (Shelton), *285*
Teenagers, HIV, and AIDS (Lyon and D'Angelo), *184*
Teen courts, *419*
Teen Dads: Rights, Responsibilities & Joys (Lindsay), *274*
TeenDriving.com, *285*

Teen Guide Job Search (Wilkes and Hamilton-Wilkes), *157*
Teen Mom: You're Stronger Than You Think (Goyer), *274*
Teen parents,
  child support payments and, *27, 29*
  continuing education programs for, *55*
  employment and, *160, 162*
  resources for, *274*
  responsible for child support payments, *27*
  rights of, *270, 271*
  school programs for, *53*
Teen pregnancy, See Pregnancy,
TeensHealth (website), *198*
Telephone harassment, *340, 342*
Television cameras in the courtroom, *393*
Temple, Joshua Aaron, *131*
Temporary Assistance for Needy Families (TANF), *271*
Tennessee, *271*
Tenth Amendment, *48*
Termination of parental rights, *415, 462*
Testimonial evidence in court cases, *395*
Texas, *124, 169, 304, 337*
  baby (text messaging service), *212*
Texting or text messages,
  cheating and, *136*
  cyberbullying and, *108*
  school personnel reading, *136, 138*

sexting, *140, 142, 432*
Texting while driving (TWD), *280, 283*
That's Not Cool (website), *112*
Third Amendment, *48*
Thornburg, Jennifer, *249*
Threats using electronic communication, *115, 117, 120, 121, 131*
Tinker test, *66, 68, 70, 108, 314*
Tinker v. Des Moines: Free Speech for Students (Gold), *88*
Tinker v. Des Moines Independent Community School District, *66, 68, 70*
Tips, *167, 169*
Title IX, *92, 95*
Title VII, Civil Rights Act, *306, 323*
To Kill a Mockingbird (film), *402*
Traffic laws, *274, 276*
Transfer to adult court, *421, 423, 425, 462*
Transgender students,
  See also Lesbian, gay, bisexual, and transgender (LGBT) people,
  bathrooms and, *316, 318*
  Boy Scouts of America and, *318*
  crowned prom queen, *316*
  first elected to state legislature, *318*
  sexual violence and, *323*
  Title VII of the Civil Rights Act and, *323*
  violence against, *323*

Traveling across national borders, *334, 337*
Trespassing, *370, 372*
The Trevor Project, *219*
Trial courts, *391, 393*
Tribal courts, *391*
Truancy, *55, 57, 362*
Trump, Donald, *327*
12 Angry Men (film), *402*
26th Amendment, *258*

U

Undocumented children, *325, 327, 329*
Uniform, work, *160*
Unreasonable searches and seizures, *42, 73, 75, 77*
US Citizenship and Immigration Services, *9*
US citizenship test, *57, 59*
US Constitution, *59, 61, 263, 265*
  See also Bill of Rights; First Amendment; Fourth Amendment; Second Amendment,
US Department of Health and Human Services, *11, 193, 212, 237*
US Department of Justice, *323*
US Food and Drug Administration (FDA), *223*
US Supreme Court, See Supreme Court,
Utah, *280, 283*

V

Vaccinations, *50*
Vandalism, *63, 375, 377*
Van Deven, Mandy, *311*
Velásquez, Liliana, *329*
Verdict, *395, 400*
Verdi, Jessica, *184*

Vermont, *230*
Vernonia School District, Oregon, *82*
Viable fetus, *201*
Violence,
  fights, *368, 370*
  gun, *63, 256*
  juvenile crime, *352, 355*
  rape, *205, 207, 210*
  in schools, *66, 73*
  school shootings, *63, 256*
Virginia, *253, 405*
Virgin Islands, *280*
Visitation, *18, 23, 25, 270*
Visual Arts Rights Act (VARA) (1990), *377, 379*
Viveros, Andii, *316*
Voting, *256, 258, 261*
Voting Rights Act (1965), *258*

W

Wages, *167, 169*
Warrantless searches, *77, 133, 142, 416*
Warrants,
  search warrants, *77, 80, 142*
Washington (state), *105, 230*
Weapons, *251, 253, 256*
Weier, Anissa, *425*
Weisman, Deborah, *91*
What Color Is Your Parachute? for Teens (Christen), *157*
When Divorce Hits Home (Joselow and Joselow), *21*
When Nothing Matters Anymore (Cobain), *217*
Where Are My Birth Parents? (Gravelle and Fischer), *9*
Whitaker, Ashton, *316*
Whitaker v. Kenosha Unified School District (2017), *316*
White, Ryan, *101*

Wilkes, Donald, *157*
Willow Canyon High School, Arizona, *253*
Wisconsin, *115, 334*
Wolf, Aniya, *316*
Women, Infants, and Children (WIC) program, *271*
Words Wound (Patchin and Hinduja), *112*
Work,
  See Employment (place of),
Workers' compensation, *160*
Wynn, Taylor, *133*

Y

Young Worker Health and Safety Website, *157*
Your Pregnancy and Newborn Journey (Lindsay and Brunelli), *274*
Youth Challenge, *53*
Youthful Drunk Driver Visitation Program, *278*
Youth@Work Initiative, *164*
YouTube, *110, 117, 129*

Z

Zarda v. Altitude Express (2018), *306*
Zero-tolerance policy on weapons, *253*

www.ingramcontent.com/pod-product-compliance
Lightning Source LLC
Chambersburg PA
CBHW011746220426
43667CB00020B/2922